Pop Music, Culture and Identity

Series Editors
Steve Clark
Graduate School Humanities and Sociology
University of Tokyo
Bunkyo-ku, Tokyo, Japan

Tristanne Connolly
Department of English
St Jerome's University
Waterloo, ON, Canada

Jason Whittaker
School of English & Journalism
University of Lincoln
Lincoln, Lincolnshire, UK

Pop music lasts. A form all too often assumed to be transient, commercial and mass-cultural has proved itself durable, tenacious and continually evolving. As such, it has become a crucial component in defining various forms of identity (individual and collective) as influenced by nation, class, gender and historical period. Pop Music, Culture and Identity investigates how this enhanced status shapes the iconography of celebrity, provides an ever-expanding archive for generational memory and accelerates the impact of new technologies on performing, packaging and global marketing. The series gives particular emphasis to interdisciplinary approaches that go beyond musicology and seeks to validate the informed testimony of the fan alongside academic methodologies.

More information about this series at
http://www.palgrave.com/gp/series/14537

Susanna Scarparo
Mathias Sutherland Stevenson

Reggae and Hip Hop in Southern Italy

Politics, Languages, and Multiple Marginalities

Susanna Scarparo
The Australian National University
Canberra, ACT, Australia

Mathias Sutherland Stevenson
Faculty of Arts
Monash University
Melbourne, VIC, Australia

Pop Music, Culture and Identity
ISBN 978-3-030-07204-9   ISBN 978-3-319-96505-5 (eBook)
https://doi.org/10.1007/978-3-319-96505-5

© The Editor(s) (if applicable) and The Author(s) 2018
Softcover re-print of the Hardcover 1st edition 2018
This work is subject to copyright. All rights are solely and exclusively licensed by the Publisher, whether the whole or part of the material is concerned, specifically the rights of translation, reprinting, reuse of illustrations, recitation, broadcasting, reproduction on microfilms or in any other physical way, and transmission or information storage and retrieval, electronic adaptation, computer software, or by similar or dissimilar methodology now known or hereafter developed.
The use of general descriptive names, registered names, trademarks, service marks, etc. in this publication does not imply, even in the absence of a specific statement, that such names are exempt from the relevant protective laws and regulations and therefore free for general use. The publisher, the authors and the editors are safe to assume that the advice and information in this book are believed to be true and accurate at the date of publication. Neither the publisher nor the authors or the editors give a warranty, express or implied, with respect to the material contained herein or for any errors or omissions that may have been made. The publisher remains neutral with regard to jurisdictional claims in published maps and institutional affiliations.

Cover illustration: MartinM303

This Palgrave Macmillan imprint is published by the registered company Springer Nature Switzerland AG
The registered company address is: Gewerbestrasse 11, 6330 Cham, Switzerland

Acknowledgements

While Mathias has been an avid collector of reggae music since his early teenage years, his awareness and interest in Italian reggae culture have their roots in his first study trip to Italy in 2001, when he attended the 2001 Rototom Sunsplash festival in Osoppo and witnessed Sud Sound System and Africa Unite perform live. Mathias introduced Susanna to Italian reggae and hip hop, and his enthusiasm for this music, coupled with her interest in Italian politics and culture, and their shared love of southern Italy, led them to develop the idea of working together on this book. Building on research from Mathias' PhD thesis, "The Politics of 'Connective Marginalities' in Italian Reggae Culture," to which Susanna contributed as main supervisor, our book includes also new research on Sardinia and Apulia and a greater focus on hip hop and recent developments in other parts of Italy.

During our research, fieldwork, and trips to Italy, the authors have been privileged to receive the collaboration of various insiders, experts, and protagonists, who extended them their friendship, provided invaluable advice and moral support, and granted interview access. In this regard, we would like to acknowledge specifically the following people: Francesco "Catchy" Salteri, Mimmo "Superbass" Pizzutilo, Antonella "Rosapaeda" Di Domenico, Antonio "Treble" Petrachi, Federico Capone, Stefano "il Generale" Bettini, Alessandra Nardi, Antonio "DJ War" Conte, Piero "Militant P" Longo, Pier Tosi, Steve Giant, Paolo "Sego" Occidentale, Renato Amata, Bob Quadrelli, Quilo, Randagiu Sardu, and Claudia Aru.

In addition to those mentioned above, Mathias would like to acknowledge the following friends for their Italian hospitality over the years: Rino,

vi ACKNOWLEDGEMENTS

Christa and Francesco Paone, La Simo, Manuela Barone, Viviano "Gamba the Lenk" Pulvirenti, Baracca Sound, Eddi Romano, Rome's Red, Gold, and Green crew, Nico Royale, and the Imperiale family at the B&B la Vecchia Corte in Salento.

Finally, Mathias wishes to thank his parents, Michael, Frances, and Susan, for their material and emotional support and for always stimulating his passions and interests, his brother Gabriel for his musical insights, and his dear partner Vivi for her ongoing love.

Susanna thanks her brother Massimiliano Scarparo and sister-in-law Dorotea Caddeo for their generous support during her time in Sardinia. Dorotea Caddeo also provided invaluable advice and assistance with translations from Sardinian *Campidanese* language. Susanna also thanks her son Claudio, her brother Massimiliano, and her husband Stephen for accompanying her to gigs and sharing the fun! Lastly, Susanna wishes to thank her husband Stephen for his love and enduring support.

CONTENTS

1 Introduction   1

2 The Roots and Routes of Reggae from Jamaica to Italy   17

3 "Inna Different Stylee": The Renaissance of Youth Culture
   and Politics in Bari   45

4 Sud Sound System and the Revival of Salentine Language,
   Culture, and Identity   85

5 The Rise of the Posses and the Power of the Word   127

6 Southern Echoes of the Posses in Sardinia: Sa Razza   163

7 The Legacy of the Posses Beyond Genres and Across
   Generations: Randagiu Sardu, Mama Marjas, Claudia Aru   193

8 Conclusion   223

Index   233

vii

CHAPTER 1

Introduction

A connection between music and politics in Italy has been evident since Giuseppe Verdi's popular chorus "Va Pensiero," known in English as "The Chorus of the Hebrew Slaves," from his 1842 opera *Nabucco*, became known as the anthem for the Italian unification. From that point onwards, this connection between music and politics was to be seen in anarchist ballads, such as "Addio Lugano bella" (Pietro Gori, 1894); socialist hymns, such as "Bandiera rossa"; and songs of emigration, such as "Mamma mia dammi cento lire" (Carrera 2001, p. 352). Whereas the Fascist regime used propaganda songs very effectively (Carrera 2001, p. 353), political songs in post-war Italy became closely linked with the intellectual singer-songwriters that emerged during the social unrest of the 1960s and 1970s, providing the musical background to the youth movements of the time. Despite the continuing prevalence of singer-songwriters, the 1980s ushered in the closely related styles of reggae and hip hop as new forms of rebel and protest music that were opposed to racism, committed to pacifism, and open to multilingual experimentation, in particular the use of dialects and local languages.

Adopting a cultural studies approach, and combining analysis of personal recollections, interviews, lyrics, and video clips, this book explores the cultural politics of these musical forms in Italy from the beginning of the 1980s to the present. Specifically, we examine ways in which imported musical forms, such as reggae and hip hop, have been synthesized within

© The Author(s) 2018
S. Scarparo, M. S. Stevenson, *Reggae and Hip Hop in Southern Italy*, Pop Music, Culture and Identity,
https://doi.org/10.1007/978-3-319-96505-5_1

1

2   S. SCARPARO AND M. S. STEVENSON

locally distinctive Italian contexts, emphasizing a transcultural process that foregrounds non-institutional politics and marginal subjectivities. In line with our understanding of the transcultural qualities of music, at various stages, our discussion also moves beyond the confines of reggae and hip hop to explore other interconnected southern Italian musical syntheses created out of this dialogue between the local and the global.

Focusing on groups and solo artists located predominantly in the southern Italian regions of Apulia and Sardinia, we discuss the modes of production and distribution of their music alongside their lyrics and video clips, paying particular attention to the ways in which these artists use and mix dominant and minor languages through music. To this end, we emphasize the linguistic aspects of cultural marginalization as well as marginalities linked to geographical location, gender, and social and political identification. Furthermore, we maintain that the ubiquitous youth connection assumes a particular resonance in Italy due to the historical lack of "official" power that Italian youth have held within social, political, and economic spheres, as well as Italy's various and sustained manifestations of cultural and political youth opposition since the late 1960s.

A key event in reggae's emergence in Italy can be traced back to Friday, June 27, 1980. On this day, approximately 100,000, predominantly young, Italians from all over the peninsula gathered at Milan's San Siro Stadium to attend the much-anticipated concert by reggae's transnational star and global icon, Bob Marley (Buda 1980, p. 8). The event was immortalized in song by the popular Roman singer-songwriter Antonello Venditti in his 1984 reggae-inspired "Piero e Cinzia" (Piero and Cinzia, Heinz Music). Based on the melody to Marley's international hit, "No Woman No Cry" (Island Records, 1974), Venditti's lyrics poignantly evoke the event:

> E lo stadio era pieno,
> E sì che Milano, quel giorno era Giamaica,
> E venne la notte da centomila fiammelle,
> La musica correva come un filo, su tutta la mia pelle.
> (And the stadium was full,
> And so that day Milan was Jamaica,
> And then came the night of one hundred thousand lighters,
> The music ran all over my body like an electric wire.)[1]

The label "reggae" denotes the distinct beat that was popular on the Caribbean island from the late 1960s to the early 1980s (Chang and Chen

---

[1] Unless otherwise stated, all translations from Italian to English are our own.

1998, p. x) but is also used as an umbrella term to describe a range of styles and subgenres, including ska, rocksteady, roots reggae, dub, rub-a-dub, and raggamuffin/dancehall, which have developed and spread throughout the globe since its inception. Crucially, key aspects of the musical culture of Jamaica, such as the use of megawatt sound systems, the foregrounding of drum and bass, the practice of toasting/rapping over rhythm tracks, the technique of the remix, and the concept of the rave party, have become crucial to global hip hop, as well as to dance music and popular music more generally. Of specific importance for this book, we stress that Jamaican sound system culture was fundamental for the development of hip hop and rap, leading to "reggae-inflected global hip-hop confluences" (Marshall and Radano 2013, p. 738). In order to emphasize the specific resonance of these global confluences between reggae and hip hop in Italy, and also to rightfully acknowledge the seminal influence of reggae on hip hop, we will occasionally apply the term "reggae-inflected hip hop" when discussing the Italian context.

Gilles Deleuze and Félix Guattari emphasize that music "has always sent out lines of flight, like so many 'transformational multiplicities,' even overturning the very codes that structure" it (1987, pp. 11–12). Therefore, "musical form, right down to its ruptures and proliferations," is comparable to a "rhizome" (1987, p. 17). The philosophical concept of the rhizome provides an ideal metaphor for the way in which reggae and reggae-inflected hip hop have transcended geographical and cultural borders to formulate syncretic cultural forms, identities, and languages. Furthermore, the way in which the rhizome "ceaselessly establishes connections between semiotic chains, organizations of power, and circumstances relative to the arts, sciences, and social struggles" (Deleuze and Guattari 1987, pp. 7–8) encapsulates both the transnational and intertextual transferal of reggae's metaphors and meanings together with the broad resonance of their sociopolitical messages and practices.

Although reggae's popularization across the world is largely due to its commercialization, which might be understood to have undermined its potential for radical protest, its international impact cannot be superficially reduced to commercial exploitation alone (Manuel et al. 1995, p. 144). For all its collusion with commercialism, reggae resonates as a sound of resistance "precisely because it circulates as a black, modern form without an explicit degree of complicity with empire" (Marshall and Radano 2013, p. 738). As such, it galvanizes minority discourse "from West Africa to East Asia without the same taint as American black music" (Marshall and Radano 2013, p. 738).

Indeed, in many countries, reggae has been adopted as a form of opposition to commercial and cultural homogenization and has also provided the soundtrack to many liberation movements (Chang and Chen 1998, p. 3). For example, apartheid-era black South Africans (see Lucky Dube), refugees from Sierra Leone (see Sierra Leone's Refugee All Stars), white working-class youth in Britain (see The Clash), Maoris in New Zealand (see Dread Beat and Blood), and indigenous Australians (see No Fixed Address) have all synthesized reggae in culturally distinctive ways. This multiplicity of (reggae) music, and its capacity to promote transcultural and interlinguistic dialogue, can also be seen in various other examples, such as the British vocalist named Apache Indian, who created a *bhangra-muffin* sound fusing Indian bhangra and the Hindi language with Jamaican raggamuffin and Patois in the early 1990s.

Hence, as a form of popular cultural expression that permeates borders, makes social and emotional connections, and adapts to new local situations, reggae music readily lends itself to processes of *transculturation*. The anthropologist and scholar of Afro-Cuban culture, Fernando Ortiz, coined the term transculturation to describe the merging and converging of cultures and the consequent generation of new cultural phenomena, or *neoculturation* (see 1995, pp. 97–103). For Ortiz, "the word transculturation better expresses the different phases of the process of transition from one culture to another because this does not consist merely in acquiring another culture, ... acculturation" but also in "deculturation" or "the loss or uprooting of a previous culture" (1995, p. 102). The prefix *trans* can be understood to denote movement, or a process of moving across or beyond, but also a process of cultural *transferal* and *transformation*.

Although it was not the first instance of reggae in Italy, the seeds of reggae's cultural transferal and transformation in Italy can be most explicitly linked back to Marley's abovementioned concert in 1980. The music critic Gino Castaldo has referred to the concert as the end of an era of great youth hope that was being snuffed out (in FusoElektronique 2011). Indeed, the concert at San Siro coincided with the fragmentation of the mass (youth) movements of the Left, which had taken root during the protests and strikes of 1968 and 1969 and spanned throughout the 1970s.[2] With the rise of Silvio Berlusconi's commercial television empire

---

[2] For a detailed discussion of the collective movement(s) of the late 1960s and the 1970s, and of their cultural politics, see Ginsborg 1990, pp. 298–405; Lumley 1991; Katsiaficas 1997, pp. 6–57; Bull and Giorgio 2006; Guarnaccia 2010; Valcarenghi 2007; Bertante 2005; Voglino et al. 1999; Vecchio 2007.

from 1980 onwards, the control of cultural capital, economic resources, and communication became intertwined with political power. The commercialization of culture and the manipulation of mass information set in motion by Berlusconi's television revolution homogenized cultural diversity and smothered independent and pluralist voices to establish a neoliberal "common sense" (to use Gramsci's term) based on acritical consumption.[3] Moreover, the 1980s were marked by deindustrialization and the restructuring of the economy along neoliberal lines, developments which were to be amplified by a widespread sense of political apathy and individualism, commonly referred to as the *riflusso* (retreat/withdrawal).

Paul Ginsborg describes the *riflusso* as the "great retreat into private life, the abandonment of collective action, [and] the painful coming to terms with failure" (1990, p. 383). According to Robert Lumley, at the conclusion of the 1970s, those in the youth movements were faced with the difficult choice of either withdrawing into private life or supporting the armed political organizations (1991, p. 307). This newfound difficulty in practising non-violent forms of alternative politics highlighted "a more general crisis of oppositional politics" (Lumley 1991, pp. 307–08), leading to the fragmentation of the movement(s) of the 1970s. In this climate of disillusionment, Bob Marley's historic concert at San Siro represented a symbolic moment in a new phase of autonomous youth cultural politics.[4] As reggae musician and promoter Mimmo Pizzutilo argues, the event "was a clear sign of how one era had finished and another had begun" and demonstrated that "the counter-culture wasn't dead, but continued on in new forms" (Personal interview).

Thus, the timing of Bob Marley's concert at the beginning of the 1980s was critical, since it catapulted reggae into the collective consciousness at a transformative historical moment in Italy and facilitated its adoption as a creative form of expression within Italian contexts. These contexts were to

---

[3] By "common sense," Gramsci refers to what he calls "the traditional popular conception of the world" which, he points out, is "unimaginatively called 'instinct'" (1997, p. 199) even though it is, in fact, "part of the historical process" (1997, p. 326). Common sense, thus, is "an ambiguous, contradictory and multiform concept" (1997, p. 423) which, although not ideologically coherent, creates situations of inequality and oppression that are accepted as natural and that are lived uncritically (Gramsci 1997, pp. 420–23; Gramsci 2000, pp. 347–49, 421).

[4] When using the term "youth," we refer to an approximate age range of 16–30 years. Our use of the term also implies both a sense of separation from and a rejection of the "parent" or dominant culture.

6   S. SCARPARO AND M. S. STEVENSON

mark a direct line of continuity with the 1970s but also a renewal of youth politics through new expressive musical forms such as reggae and later reggae-inflected hip hop.

Analogously to the Italian singer-songwriters and folk singers of the late 1960s and 1970s, who intellectualized, vocalized, and popularized the sociopolitical themes relating to the student and workers' movements of the period, the reggae and reggae-inflected hip hop practitioners we discuss in this book, starting from the 1980s, use music and musical culture as a vehicle for social and political aggregation, critique, and practice. However, despite such elements of continuity, their adoption and trans-culturation of reggae, and later reggae-inflected hip hop, also reflected a shifting understanding of Italian popular music which established more overt transnational links motivated by worldwide protest against racism, war, colonialism, and environmental exploitation.

These antagonistic qualities of Italian reggae culture are embedded in the politics of its connective marginalities, a concept we borrow from Halifu Osumare and that we use to explain how reggae's peripheral origins, and by and large non-hegemonic channels of dissemination, allow for disparate yet parallel marginalized groups to build tangible and symbolic alliances in an attempt to resist the dominant practices of cultural, economic, and political power. In Italy, such alliances have articulated counter-hegemonic meanings, narratives, and voices, whilst bringing to light the synthesis between global and local elements which leads to the formation of *glocal* cultural forms.[5]

Our conceptualization of connective marginalities in Italian reggae, and reggae-inflected hip hop culture, takes as a point of departure Osumare's discussion of the various social and historical realms that form the context for hip hop's diffusion amongst global youth. Central to her connective marginalities framework is the way in which "the global meanings of blackness may signify parallel issues of marginality and difference already marked in other countries" (2007, p. 62) and how blackness therefore becomes "a global sign in the contested construction of identities and meanings" (2007, p. 68). Thus, through its association with blackness, or what she terms its "Africanist aesthetic," hip hop culture

---

[5] The term glocalization (the combining of the global with the local) was first used in English by the sociologist Roland Robertson to explain the process of globalization by which imported social categories and practices assume a local character in their new setting (1995, pp. 25–44).

"instigates global connections of understanding about various peoples' marginal status at the local level" (2007, p. 64).

According to Osumare, these connective marginalities of hip hop are "resonances of social inequities that can manifest as four particular configurations in different parts of the world—youthful rebellion, class, historical oppression, and culture" (2007, p. 63). Low-class status is nominated as the next largest social sphere of connectivity, and is measured in terms of "financial wealth, political power, and family status," and is particularly common to ethnic and immigrant groups (Osumare 2007, p. 70). Historical oppression represents the second-largest connective sphere and "explains the social status of a group that identifies with a long history of purposeful subjugation" (Osumare 2007, p. 71). And, finally, the "generational link of 'youth' is present in every global example" and therefore represents the largest connective marginality (Osumare 2007, p. 71).

Alongside Osumare's definition, our conceptualisation of connective marginality in this book is informed by our interpretation of the fraught dynamics involved in the North versus South divide that characterizes Italian politics and culture. This divide dates back to the unification of Italy in the nineteenth century and to the political and cultural movement, commonly known as the *Risorgimento* (rebirth), that promoted the bringing together of the diverse states of the Italian peninsula, including the islands of Sardinia and Sicily, into a single state. The North/South divide is constructed along ethnic, economic, and post-colonial categories, whereby the South is positioned as being historically, culturally, and economically closer to Africa than Europe. Moreover, many in the South, and particularly in the island of Sardinia, interpret their place within Italy as a result of colonial exploitation and oppression. It is through this context that we deploy the framework of connective marginalities in relation to the adoption of reggae and hip hop in the South of Italy, as exemplified, predominantly, by groups and artists from Apulia and Sardinia.

The reason to focus primarily on these two regions is threefold. First, groups from Apulia pioneered the use of local languages and the fusion of local musical styles within reggae and reggae-inflected hip hop. Second, both regions are often overlooked in discussions about the South of Italy, which tend to place more emphasis on Naples, and its surrounding region, and Sicily. Third, particularly in relation to Sardinia, the effects of colonial exploitation, linguistic repression, and cultural devaluation enact a process of connective marginality with the post-colonial and "Africanist aesthetic" (Osumare 2007, p. 70) of reggae and hip hop.

Moreover, as Paul Gilroy has argued in relation to the British context, the appropriation of music styles and forms, which "had both informed and recorded black struggles in other places," has helped to create a "new metaphysics of blackness" in Europe and elsewhere (1993, p. 83). Such metaphysics of blackness, defined by shared experiences of racial discrimination, found expression within "the underground, alternative, public spaces constituted around an expressive culture that was dominated by music" (Gilroy 1993, p. 83). The "political language of citizenship, racial justice, and equality," which according to Gilroy was "one of several discourses which contributed to this transfer of cultural and political forms and structures of feeling" (1993, p. 83), has resonated powerfully within the Italian context of regional identities divided along perceived racial and ethnic lines.

Consequently, the localization of reggae in Italy, which, as Venditti sings in the above-cited "Piero e Cinzia," had the power to transform symbolically the northern Italian city of Milan into the culturally and geographically distant (and decidedly "southern") island nation of Jamaica, also coincided with a new openness to foreign, and particularly black, musical forms. In fact, reggae's indigenization in Italy represented for the first time a black, dance-oriented musical form originating outside Britain or America had been consciously adapted and invested with political significance in that country. In turn, this process was to feed new and diverse understandings of cultural identities and cultural expressions throughout the nation, especially in the marginalized South. Whereas the singer-songwriters and the political movements which identified with them of the late 1960s and 1970s had been largely concentrated in Italy's more economically rich North and Centre, the post-colonial politics and aesthetics of reggae found particularly fertile terrain in Italy's disadvantaged *Mezzogiorno* (southern Italy), where they were used to reflect on and challenge a pervasive sense of marginalization.[6]

Through our discussion of select examples of the multilingual music production of groups and solo artists from Apulia and Sardinia, we argue that, through their music, they resist the marginalization of the South and create new alliances and transcultural exchanges that engage critically, but

---

[6]Franco Fabbri and Goffredo Plastino's 2014 edited collection of essays *Made in Italy* provides a comprehensive account of Italian popular music, including discussions of select singer-songwriters and an analysis of the significant 1970s Neapolitan scene (see Chap. 5). This collection, however, does not include chapters on reggae or reggae-inflected hip hop.

INTRODUCTION 9

also productively, with the social, political, and economic challenges and opportunities offered by globalization. Hence, we claim that this music production represents one of Italy's most significant forms of creative political expression since the 1970s and a means of challenging hegemonic politics and culture. Specifically, we argue that the adoption and adaptation of reggae and reggae-inflected hip hop have provided southern Italian youth with the cultural means through which they have questioned and reinvented the counter-cultural and counter-hegemonic practices of the 1970s.

Regrettably, however, the endemic sexism and misogyny of Jamaican popular music, and the male-dominated music industry more generally, contributed to the lack of female performers in the Italian context. With the exception of Antonella Di Domenico, who was the lead singer and base-guitarist of the pioneering reggae band Different Stylee, it was not until the unparalleled success in the mid-2000s of the Apulian reggae performer Mama Marjas (Maria Germinaro, discussed in Chap. 7) that women started to become protagonist of Italian reggae and reggae-inflected hip hop.

This book is largely motivated by the lack of in-depth research and knowledge surrounding Italian reggae and its influence on the development of hip hop scenes in southern Italy; to use an expression oft-used in reggae, "the half has never been told."[7] Whilst the literature in the Italian language specifically dedicated to Italian reggae might be generously described as sparse, in English it is practically non-existent. There has, however, been some important Italian and English language research dedicated to hip hop and the so-called posse era, roughly between 1989 and 1994, in which there was a nationwide emergence of a multitude of col-

---

[7] To date, the only published texts dedicated at length to the topic remain Goffredo Plastino's reading of southern Italian rap and raggamuffin, *Mappa delle voci: Rap, raggamuffin e tradizione in Italia*; Rankis Nano's first-hand account of the autonomous Roman reggae scene, *Come again: vibrazioni dal basso*; Federico Capone's discussion of Salentine reggae and hip hop in *Hip hop, reggae, dance, elettronica*; Tommaso Manfredi's crucial documentation of the history of reggae in Apulia based on interviews with key protagonists, *Dai Caraibi al Salento*; and a brief yet historically rich appendix on Italian reggae's phases of evolution in *Paperback reggae*, written by two insiders: veteran vocalist Stefano Bettini (aka il Generale) and reggae journalist and radio presenter Pier Tosi. Two documentary films containing key interviews were released in 2011: Mattia Epifani's *Rockman*, a poetic rendering of Manfredi's account of reggae's Apulian evolution centring on the magnetic figure of Piero Longo (aka Militant P), and Giovanni De Gaetano's *Pull It Up: An Italian Story*, which narrates the evolution of Italy's dancehall and sound system culture from the early 1990s to the present.

10 S. SCARPARO AND M. S. STEVENSON

lectives, groups, and vocalists practising reggae, raggamuffin, dub, and hip hop (often in hybridized forms).[8] This narrow focus has largely neglected the fundamental role that reggae (along with punk) played throughout the 1980s and 1990s, not only in establishing a network of interconnected, autonomous, and antagonistic music scenes associated with the *centri sociali organizzati autogestiti* (organized self-managed social centres), *radio libere* (free radios), and fanzines, but also in introducing a self-consciously "black" musical aesthetic into politicized youth contexts for the first time.

This limited recognition of the foundational role played by reggae is reflected in the fact that many of those authors writing about the posse era have tended to group its Jamaican-derived expressions under the umbrella of hip hop or rap.[9] Given the historical connections between reggae and hip hop, together with their aesthetic, technical, and performative similarities, and the genre-blurring fusions which took place during the posse era, at times this confusion is justified. Nonetheless, this tendency to conflate reggae with hip hop also speaks to the hegemony of Afro-American musical traditions over those of the Afro-Caribbean and can be understood as yet another instance of the failure to recognize and give legitimacy to the global influence of Jamaican popular music and its interactions within vari-

---

[8] In our discussion throughout this book, we group the subgenres of "raggamuffin/dancehall" and "dub" under the umbrella term "reggae" unless referring to them separately. For English language discussions of Italian hip hop, see Mitchell 1995, 1996, 2000, 2001; Verdicchio 1997, 2006; Wright 2000; Plastino 2003; Anselmi 2002; Dawson and Palumbo 2005; Santoro and Solaroli 2007; Lutzu 2012; Plastino and Sciorra 2016. For scholarship in Italian, see Branzaglia et al. 1993; Pacoda 1996, 2000, 2011; Campo 1995.

[9] As is widely known, hip hop originated in the early 1970s, in decaying South Bronx neighbourhoods where unemployment rates among young blacks and Latinos were sky-high, running between 60 and 80 per cent (Higgins 2009, p. 16). The new ethnic groups who made the South Bronx their home in the 1970s, North American blacks, Jamaicans, Puerto Ricans, and other Caribbean people with roots in post-colonial contexts, began building their own cultural networks, which would prove to be resilient and responsive in the age of high technology (Rose 1994, pp. 33–34). Hip hop, which encompasses four elements—DJ'ing (the manipulation of pre-recorded music), breakdancing, rapping/MC'ing, and graffiti writing—gave voice "to the tensions and contradictions in the public urban landscape during a period of substantial transformation in New York" and attempted "to seize the shifting urban terrain, to make it work on behalf of the dispossessed" (Rose 1994, p. 22). In our discussion throughout this book, we use the term hip hop and rap interchangeably.

INTRODUCTION   11

ous local contexts, including those of Italy.[10] By contrast, this book seeks to give reggae centre stage by retracing the major steps in its evolution and dissemination in Jamaican, British, and US contexts in order to bring to light its centrality to the post-1970s continuation and renewal of youth cultural politics in Italy, including its influence on hip hop.

In so doing, we establish a narrative along historical as well as thematic lines. In Chap. 2, we outline the social, cultural, and political context of Jamaican popular music and its routes to Italy via the UK. We also identify reggae's origins in the "sound system" as crucial to its capacity to act as a medium outside dominant channels of information. As discussed in the chapter, the unique sociocultural dynamic of the sound systems gave rise to a grassroots and distinctive musical culture from the early 1960s, which was in turn disseminated in London (and later New York) through the transnational flows of migration and the commercial music industry. Furthermore, we discuss how the international commodification of reggae, and its marketing by the industry as rebel music through such figures as the Wailers and Bob Marley, was also a crucial element in its global dissemination and broad resonance as a form of protest music in Italy.

Chapter 3 focuses on what was arguably Italy's most distinctive and influential early reggae scene, located in the southern town of Bari. This Bari context demonstrates the manner in which reggae music and culture were locally recontextualized within the fragmented and fading collective counter-culture of the late 1970s. More specifically, we interpret the localization of reggae by marginalized youth as a process of creative synthesis that fused together elements of Italy's preceding political youth subculture with practices and idioms originating in Jamaican and British reggae culture and in British and Italian punk culture (the sound system, dub reggae, and fanzines). Moreover, we maintain that this process of glocalization and transculturation established a "politics of the everyday," as well as new forms of identity based on *difference* from the cultural mainstream. Through this ethical and aesthetic process of self-differentiation, this southern Italian youth succeeded in establishing connections and alliances with the other (trans)local Italian reggae scenes of the time and with other marginalized groups both at home and abroad.

---

[10] Russell Potter comments that "what is less often noted is the strong similarity between the rhetorical and narrative conventions of ska and reggae with those of hip hop" (1995, p. 38). For other studies about the influence of reggae on hip hop, see Higgins 2009 and Jones 1988.

Chapter 4 is a chronological and thematic continuation of Chap. 3. In this chapter, we detail the social and cultural factors surrounding reggae's distinctive glocalization in the Apulian province of Salento through its first and most longevous reggae-raggamuffin crew, Sud Sound System. We argue that the resonance of reggae in Salento stemmed from its emphasis on black cultural identity through the concepts of "roots and culture," which spoke directly to the sociocultural condition of Salentine youth of the 1980s. Because of this resonance, raggamuffin reggae provided an accessible and creative vehicle for marginalized Salentine youth to produce autonomous spaces and reinvent a southern cultural identity that could challenge the homogenizing tendencies of the *riflusso* and the corrosive influence of organized crime. Indeed, Sud Sound System's use of the Salentine dialect and citation of local traditions established a syncretic and transcultural musical language which led to what has been termed a "Salentine renaissance" (Pacoda 2011, p. 7).

In Chap. 5, we examine the autonomous origins and early contexts of the reggae-inflected hip hop posse movement (independent music groups/ collectives), paying particular attention to its crucial association with *la Pantera* (the first major student movement since the late 1970s), the autonomous spaces and practices of the *centri sociali* (self-managed social centres usually located in squatted abandoned buildings) and *radio libere* (free to air and self-managed radio stations), and the pioneering reggae scenes and anarcho-punk movement of the 1980s. We argue that the posses both continued the musical rejuvenation of youth politics, which had originated in the early 1980s through the work of groups such as Different Stylee, and represented a popularization of political music in Italy on a scale not seen since the 1970s.

Focusing on Sardinia, in Chap. 6 we discuss the lasting influence of the posse movement in the South. In particular, we examine the political use of reggae and hip hop as a form of cultural expression that critiques power structures, foregrounding marginal voices and languages. Our discussion includes the historical role played by posse era group Sa Razza in the early to mid-1990s and their ongoing influence in the present. A number of Sa Razza's members are still active, and they have collaborated with next-generation artists and collectives, such as Randagiu Sardu and Claudia Aru, who are included in our discussion of the intergenerational legacy of the posses since the early 2000s in Chap. 7.

In this chapter, we discuss artists who, in our view, demonstrate distinctive ways in which the reggae and posse era have continued into the present in Apulia and Sardinia. The artists we include in this chapter share a commitment to self-production and an eclectic reimagining and intercultural interpretation of reggae and hip hop. Significantly, they demonstrate how reggae and the music of the posses evolved into more gender-inclusive and self-consciously hybrid music styles. Through our discussion of the independent contexts of production and our analysis of the linguistic, thematic, and visual styles of the "rappamuffin" musician, Randagiu Sardu, and the self-produced singer-songwriter, Claudia Aru, both from Sardinia, and the Apulian reggae performer, Mama Marjas, Chap. 7 aims to demonstrate how these artists consciously reinterpret the legacy of the posses by celebrating their geographic, gendered, linguistic, social, and political marginalities.

It is not coincidental that two of the artists included in this chapter are female performers. Indeed, they are examples of the increased female presence in the music industry in general and more specifically, as is the case with Mama Marjas and Claudia Aru, respectively, the reggae context and the Sardinian independent musical context. Mama Marjas, in particular, claims direct lineage to both the male-dominated posses, such as 99 Posse, and iconic reggae female singers such as Judy Mowatt, Marcia Griffiths, and Rita Marley. Celebrating their femininity and focusing on female-centric themes in their songs, both Mama Marjas and Claudia Aru highlight their marginality through a cultural politics based on diversity, multilingualism (including the deliberate use of local southern dialects and languages), and the transcendence of dominant and fixed notions of gender and cultural identity.

Works Cited

Anselmi, William. 2002. From Cantautori to Posse: Sociopolitical Discourse, Engagement and Antagonism in the Italian Music Scene from the Sixties to the Nineties. In *Music, Popular Culture, Identities*, ed. Richard Young, 17–45. Amsterdam: Editions Rodopi. Print.

Bertante, Alessandro. 2005. *Re nudo. Underground e rivoluzione nelle pagine di una rivista*. Rimini: NdA Press. Print.

Bettini, Stefano, and Pier Tosi. 2009. *Paperback reggae: Origini, protagonisti, storia e storie della musica in levare*. Firenze: Editoriale Olimpia. Print.

Branzaglia, Carlo, Pierfrancesco Pacoda, and Alba Solaro. 1993. *Posse italiane: Centri sociali, underground musicale e cultura giovanile degli anni '90 in Italia*. Firenze: Editoriale Tosca. Print.

Buda, Massimo. 1980. I centomila figli di capitan Marley. *l'Unità*, June 29. Print.

Bull, Anna Cento, and Adalgisa Giorgio, eds. 2006. *Speaking Out and Silencing: Culture, Society and Politics in Italy in the 1970s.* London: Legenda. Print.

Campo, Alberto. 1995. *Nuovo? Rock?! Italiano!* Firenze: Giunti. Print.

Capone, Federico. 2004. *Hip hop, reggae, dance, elettronica.* Roma: Stampa Alternativa. Print.

Carrera, Alessandro. 2001. Italy's Blues. Folk Music and Popular Song from the Nineteenth Century to the 1990s. *The Italianist* 21 (1): 348–371. Print.

Chang, Kevin O.B., and Wayne Chen. 1998. *Reggae Routes: The Story of Jamaican Music.* Philadelphia: Temple University Press. Print.

Dawson, Ashley, and Patrizia Palumbo. 2005. Hannibal's Children: Immigration and Antiracist Youth Subcultures in Contemporary Italy. *Cultural Critique* 59 (1): 165–186.

De Gaetano, Giovanni, dir. 2011. *Pull It Up: An Italian Story.* Nine Lives. Film.

Deleuze, Gilles, and Félix Guattari. 1987. *A Thousand Plateaus.* London: Continuum. Print.

Epifani, Mattia, dir. 2011. *Rockman.* Goodfellas. DVD.

Fabbri, Franco, and Goffredo Plastino, eds. 2014. *Made in Italy: Studies in Popular Music.* New York and London: Routledge. Print.

FusoElektronique. 2011. Stelle. Speciale Bob Marley—Parte 1. Rai. Documentary. *YouTube*, May 15. https://www.youtube.com/watch?v=w_7xgQqPtrw. Accessed 7 July 2011.

Gilroy, Paul. 1993. *The Black Atlantic: Modernity and Double Consciousness.* London: Verso. Print.

Ginsborg, Paul. 1990. *A History of Contemporary Italy: Society and Politics 1943–1980.* London: Penguin. Print.

Gramsci, Antonio. 1997. *Selections from the Prison Notebooks of Antonio Gramsci.* Ed. and Trans. Quentin Hoare and Geoffrey Nowell Smith. New York: International Publishers. Print.

———. 2000. *The Gramsci Reader: Selected Writings, 1916–1935.* Ed. and Trans. David Forgacs. New York: New York UP. Print.

Guarnaccia, Matteo. 2010. *Re Nudo Pop & altri festival: Il sogno di Woodstock in Italia, 1968–1976.* Milano: Vololibero. Print.

Higgins, Dalton. 2009. *Hip Hop World.* Berkeley, CA: Groundwood Books. Print.

Jones, Simon. 1988. *Black Culture White Youth: The Reggae Tradition from JA to UK.* London: Macmillan. Print.

Katsiaficas, Georgy. 1997. *The Subversion of Politics: European Autonomous Social Movements and the Decolonization of Everyday Life.* Oakland: AK Press. Print.

Lumley, Robert. 1991. *States of Emergency: Cultures of Revolt in Italy from 1968 to 1978.* London and New York: Verso Books. Print.

Lutzu, Marco. 2012. *Su RAAP:* Sardinian Hip Hop Between Mass Culture and Local Specificities. *Journal of Mediterranean Studies* 91 (2): 349–366. Print.

INTRODUCTION 15

Manfredi, Tommaso. 2008. *Dai Caraibi al Salento: Nascita, evoluzione e identità del reggae in Puglia.* Lecce: AGM. Print.

Manuel, Peter, Kenneth Bilby, and Michael Largey. 1995. *Caribbean Currents. Caribbean Music from Rumba to Reggae.* Philadelphia: Temple University Press. Print.

Marshall, Wayne, and Ronald Radano. 2013. Musical Antinomies of Race and Empire. In *The Cambridge History of World Music*, ed. Philip V. Bohlman, 726–743. Cambridge: Cambridge University Press. Print.

Mitchell, Tony. 1995. Questions of Style: Notes on Italian Hip Hop. *Popular Music* 14 (3): 361–376. Print.

———. 1996. *Popular Music and Local Identity: Rock, Pop and Rap in Europe and Oceania.* London and New York: Leicester University Press. Print.

———. 2000. Doin' Damage in My Native Language: The Use of 'Resistance Vernaculars' in Hip Hop in France, Italy, and Aotearoa/New Zealand. *Popular Music and Society* 24 (3): 41–54. Print.

———. 2001. Fightin da Faida: The Italian Posses and Hip Hop in Italy. In *Global Noise: Rap and Hip Hop Outside the USA*, ed. Tony Mitchell, 194–222. Middletown: Wesleyan University Press. Print.

Nano, Rankis. 1997. *Come again: vibrazioni dal basso.* Roma: Edizioni XOA autoproduzioni. Print.

Ortiz, Fernando. 1995. *Cuban Counterpoint: Tobacco and Sugar.* Trans. Harriet De Onis. Durham and London: Duke University Press. Print.

Osumare, Halifu. 2007. *The Africanist Aesthetic in Global Hip-Hop: Power Moves.* New York: Palgrave Macmillan. Print.

Pacoda, Pierfrancesco. 1996. *Potere alla parola: Antologia del rap.* Milan: Feltrinelli. Print.

———. 2000. *Hip Hop Italiano: Suoni, parole e scenari del Posse Power.* Torino: Einaudi. Print.

———. 2011. *Salento, amore mio: Viaggio nella musica, nei luoghi e tra i protagonisti del rinascimento salentino.* Milano: Kowalski. Print.

Pizzutilo, Mimmo. 2012. Personal Interview. August 13.

Plastino, Goffredo. 1996. *Mappa delle voci: Rap, raggamuffin e tradizione in Italia.* Roma: Meltemi. Print.

———. 2003. Inventing Ethnic Music: Fabrizio De André's *Crueza de mä* and the Creation of *Musica Mediterranea.* In *Mediterranean Mosaic: Popular Music and Global Sounds*, ed. Goffredo Plastino, 267–286. New York: Routledge. Print.

Plastino, Goffredo, and Joseph Sciorra, eds. 2016. *Neapolitan Postcards: The Canzone Napoletana as Transnational Subject.* New York: Rowman & Littlefield. Print.

Potter, Russell A. 1995. *Spectacular Vernaculars: Hip Hop and the Politics of Postmodernism.* Albany: State University of New York Press. Print.

Robertson, Roland. 1995. Glocalization: Time-Space and Homogeneity-Heterogeneity. In *Global Modernities*, ed. Mike Featherstone, Scott Lash, and Roland Robertson, 25–44. London: Sage Publications. Print.

Rose, Tricia. 1994. *Black Noise: Rap Music and Black Culture in Contemporary America*. Hanover: University Press of New England. Print.

Santoro, Marco, and Marco Solaroli. 2007. Authors and Rappers: Italian Hip Hop and the Shifting Boundaries of Canzone d'Autore. *Popular Music* 26 (3): 463–488. Print.

Valcarenghi, Andrea. 2007. *Underground: A Pugno Chiuso!* Rimini: NdA Press. Print.

Vecchio, Concetto. 2007. *Ali Di Piombo*. Milano: Rizzoli. Print.

Verdicchio, Pasquale. 1997. *Bound by Distance: Rethinking Nationalism through the Italian Diaspora*. Madison, NJ: Fairleigh Dickinson University Press. Print.

———. 2006. Horizontal Languages and Insurgent Cultural Alignments: National Popular Culture and Nationalism. *This Nothing's Place*. March 1. http://light-zoo.blogspot.com.au/2006/03/horizontal-languages-and-insurgent.html. Accessed 4 Mar 2011.

Voglino, Alex, et al. 1999. *Miserabili quegli anni: Dalla contestazione al terrorismo: Analisi critica degli anni Settanta*. Firenze: Tarab. Print.

Wright, Steve. 2000. 'A Love Born of Hate': Autonomist Rap in Italy. *Theory, Culture & Society* 17 (3): 117–135. Print.

DISCOGRAPHY

Bob Marley and the Wailers. 1974. No Woman No Cry. *Natty Dread*. Island Records. LP.

Venditti, Antonello. 1984. Piero e Cinzia. *Cuore*. Heinz Music. LP.

CHAPTER 2

The Roots and Routes of Reggae from Jamaica to Italy

Reggae's capacity for recontextualization and transculturation in Italy from the late 1970s/early 1980s must be understood in relation to its sociocultural and historical origins in Jamaica. Notwithstanding its population of a little over 2.5 million, Jamaica has "conquered the world" with its popular music (Manuel et al. 1995, p. 143), a remarkable feat when one considers that only major economic superpowers, such as the US and Britain, have been able to do the same. Generically known as reggae, Jamaican popular music resonates widely as both rebel music and exotic soundtrack, influencing music styles and music scenes in almost every corner of the globe (Chang and Chen 1998, p. x; Marshall and Radano 2013, p. 738; Hebdige 1979; Manuel and Marshall 2006; Veal 2007; Barrow and Dalton 2004, p. x).

Fernando Ortiz applied the term transculturation to the cultural synthesis arising from colonization and the geographical movement of peoples, and these very dynamics were central to the evolution of reggae in Jamaica. Reggae's spread and adaptability is a logical extension of its transnational and syncretic origins and its evolution through processes of creolization and cultural exchange. The inherent political characteristics of reggae stem from its anti-colonial foundations (as exemplified by Peter Tosh's 1973 song "Here Comes the Judge") and its roots in the culture of the sound system.

© The Author(s) 2018
S. Scarparo, M. S. Stevenson, *Reggae and Hip Hop in Southern Italy*, Pop Music, Culture and Identity,
https://doi.org/10.1007/978-3-319-96505-5_2

Christine Ho and Keith Nurse assert that "Caribbean popular culture is a counter-culture or counter-narrative that challenges hegemonic structures and ideologies, deploying aesthetic forms to contest inequality, social injustice and cultural deprivation" (2005, p. xiii). All Caribbean forms of music share a history of colonialism, slavery, class conflict, and twentieth-century US imperialism. Consequently, they have evolved through a complex process of creolization, which has combined African and European traditions, and have incorporated "elements of cultural resistance as well as dominant ideology" and "local traditions as well as those borrowed from international styles" (Manuel et al. 1995, p. 2). Modern Jamaican popular music, in particular, was heavily influenced by American black music, such as jazz and R&B, to the extent that American black music "has remained a common touchstone for generations of Jamaican musicians and audiences" (Marshall and Radano 2013, p. 737). Indeed, as Marshall and Radano point out, "the seductive projections of black pride and power via American soul and funk, later picked up by hip-hop, have left an audible mark on reggae" (2013, p. 737). In turn, "reggae's distinctive filtering of American racial ideologies has helped to propagate further and reinvent those ideologies" (Marshall and Radano 2013, p. 737). Even before its international dissemination, therefore, the music of Jamaica was the product of cultural transplantation, exchange, and hybridization. This multifaceted process of cultural synthesis, which underlies the foundation of reggae and facilitates its international recontextualization, is one of transculturation, a process whereby cultural forms literally move through time and space and interact with other cultural forms and settings to produce new forms (Lull 2000, p. 242).

The processes of transculturation that gave rise to Jamaican popular music were firmly grounded in the dynamics of colonialism and creative resistance to it. The British plantocracy attempted to eradicate African cultural expressions "through a mixture of legislation, conversion, and coercion" (Veal 2007, p. 26). However, as Simon Jones makes clear, the cultural responses of the slaves to such oppression became "the raw material out of which their resistances were manufactured" (1988, p. 5). The evolution and use of language in the Caribbean also provide another fundamental example of how creolization was forged out of the dialectic of resistance. Because the various West African languages spoken by the slaves were forbidden, they were modified and combined with European idioms to form, over a number of generations, "a comprehensive creole vernacular or patois ... of resistance" (Jones 1988, p. 6).

Alongside its rich and varied African influences, Jamaican popular music incorporated European elements from the very beginning. The high mobility of Jamaicans, who since the nineteenth century have travelled around the Caribbean, South America, and North America, resulted in the further absorption and adaptation of diverse elements of foreign music. Officially considered the first stage in the development of Jamaican popular music, mento was a lively song and dance form performed by troubadours carrying news and social commentary (Chang and Chen 1998, p. 14). Mento blended European social dance music, such as the quadrille, with African-derived stylistic features and imported Trinidadian and Cuban elements.

Due to this vast array of influences, by the 1940s Kingston had become a rich musical melting pot. Each section of the town had its own type of music, from the preaching and drumming of the syncretic religious groups to the bawdy refrains of the mento singers and the music of New Orleans-style street musicians (Stolzoff 2000, p. 37). Furthermore, the presence of American military bases in Jamaica during the Second World War resulted in American R&B becoming the preferred music of lower-class black Jamaicans (Bettini and Tosi 2009, p. 17).

Modern communications technology, the culture industries, and human mobility also facilitated the synthesis of diverse cultural forms. The increasing communal use of radios reinforced the American influence, since the only music transmissions in Jamaica originated in southern American states, such as Florida and Tennessee. Moreover, the flow of American sound equipment and records into Jamaica, and the seasonal migration of Jamaicans to the American South, Cuba, Panama, and Costa Rica, formed a "cultural bridge" which "became a catalyst for the creation of hybrid musical styles" (Stolzoff 2000, p. 38).

The most significant factor in the evolution of a popular Jamaican protest music, which shifted the field of cultural production away from "uptown" (the Eurocentric, wealthy, white and brown, privileged, ruling minority) to "downtown" (the local, poor, black, underprivileged, subaltern majority), was the rise of sound system or dancehall culture. Without sound system culture, the Jamaican recording industry and indigenous forms of Jamaican popular music would not have evolved in the manner in which they did, if at all. Furthermore, the counter-hegemonic cultural politics of reggae are inextricably linked with the autonomous and organic culture of the sound system, and the dissemination of sound system culture in the UK and the US by Jamaican immigrants was a key factor in reggae's spread.

Thus, sound system culture is vital for an understanding of both the counter-hegemonic origins and qualities of reggae culture and its adaptability into multiple, decentred, and underground locations and spaces around the globe. In the 1970s, for example, the Jamaican sound system powerfully resonated within the multiethnic and economically ravaged ghettoes of the Bronx after it was introduced by the Jamaican-born DJ, Clive "Kool Herc" Campbell, becoming a major catalyst for the birth of hip hop. Most importantly for our argument, the experience and emulation of sound system styles and practices were crucial to the evolution of Italian reggae culture.

The sound system emerged in Jamaica in the 1950s as a response to the exodus of Jamaica's trained musicians from Kingston and the increasing unreliability of US radio frequencies (Stolzoff 2000, p. 41). Large mobile discotheques consisting of a turntable connected to a valve amplifier and two or more large speakers, the sound systems filled the musical void and became the basis of a resourceful dancehall scene. The sound systems allowed people who were previously excluded due to their social class to enter the field of dancehall promotion for the first time (Stolzoff 2000, p. 42). They also became "community record players" for those who were unable to afford a private stereo (Chang and Chen 1998, p. 20), making dance entertainment widely available to members of the black lower classes (Stolzoff 2000, pp. 42–43).

Although British rule ended in 1962, the social and political structures of colonialism remained in place. The new ruling class in Jamaica encouraged its citizens, especially the "brown" middle class, to embrace European values and emulate British culture (King 2002, p. 69). However, a prevailing mood of nationalistic pride encouraged in the arts "an increasing openness toward indigenous cultural expressions and stimulated a certain amount of conscious musical experimentation with rural folk forms" (Manuel et al. 1995, p. 157). Hence, Jamaican-produced R&B began to incorporate and blend elements of mento and Afro-Jamaican religious music. Through this process of transculturation, the local R&B sound gradually evolved into something uniquely Jamaican: ska. Ska music came to be characterized by a driving combination of marching drum and bass, with the drum accentuating the second and fourth beats and the guitar emphasizing the second, third, and fourth beats (Chang and Chen 1998, p. 30). This offbeat emphasis was to become a defining feature of Jamaican popular music.

As a vibrant, popular cultural force and a key vehicle of political expression for the black working class, ska was held in contempt by middle class Jamaicans. The state-controlled media sought to suppress it, but, through the popularity of the sound system, ska soon "undermined the domination of white American popular music in the island's 'official' musical culture" and challenged "the cultural hegemony of the colonial bourgeoisie" (Jones 1988, p. 21). Thus, since Jamaican popular music developed through this close relationship between the sound system and its audience, it can be understood as an organic and counter-hegemonic form of cultural production.

THE INTERNATIONALIZATION AND TRANSCULTURATION OF JAMAICAN POPULAR MUSIC

Mediated by the musical subculture of Jamaican and Afro-Caribbean immigrants, Jamaican popular music's intercultural crossover to the UK generated a process of connective marginality between white and black working class youth.[1] In turn, this transcultural alliance led to reggae's broader and more sustained crossover success and ultimately to its appreciation and adoption in Italy. Indeed, Britain's considerable cultural influence on Italy, particularly in relation to the shaping of popular musical tastes, and its relative geographical proximity distinguish it as the most crucial nexus in reggae's route from Jamaica to Italy.

The first instance of Jamaican popular music's internationalization dates back to the 1950s, with the crossover success of Harry Belafonte in the US. However, the first and most significant foreign location where Jamaican music took root was Britain. The first "Jamaican" song to have an international commercial impact was Millie Small's infectious ska recording, "My Boy Lollipop" (Fontana, 1964). Cut in London and exhibiting a diluted and "treble-oriented sound far removed from the vigorous, bass-dominated recordings emanating from Jamaica" (Jones 1988, p. 58), it sold over six million records worldwide. Helping to launch

---

[1] For a discussion of solidarity between black and white working class youth in Britain, see Dawson 2005 and 2007. Dawson defines the influence of Jamaican ska on British punk and the fusion of rock and reggae, known as two-tone music, as "polycultural musical styles and highly politicized messages that appealed to their racially diverse audiences" (2005, p. 8). Dawson also points out that sound systems and the dancehalls became central components of black youth culture during the post-war period and, by the mid-1970s, "sound systems had begun playing the dread rhythms of reggae" (2007, pp. 85–86).

Chris Blackwell's Island Records into mainstream popular music, and laying the foundation for the subsequent crossover success of Bob Marley on the same label, the success of this single was crucial to reggae's international explosion in the 1970s (Jones 1988, p. 58). The success of "My Boy Lollipop" also encouraged pioneering Jamaican musicians to migrate to the British capital, which led to the more rapid expansion of its burgeoning reggae scene (Chang and Chen 1998, p. 35).

The song's popularity also signalled a vital moment in Jamaican popular music's diffusion throughout Europe, with covers of the song appearing in France, Germany, and Italy. In Italy, the song was covered under the title "Tu Sei Pallido" (You Are Pale) by two mainstream artists, Margherita (1964) and Rita Pavone (1965). These Italian interpretations, however, demonstrated a disconnect from the sociocultural specificity of Jamaican music. For example, the record sleeve of the Margherita version erroneously indicated ska's point of origin as being the US and England. This neglect of the peripheral Jamaican sociocultural context of ska reflected the contemporary Anglo-American cultural hegemony over Italian music. It was also indicative of the Italian music industry's conscious detachment of foreign music from its cultural and social context in order to facilitate mass consumption.

As Umberto Fiori explains, the history of foreign musical styles in Italy is one of delays and misunderstandings (1984, p. 262). Lacking the means by which to respond immediately to rapid changes in the composition of the foreign market, in the 1950s artists as varied as Elvis Presley, Pat Boone, and Harry Belafonte were mixed indiscriminately in Italy under the banner of rock (Fiori 1984, p. 262). As was the case with "Tu Sei Pallido," the integration of foreign music in Italy during the 1960s was carried out in the form of Italian language covers of British and American beat and garage rock songs, whereby the use of Italian was predominantly a means to assist consumption. Reflecting these commercial concerns, the Italian record producers did not actively promote the development of homegrown Italian rock, instead preferring to experiment sporadically with it by having groups such as Equipe 84 and The Rokes record musically identical Italian language covers of American or British hits. Consequently, Italian rock music was little more than a disconnected thread of modern tendencies within the field of *musica leggera* (pop music) conceived solely for entertainment (Fiori 1984, pp. 270–71).

This top-down dynamic in Italian popular music, characterized by occasional experimentation with foreign styles, meant that Jamaican music was destined to remain an exotic yet socially and culturally detached curiosity within the conservative commercial market of the time. Consequently, "Tu Sei Pallido" was only followed by sporadic releases in Italy that superficially cited Jamaican music. Of the few other Jamaica-inspired singles of the period, Peppino di Capri's original 1966 ska release, "Operazione Sole" (Operation Sun, Carisch), was the only one which made any attempt to engage with the music's origins. Nevertheless, its lyrics—"Da lontano questo ballo giamaicano / ... Lì la gente lo chiama ska / Qui nessuno lo sa / Prima o poi ci conquisterà" (This Jamaican dance from afar / ... There the people call it ska / Here nobody knows it / Sooner or later it will win us over)—demonstrate that di Capri viewed ska simply as an exotic and novel dance that he could exploit domestically. Indeed, di Capri proposed "Operazione Sole" on the 1966 edition of the *Un disco per l'estate* televised summer song contest, but its failure to make it through to the next phase confirmed that the optimism of the lyrics was misplaced, and his foray into Jamaican sounds remained a one-off.

By contrast, the sociological and cultural circumstances in Britain were markedly different from those in Italy. As Dick Hebdige explains, the establishment of sizeable immigrant communities in Britain's working class areas during the early 1960s meant that a level of contact and rapport had begun to develop between black and white working class youth (1979, p. 52). Simon Jones explains that for many young whites in this period, "Jamaican music's appeal lay precisely in its esoteric qualities" and the appreciation and "'discovering' of what was felt to be an 'underground' form" (1988, pp. 88–89). By the latter half of the decade, there was a white interest in the newly formed "rude boy" subculture of the Afro-Caribbean youth.

The rude boy youth movement had emerged in Jamaica in the mid-1960s during a period of increasing political, social, and economic instability. The political hegemony of the dominant classes came under increasing attack as the Rastafarians[2] asserted their radical black consciousness, and disenfranchised young Jamaicans from the ghetto began to rebel (King 2002, pp. 26–27). The rude boy style exalted the angry, young, tough kids of West Kingston (Potter 1995, p. 38), who were unskilled and did not belong to organized groups, but developed rituals and ideas in line

---

[2] Inspired by the proclamations and activism of Marcus Garvey, the Rastafarians believe that Ras Tafari, who was crowned Emperor Haile Selassie I in Ethiopia in 1930, is "the living incarnation of Negus, the black man's true God" (Gunst 2003, p. 75). Rastafari also proposes repatriation to the Holy Land of Ethiopia for members of the African diaspora.

with, but also distinct from, the Rastafarians (Thomas 2004, p. 73). Nonetheless, by 1968 Rastafari's "emphasis on African roots, black redemption, and social awareness began to displace the rude boy variety of socioeconomic and political critique" (Thomas 2004, p. 77). A new generation of rude boys became influential again in the 1980s following the death of Bob Marley. As Deborah Thomas explains, "where previous reggae music had emphasized social critique and a belief in redemption, early dancehall music reflected a ghetto glorification of sex, guns, and the drug trade" (2004, pp. 80–81).

The term "rude boy" (pronounced "rude *bwoy*") eventually applied to anyone against the system and its numerous oppressions (Jones 1988, p. 80). The rude boy swagger and attitude were adopted by black British youth (Jones 1988, p. 89). In Britain, the term "rude boy" is still associated with street and urban culture. Jamaica's rude boy movement also coincided with a change in Jamaican popular music, as ska evolved into rocksteady, a stylistic phase which lasted for less than three years (from 1966 to 1968). Like all Jamaican popular music, rocksteady was a synthesis of diverse stylistic influences, both Jamaican and American. Despite its much slower tempo, rocksteady, like ska, was played in the offbeat rhythm. However, the marching basslines of ska became deeper and sparser, playing a repeated pattern that syncopated the rhythm. The bass used was now electric and it "'boomed' like a cannon" (King 2002, p. 42), while the jazz-inspired horns of ska took a back seat. From this point onwards, the increasing influence of drum and bass became the defining feature of Jamaican popular music and one of its primary points of foreign appeal. The vocals also gained prominence and song lyrics became increasingly concerned with the social realities of the day (Chang and Chen 1998, p. 40).

As Jamaican music evolved from rocksteady to reggae in 1968, the British skinhead subculture emerged. The skinheads expressed a "'lumpen' identity" by drawing on "the cultures of the West Indian immigrants and the white working class" (S. Jones 1988, p. 55). Although later engaging in systematic racist violence against blacks, for approximately four years (until Rastafarian themes and attitudes came to permeate reggae), the skinheads constituted a white audience "for the faster, more jerky sounds then emerging from the Kingston studios, as well as records produced nearer at hand and (partly) aimed at them" (Barrow and Dalton 2004, p. 385).[3]

---

[3] A seminal example of British reggae's active courting of the white skinhead audience was the band Simaryp, which released the hit album, *Skinhead Moonstomp*, in 1970 on the Trojan label.

It was in 1968 that Toots Hibbert first popularized the term reggae with his song, "Do the Reggay" (Pyramid). In musical terms, reggae was similar to rocksteady; the bassist played a *riddim* (Patois for rhythm) based on a repetitive pattern of notes followed by a brief pause or rest. The continuing emphasis on the offbeat was achieved through the guitar and keyboard, and the drummer performed the traditional timekeeping role whilst improvising with rim shots and cymbal accents. Advancements in recording techniques further enabled the foregrounding of the drum and bass, which became the foundation for the contemporary reggae sound (King 2002, p. 64). Although reggae's tempo was fast during its early phase, it eventually slowed down and was driven by a two-chord pattern (King 2002, p. 64). Another feature which distinguished reggae, and for that matter ska and rocksteady, from other popular music was the strong emphasis on the third beat of the bar, often referred to as the "one drop," as opposed to the first beat, or the "downbeat."[4]

These musical and rhythmic orientations of reggae were far removed from those of mainstream British pop culture, and their appeal lay in their danceable rhythms. Together with its exotic rhythmic appeal, reggae's "rough-and-ready qualities suited the aggressively proletarian sensibilities of skinhead style and culture" (Jones 1988, p. 90). Thus, the idiosyncratic and raw musical form of early reggae was as important as its black sociocultural origins in the formation of a syncretic and oppositional white working class youth culture.

Indeed, throughout many sections of the music industry there were deep prejudices towards Jamaican music during the late 1960s and early 1970s, and for middle class rock fans reggae was simply uneducated "'yobbo' music" (Jones 1988, p. 61). The mutual contempt in which rock and reggae fans held one another "symbolised the class divisions and the uneven appropriations of black music within white youth-culture during this period" (Jones 1988, p. 90). Since progressive rock wanted to distinguish itself from pop and "black" music, most rock fans considered reggae to be an exemplar of bad taste, while for the skinheads, "reggae was everything that progressive rock was not, rhythmic, spontaneous, unpretentious, supposedly 'crude' and unmistakably working-class in origin" (Jones 1988, 90).

Whilst in Britain reggae was establishing these sociological connective marginalities, in Italy this was far from the case. Raffaella Carrá, who was

---

[4] If you count the beats in half-time, the emphasis of the drums falls on beats 2 and 4.

one of the leading symbols of the mainstream culture industry, performed Italy's first musical citation of reggae in 1970, rendering explicit the socio-cultural contrasts between Britain and Italy. Carrá's "Reggae Rrrrr!" (RCA Italiana) was a cover of an obscure funky reggae single by a South African group named Zorro Five. The original, named "Reggae Shhh!" (Decca 1970), had been an underground hit on the mod/skinhead scene in London. While the manner in which this marginal song made its way into Italy's cultural mainstream is not widely known, this example of cultural transferal was further evidence of Italy's dependency on Britain for the introduction of new musical styles.

As well as releasing "Reggae Rrrrr!" as a single on the US-owned RCA label, Carrá performed the song on Rai's television variety programme, *Canzonissima*. Whereas Peppino di Capri's "Operazione Sole" had some-what reductively introduced ska to Italian audiences as a dance from Jamaica, during the programme Carrá introduced reggae as a popular dance fad from the discos of the US and London (see amicoamante255 on YouTube). The link to dance was further reinforced by the lyrics of Carrá's version—"You lose weight with reggae / You grow a metre with reggae / You feel more beautiful with reggae"—and the humorous "reggae dance" that accompanied her television performance. "Reggae Rrrrr!" also hints more widely at the sharp differences between Italy and Britain in terms of the social and political aspects of youth music consumption. Whereas in London reggae had already been adopted within counter-hegemonic youth subcultures, Italy's first reggae song was the product of the cultural mainstream.

In the early to mid-1970s, Trojan Records (Island Records' reggae co-label) helped to develop an autonomous "roots market" within Britain's black communities (Jones 1988, p. 38). By 1972, reggae music became more openly committed to issues of black identity and Rastafari, and its slower, heavier, and more hypnotic rhythms, coupled with its increased use of Jamaican Patois, reflected this increasing Afrocentrism. Reggae's militant focus on issues of black identity, along with wider social and economic issues affecting the working class, clashed with the increas-ingly nationalistic skinhead subculture (Letts 2016; Hebdige 1979, pp. 58–59).[5]

---

[5] For an excellent account of the often-contradictory politics and aesthetics of the skinhead subculture, see Don Letts' documentary, *The Story of Skinhead with Don Letts*.

By this time, reggae had been firmly established in the British market and was well on its way to becoming an international force. Two developments in 1972, both of which were heavily mediated by the recording industry, further accelerated this process. *The Harder They Come* (1972), Perry Henzell's internationally distributed film starring singer Jimmy Cliff, provided a fresh and accurate representation of the harsh realities of Jamaica's corrupt recording industry and of the country's prevailing social conditions. More importantly, the film's soundtrack (released in the UK on Island Records) became one of the highest selling international reggae albums of all time. Both the film and its soundtrack helped to turn white middle class kids on to reggae (Barrow and Dalton 2004, p. 88).

Furthermore, towards the end of 1973, Island Records released the first reggae record made with a rock audience specifically in mind: Bob Marley and the Wailers' first internationally successful album, *Catch a Fire*.[6] Island's owner, Chris Blackwell, actively courted the rock press in his attempt to market reggae as the next big thing, and he added rock elements through overdubs and a novelty sleeve. In the charismatic, rebellious, and dreadlocked Marley, who had a white English father, Blackwell discerned a highly marketable persona with crossover appeal (Chang and Chen 1998, p. 52). In his own words, Blackwell marketed Marley and reggae internationally to "'white, liberal college oriented-type people who were interested in it because of its sociological aspects as well as its rhythm'" (in Connell and Gibson 2004, p. 346). Although Marley was to make some stylistic compromises, his songs maintained a political militancy and a counter-cultural quality which appealed deeply to young whites (King 2002, p. 94). Consequently, Island Records' campaign with Bob Marley rendered a radical yet musically cosmopolitan form of Jamaican music fit for mass white consumption.

Defying conventional wisdom, Blackwell and his imitators, such as Richard Branson (Virgin), successfully marketed reggae by "celebrating the ganja-smoking Rastafarian as a universal symbol of rebellion and protest" (King 2002, p. 96). The image of the rebellious and revolutionary reggae artist that was marketed to the rest of the world led to reggae's international adoption as protest music. Hence, although radically political music was traditionally considered less commercially viable, Anglo-American record companies successfully sold reggae to white

---

[6] At this time, the group included Peter Tosh and Bunny Wailer and was known simply as "the Wailers."

28 S. SCARPARO AND M. S. STEVENSON

American college students and European youths as a new "rebel music." Despite being marked by a more sophisticated and polished studio sound, the radical messages of reggae remained undiluted. Song lyrics continued to critique Jamaica's social and economic conditions, such as unemployment, inadequate housing, and political violence, whilst reflecting an awareness of international issues (King 2002, pp. 90–91).[7]

Moreover, despite the fact that commercial forces were behind its internationalization, reggae continued to be a product of the dialectic between artists and audience, sound system and crowd that originated in Jamaica (Jones 1988, p. 31). Indeed, sound system reggae was transported to the UK by the wave of Jamaican migrants in the 1960s and 1970s, and so, by the time reggae reached other European countries such as Italy, its form and content remained fundamentally the same. Furthermore, Daniel Fischlin explains that while virtually every popular musical form associated with rebellion has been commodified, musicians continue to resist conformity and commercialization by transmitting "the sounds and ideas that produce resistance, critique, and a differential relation to hegemony" (2003, p. 14). As George Lipsitz maintains, "the circuits and flows of commerce created in the wake of flexible capital accumulation create new circuits and flows for culture and politics as well" (1994, p. 6). Such transnational commercial flows facilitated the diffusion of the radical political, social, and spiritual message of reggae, and, mediated by the British context, both international reggae and sound system reggae were eventually to tap into the collective and oppositional sensibilities of a specific Italian youth demographic.

REGGAE AND THE MUSIC POLITICS OF BRITISH YOUTH DURING THE 1970s

Discussing the different British and Italian cultural contexts in relation to the centrality of autonomous politics to Italy's youth culture, Robert Lumley argues that "[w]hile in Britain youth protest was primarily expressed through music, dress and a reworking of youth subcultural

---

[7]As already mentioned, the fact that reggae became a highly mobile international commodity invested it with a broader and deeper level of political impact, since its oppositional attitudes and messages were to resonate with a variety of marginalized groups around the world. In Australia, for example, Bob Marley's 1979 visit helped to launch a "Black Power" movement amongst its indigenous activists (Lipsitz 1994, p. 13).

THE ROOTS AND ROUTES OF REGGAE FROM JAMAICA TO ITALY 29

forms …, in Italy a youth subculture had to be invented out of the raw materials of a political subculture (versions of 'autonomy'), with imported elements added" (1991, pp. 305–06). Thus, in the Italian context, "cultural spaces and activities were quickly consumed or converted under the pressures of political action," and "'alternative' practices were invariably 'oppositional' and politicized" (Lumley 1991, p. 306). Consequently, during the 1970s, Italy's intense and often volatile political landscape directly influenced the nature of musical production and consumption, and despite its growing international popularity and its protest quality, reggae music remained at the margins of Italy's youth counter-culture until the late 1970s.

The Italian counter-culture remained suspicious of reggae's loose association with the discos and its relationship with the international rock industry (Bettini and Tosi 2009, p. 229). Consequently, the international popularity of a number of reggae covers by renowned artists like Johnny Nash ("Stir It Up," CBS, 1972), Eric Clapton ("I Shot the Sheriff," RSO, 1974), and The Rolling Stones ("Cherry Oh Baby," Rolling Stones Records, 1976) did not lead to reggae making a significant impact in Italy during the early 1970s. Only the occasional Bob Marley song, in particular "No Woman No Cry" (Island, 1974), which was covered by the German disco group Boney M, was able to make any inroads (Bettini and Tosi 2009, pp. 229–30). However, despite initially creating a barrier to reggae's acceptance, the unique dialectic between music and politics that developed in Italy during this period, discussed below, would later influence the manner in which reggae was received, disseminated, and reproduced in this country.

Unlike in other European countries, student protests in Italy went on for long after 1968, joining forces with workers' demonstrations in 1969 and forming the basis of a vast anti-fascist movement (see Lumley 1991; Ginsborg 1990; Katsiaficas 1997). The revolutionary Marxist *movimento* (student movement), which lasted throughout the 1970s and climaxed in 1977, was accompanied by a new assertion of "youth identity" based on "exclusion, marginality, and deviance" (Lumley 1991, p. 296) and was based on new ideas about the political potential of popular culture and modes of cultural consumption. Alienated both from institutional politics and the structures of labour, a prominent desire of the youth movement was to *stare insieme* (be together) and enjoy oneself (Ginsborg 1990, pp. 381–82). In turn, this new attitude was to influence directly the dynamic between leisure, consumption, politics, and culture. Widespread unemployment was a contributing factor in this politicization of free time and the renewal and expansion of the entertainment sector (Grispigni 1996, p. 50).

The production of alternative forms of information, or counter-information, was a defining characteristic of the *movimento*, and the influential magazines *Erba Voglio* and *Re Nudo* were central in this regard. The collective behind *Re Nudo* dealt directly with the realm of music, popularizing "the struggle to reappropriate free time" through the process of *autoriduzione* (the collectively enforced reduction of ticket prices or the forcible claiming of free entry) and the creation of free, self-managed events and spaces, such as festivals and counter-cultural centres (Lumley 1991, pp. 297–98). Often taking their cue from feminism, "the counter-culturalists directed their fire at the moralism which underpinned the left-wing militants' sacrifice of the 'private' in the name of the 'public' sphere" (Lumley 1991, p. 298). The pages of *Re Nudo* repeatedly reinforced the political importance of free time and the politics of the personal: "Let's ensure that free time becomes freed time!"; "The revolution has begun. The revolution is the new way of living"; "the revolution is a daily process, … every choice of ours must be the product of a revolutionary choice" (Valcarenghi 2007, pp. 113, 107, 135).

Re Nudo provided the most significant and groundbreaking example of an attempt to establish a revolutionary Italian youth counter-culture through the synthesis of foreign models, specifically those from the American counter-culture, with the local politics of the non-institutional Left. *Re Nudo* summed up the aims of this project in the following manner: "may the Mao of Western Marxism grow the long hair of alternative culture" (Valcarenghi 2007, p. 134). The Italian counter-culture thus involved the politicized transculturation of foreign cultural forms, particularly rock music. Fiori explains this process in the following manner:

> The large majority of young people took the symbols and models, often indirectly, and vested them with extra meaning, translating them in terms of their own culture and their own experience. In the same way that converted pagan peoples fit the Christian religion to their existing local cults …, young Italians … both gave in to and yet resisted the process of culturalization by English and American rock …. Towards the end of the 1960s and for all of the 1970s, this process of assimilation and rejection was slowly centering … around a marxist [sic] view of class culture. (1984, p. 264)

The attempts to integrate foreign rock as a politically and culturally relevant force were evident in various declarations from *Re Nudo*, such as "Proletarian youth of Europe, ... Jimi Hendrix unites us, youth culture unites us," and "rock doesn't really need translation: its liberating violence is a type of musical Esperanto!" (Valcarenghi 2007, pp. 121–23). The political hegemonization of rock music by the counter-cultural Left formed part of a more widespread "cultural revolution" aiming to facilitate social and political change through a transformation of society's values and lifestyles.

It must be noted that the question of the relationship between music and politics had already been a focus of an influential folk revival movement in the 1960s. Franco Fabbri explains that this movement "was ideologically driven to discover struggle songs and battle hymns from the anti-fascist resistance and to find links between such songs and previous work songs" (2007, p. 412). Founded in 1964, the music magazine *Il Nuovo Canzoniere Italiano* was the driving force of the folk revival, also giving rise to the Istituto De Martino. These two groups were active in the collection and study of radical and popular songs but also in the composition and production of new ones, which "became a powerful means of communication and political propaganda" (Di Paola 2010, p. 113).

Hence, the student movements of the early 1970s inherited a large repertory of songs and provided new ones of their own, which were sung during demonstrations, before or after political rallies, in small concerts organized in schools, and during strikes (Fabbri 2007, p. 412). Paolo Pietrangeli, Giovanna Marini, and Ivan Della Mea were leading protagonists in this merging of the politicized folk tradition with the student movement, which gave rise to the so-called *nuova canzone politica* (new political song).[8]

A vital aspect of the counter-culture's politicization of popular music and of the personal realm of leisure was the numerous free open-air concerts between 1970 and 1976, which were inspired by the myth of

---

[8] For example, Ivan Della Mea sang at the university occupations of 1968 (see Valcarenghi 2007, p. 53), and Pietrangeli's explicitly anti-establishment "Contessa" (Countess, I Dischi del Sole, 1968) became the anthem of the movement of 1968. Moreover, Pietrangeli's "Valle Giulia" (I Dischi del Sole, 1968) provided a defiant first person counter-narrative of the so-called *Battaglia di Valle Giulia* (Battle of Valle Giulia), which was to be the first in a long line of violent clashes between students and police. A highly influential singer-songwriter in her own right, Marini provided backing vocals for both "Contessa" and "Valle Giulia."

Woodstock.[9] These music festivals involved considerable eating, drinking, dancing, and the consumption of marijuana and LSD "around the themes of work-refusal, a shorter working week, and demands for the immediate gratification of a series of 'needs' irrespective of work done" (Lumley 1991, pp. 300–01). The most significant of these music festivals were organized by *Re Nudo* in Milan's hinterland. *Re Nudo* linked the creative political aims of the festivals to those of the wider protest movement: "Like the house occupations, like the barricades of '68 ..., in its creative violence, the free pop festival is revolution. So let's finish separating the political moment from the existential moment, since both are revolutionary if they are experienced with creativity" (Guarnaccia 2010, p. 67). As Fiori explains, "there was a programmed exploration of all possible ways of making music," and, through the political debate which accompanied these festivals, "the marginalized, the dispersed and the sub-proletariat were brought back into active political life" (1984, pp. 265–66). Considering the profound cultural conservatism of Italy at the time, the festivals were truly subversive and were often met with moral panics and repressive measures from authorities (see Guarnaccia 2010, p. 75).

As a reflection of their revolutionary Marxist ideals, from 1973 these rock rallies assumed the title *Feste del proletariato* (Festivals of the proletariat). Held at Milan's Parco Lambro, the ambitious slogan of the first of these festivals was "Let's change life before life changes us" (*Cambiamo la vita prima che la vita cambi noi*) (Guarnaccia 2010, p. 81). However, the free-love and hedonistic optimism of these festivals, and their shift towards a more open understanding of the relationship between entertainment, culture, and politics, was counter-balanced by ideologically driven conflict and violent disturbances from militant groups. One of the most characteristic examples of the relationship between rock and politics in Italy was the *autoriduzione* of concert prices within the "free music" movement (Fiori 1984, p. 266). The idealistic ideology of this movement was that the liberating and revolutionary qualities of rock rendered it (by definition) an "anti-commodity," as well as a primary need. Using slogans like "Let's reclaim music" (*Riprendiamoci la musica*), the militant magazine, *Stampa Alternativa*, fought constantly against tour managers, record companies,

---

[9]As Fabbri explains, due to its "universal" and "tribal" nature, Woodstock "seemed to be one of the most comprehensively political images to be expressed in the sphere of rock, and yet it was at the same time sufficiently general to allow an easy remodelling in the Italian situation" (2007, p. 265).

THE ROOTS AND ROUTES OF REGGAE FROM JAMAICA TO ITALY   33

and superstars, offering its support to youth that attacked concert venues as a means to obtain *musica gratis* (music for free).

Such ideological understandings of music were also reflected in questions of musical taste. As Fiori stresses, the "search for the 'right' music was the collective problem of a whole movement" (1984, p. 68). The music on show during the festivals was varied and experimental: the Jimi Hendrix-inspired psychedelic rock of Garybaldi, the avant-garde and progressive rock of groups like Stormy Six and Area, the folk of Canzoniere del Lazio and the folk-rock of singer-songwriters such as Eugenio Finardi, and the international jazz of Don Cherry. Hence, whereas in Britain progressive rock was originally associated with a select middle class student public, in Italy it was embraced by an audience composed of different classes and cultural levels. Political and social ideals increasingly determined musical choice, and the moment of consumption was "decisive in the attribution of political significance to a given musical product" (Fiori 1984, p. 269). The recovering of popular and local/national forms, within the *nuova canzone politica* and the folk revival movement, inspired Italian rock to consciously abandon the more overtly American sounds. Instead, there was a search for the "sources of a national music," and groups such as Area, Canzoniere del Lazio, and Stormy Six substituted the melodic and rhythmic patterns of Mediterranean folk music for the blues influences in rock (Fiori 1984, p. 273).

As stated by Fabbri, the political movement impacted on the music business by encouraging singer-songwriters and bands to include more political songs in their repertory, offering a new circuit formed by a few alternative festivals and contrasting with the established music business directly (Fabbri 2007, p. 412). A significant product of this politicization of Italian music was the new progressive trend inside the field of *musica leggera* represented by the singer-songwriters known as the *nuovi cantautori*, such as Francesco Guccini, Edoardo Bennato, and Francesco De Gregori. Fiori emphasizes that the trend of the *cantautori* was able to reach a degree of political and cultural legitimization, together with commercial success, that rock had been unable to obtain (1984, p. 274). Thus, the recording companies were able to offer on the Italian market a musically conservative product that was "full of literary ambition, was vaguely political and musically not unlike certain kinds of folk-rock" (Fiori 1984, p. 274). The word-centred Italian *cantautori* (singer-songwriters) of the 1970s assumed a position of primacy in the vocalization of the movement's political themes and thus fought off the competition from foreign music (Fiori 1984, p. 275). Nevertheless, its use of simple guitar accompaniment lacked concern for producing something which was also enjoyable from a musical perspective (Liperi 1996, p. 191).

While in the US and Britain, where there was a large and oppressed black social component, the adoption of the languages and the aesthetics of Afro-American or Afro-Caribbean music was inherently oppositional, in Italy these types of music formed an integral part of a foreign culture seemingly imposed "from above" and seen to suppress local traditions (Fiori 1984, pp. 273–76). Consequently, rather than signifying political opposition, the choice of a "black" musical form could appear to be "a symptom of a colonised mentality" (Fiori 1984, p. 276). This culturally embedded perspective of black musical forms and influences initially created a barrier to the understanding and appreciation of reggae's protest elements and anti-colonial politics. Furthermore, reggae's status as "dance music" was in apparent contrast with the "cerebral" formalistic experimentations of Italian progressive rock groups and the "logocentric" *cantautori*.

In the UK, reggae music, culture, and style were now deeply embedded in the black British experience and had begun dealing directly with problems of race and class. British reggae culture, which grew around the sound systems, disseminated the cult of Rastafari and transformed it into a "style." This style "proclaimed unequivocally the alienation ... built into the lives of young working-class West Indians in the form of bad housing, unemployment and police harassment" (Hebdige 1979, p. 36). Stylistically, reggae had developed in two different directions: international reggae and dancehall/sound system reggae. Since reggae music, particularly the heavier and more "rootsy" varieties, was virtually exiled from the airwaves, the sound systems became the cultural voice of the black working class and a symbolic communal space that reinvented black identity (Hebdige 1979, pp. 38–39). Reflecting their militant cultural autonomy, the British sound systems disseminated reggae's heavier, rawer, and less diluted variations: heavy roots, dub, and deejay style.

Dub reggae and deejay style are overlapping reggae subgenres which evolved through technical innovations in Jamaica during the late 1960s and the early 1970s. Dub is the remixed version of a record with the vocals either entirely or partly removed. On the remaining rhythm track, the bass and drums are brought to the foreground, and the other instruments are fragmented and distorted through sound effects and other mixing

THE ROOTS AND ROUTES OF REGGAE FROM JAMAICA TO ITALY   35

techniques. According to Simon Jones, "[i]t is in the non-verbal qualities of dub that reggae's non-European heritage is most apparent, for its aesthetics run counter to nearly every canon of Western, popular musical taste" (1988, p. 25). Furthermore, Michael Veal maintains that dub's "low-fidelity, densely textured aesthetic, and self-consciously crude production values" deliberately create a distance from the corporate music culture and "dramatize a subcultural distance from what was thought to be 'mainstream society'" (2007, p. 258). Hence, similarly to the avant-garde strands of the 1970s Italian progressive rock, dub adopted a self-conscious and experimental approach to form that came to symbolize a rejection of hegemonic culture and, fittingly, was later adapted by specific Italian groups as a form of cultural opposition and non-conformism (see Chap. 3).

The fragmentation and superimposition of vocals inherent in dub were at least partially inspired by the performance style of the sound system deejays and selectors. In the late 1960s and early 1970s, Jamaican deejays, such as Count Machuki and King Stitt, began using their vocals to introduce a song or to energize it during slow patches.[10] This new vocal technique, called "toasting," was a method of improvising with words as well as vocal tone and timbres (Bettini and Tosi 2009, p. 22) and was a precursor to American rap. Through a new generation of deejays, such as U-Roy and Big Youth, from the second half of the 1970s, toasting was to become a more popular vocal style than singing. The musical phenomenon of the deejay is "historically rooted" in African oral traditions (Jones 1988, p. 29), and it was marked by the exaltation of Patois as the most direct and authentic form of verbal communication. As discussed in later chapters, the deejay's art of toasting was also to become a preferred vehicle for communication by groups and artists who chose to express themselves in southern Italian dialects and languages.

For black working class youth in Britain, the heavier and more "authentic" forms of reggae, such as dub, deejay style, and heavy roots, formed part of a politically significant identity based on a self-conscious sense of racial and cultural difference. Another crucial component of this counter-hegemonic cultural identity was the use of Patois alongside the adoption of the Rastafarian metaphors, discourses, and symbols of reggae. In particular, the concept of "Babylon" offered black youth a symbol

---

[10] In the reggae tradition, the MC is referred to as a "deejay" and the DJ as a "selector/operator."

through which they made sense of the dynamics of race and class that caused their subordination (Jones 1988, p. 47).[11]

By 1976, reggae was in the midst of establishing its newest, most influential, and most politically significant connective marginality to date. During a summer marked by economic gloom and racially motivated violence at the Notting Hill Carnival, the heterogeneous youth musical style of punk was being generated. This new punk culture was inherently hybrid, incorporating an "awkward and unsteady confluence of the two radically dissimilar languages of *reggae* and *rock*" (Hebdige 1979, p. 27). By 1977, those at the vanguard of the punk aesthetic were expressing a preference for the black styles of roots reggae, deejay style, and dub reggae over new wave.

A crucial figure in this new interracial connective marginality was Don Letts, a young first-generation Jamaican-Brit who gave the punks their first taste of Jamaican music by spinning heavy dub and reggae at the legendary club, The Roxy. He also gave compilation tapes to The Clash, the Sex Pistols, and Patti Smith. The affinity between punk and reggae stemmed from a mutual sense of self-conscious distance and difference from the cultural mainstream and from commonly held anti-establishment views. There were similarities between the apocalyptic discourses of punk and reggae, and, consequently, reggae gave punks a "tangible form to their alienation" and an increased "political bite" (Hebdige 1979, p. 63).

Furthermore, the uncompromising "blackness" of reggae was implicitly subversive and resonated with punk's anarchic values (Hebdige 1979, p. 64). The punks drew a connection between their marginalization and discrimination, as a result of their appearance and beliefs, and the marginalization and discrimination of the dreadlocked and subversive Rastafarians (Jones 1988, pp. 95–96). For Ashley Dawson, "the Clash's debt to reggae dub music and to the insurrectionary Rastafarian ideology is the clearest instance of such hybridization" (2005, p. 7). Similarly, *Cut* (Island Records, 1979), the first album released by pioneering all-women punk

---

[11] In Rastafarian discourse and symbolism, Babylon has an array of connotations and nuances. Adopted from the Christian scriptures, Babylon constitutes a "symbolic delegitimation of those Western values and institutions that historically have exercised control over the masses of the African diaspora" (Edmonds 1998, p. 24). In a global context, "Babylon is that worldly state of affairs in which the struggle for power and possessions takes precedence over the cultivation of human freedom and the concern for human dignity" (Edmonds 1998, pp. 24–25). For a portrayal of the sociocultural importance of dub and sound system culture in Britain, see Franco Rosso's film *Babylon* (1980).

THE ROOTS AND ROUTES OF REGGAE FROM JAMAICA TO ITALY   37

band The Slits, was heavily influenced by dub music. In turn, as Dawson points out, reggae bands such as Birmingham's Steel Pulse were influenced by punk: "performing next to punk bands like The Stranglers, their voices got angrier, guitars choppier, bass heavier, and drums rockier" (2005, p. 7).

Jones points out that the punk movement also emerged as "a reaction against rock's increasing technological sophistication, the gigantism of its live concerts and widening gap between audience and artists," and the punks understood reggae to have political and participatory aspects that were lacking in contemporary pop and rock (Jones 1988, p. 95). Moreover, the aims of punk to "expose the oppressive nature and boredom of everyday life under capitalism resonated with reggae's antipathy to commodity forms, its emphasis on 'roots' and its documentation of topical issues and current events" (Jones 1988, p. 97). Analogously to the way that the Italian youth counter-culture sought to undertake a political reclamation of free time, reggae refused to distinguish between "leisure" and "politics," and this directly influenced punk's criticism of consumerism in relation to leisure.

The synthesis between reggae and punk during the late 1970s also extended to the fields of musical production and distribution. The Clash recorded their own versions of popular roots songs, like Junior Murvin's "Police and Thieves" (Island Records, 1977) and Willie Williams' "Armagideon Time" (Studio One, 1978), and some punk groups emulated the Jamaican practice of putting dubbed versions of their songs on the B-sides of their singles. Furthermore, the influence of reggae culture was evident in punk's do-it-yourself (DIY) approach to music making, its directness of expression, and its attempts to close the gap between artists and audience. There was also a striking parallel between reggae's model of production and distribution and the emergence of an autonomous network of independent punk labels, punk zines, distributors, show promoters, and record stores (O'Connor 2008, pp. 2–4). In summary, it is widely acknowledged that reggae had as much influence on British musicians in the 1970s as the blues had had on them in the 1960s (Curtis 1987, p. 313).

Britain's punk-reggae connection provided an interesting counterpoint to the conscious politicization of music in Italy during the 1960s and 1970s. As James M. Curtis points out, British disenfranchised youth felt a strong affinity with reggae because they viewed it as a musical expression that belonged to oppressed people (1987, p. 313). The most significant

38 S. SCARPARO AND M. S. STEVENSON

manifestation of this was the formation of the Rock Against Racism (RAR) organization in late 1976. RAR was a loose political alliance of musicians, fans, media workers, and anti-racist/fascist activities which drew its strength from the connective marginalities between black and white youth stemming from Bob Marley's crossover success and from the rise of punk. RAR was a grassroots movement, which remained autonomous from the mainstream music industry, and it pioneered new links between politics and music. The group was formed in response to the growing popularity of racism that was engulfing British mainstream popular culture in the mid-1970s (Dawson 2005, p. 5). Through the "Militant Entertainment Tour," which featured 43 bands and included 23 concerts across the UK (Goodyer 2009, p. 11), RAR successfully used the appeal of music to convey its anti-racist political message to large audiences while also giving rise to the multiracial 2 Tone music movement of the late 1970s/early 1980s. In so doing, it foregrounded the use of music as a commodity that could also be a catalyst for combining entertainment with politics and political education. This view of popular music subsequently formed a distinguishing feature of Italian reggae.

REGGAE MAKES ITS MARK IN ITALY

In Italy, 1977 proved to be the climax of the autonomous youth movement, as tens of thousands of young people took to the streets of Rome and Bologna to protest against university reform. These demonstrations resulted in a repressive police response and the death of an unarmed activist in Bologna. The practice of *autoriduzione* also reached its extreme conclusion in 1977, with the launching of Molotov cocktails onto the stage by *autoriduttori* during a Santana concert in Milan, an incident which led to a moratorium on concerts by foreign artists that lasted until 1979.

Sometime between 1977 and 1978, at the culmination of the youth protest movement, reggae finally began to enter into a period of greater recognition in Italy (see Bettini and Tosi 2009, p. 230; Pizzutilo in Epifani 2011). Somewhat paradoxically, the enforced hiatus in live music mentioned above facilitated an increased awareness of reggae in Italy, since it encouraged many young Italians to travel to London and Paris, where they were exposed to a different musical culture. The decision to go to London was particularly significant for the spread of reggae, with the discovery of new musical styles and the Bob Marley explosion. Also crucial was the signing of the militant ex-Wailer Peter Tosh to the Rolling Stones record label. Tosh's first album on the Rolling Stones record label was *Bush Doctor* (1978), and it contained the rock-reggae collaboration with Mick Jagger: "(You Gotta Walk) Don't Look Back." The song was a minor hit in Britain and it gave Tosh great international media exposure. This included a performance with Jagger on the NBC's popular live comedy and variety show, *Saturday Night Live* (see midnightraverblog.com), which was transmitted to Italian television audiences on the popular Sunday afternoon programme, *L'altra Domenica*.

In the following year, Tosh played a concert at Bologna's Palasport stadium to promote his second album on the Stones' label, *Mystic Man* (1979). The *Mystic Man* album contained the subversive and ironically disco-inflected "Buk-In-Hamm Palace," which contained the lyrics: "Light your spliff, Light your chalice / Mek we smoke it ina Buk In Hamm Palace … / Don't you let disco get you down / Give a listenin' to reggae sound." However, despite the anti-disco nuances of the lyrics, the up-tempo danceability of the track rendered it popular in Italy's clubs. "Buk-In-Hamm Palace" thus provides another example of how the commodification of reggae facilitated the transmission of counter-hegemonic messages in new and unintended ways.

The most politically significant Italian citation of reggae also emerged in 1978, when Rino Gaetano, the *cantautore* of Calabrian origin famous for his satirical and ironical songs, released the album and eponymous single "Nuntereggae Più" (IT, 1978). Gaetano's idiosyncratic body of work was at odds with the commercial mainstream, and his eclectic approach marked a break with the approach of the other politically engaged singer-songwriters of the time. The title plays on the assonance between "reggae" and *reggo* in evoking the expression *non ti reggo più* (I can't bear you any longer). Although the song's rhythm was an even looser adaptation of reggae than Raffaella Carrà's "Reggae Rrrr!," its lyrical critique of Italy's hegemony (a bloc of political, economic, and media figures) rendered it a far more relevant landmark in the ensuing development of Italian reggae's protest aesthetic.

In 1979, the black British reggae band, Misty in Roots, which had played together with the punk band, The Ruts, in London at the Rock Against Racism concerts, toured Italy. These tours were accompanied by an increasing awareness that reggae and punk were allied forms of protest music in Britain, a fact reinforced through first-hand contact by Italians who travelled to Britain and there came into contact with the British reggae scenes in areas such as Notting Hill and Brixton. Furthermore, the

40 S. SCARPARO AND M. S. STEVENSON

previously mentioned Jamaican cult film, *The Harder They Come*, began to circulate in a number of Italian theatres (Bettini and Tosi 2009, p. 230). The Italian record company Dischi Ricordi had recently licensed the Island Records catalogue, and reggae began to trickle onto underground radio stations and into Italian record stores (Pizzutilo in Manfredi 2008, p. 27). Thus, despite the challenges encountered in acquiring records, a small but dedicated group of Italian reggae enthusiasts, some of whom were also developing an interest in Rastafarian culture, began to emerge (Bettini and Tosi 2009, p. 230). It is within this emerging grassroots context that Italy's first reggae band, the humorously named Puff Bong, was formed in Venice (Bettini and Tosi 2009, p. 231).[12]

Furthermore, in the summer of 1979, the Italian pop singer, Loredana Berté, had a major commercial Italian hit with the reggae-styled song, "E La Luna Bussò" (And the Moon Knocked, CGD, 1979). While its opaque lyrics hinted at metropolitan marginalization, its rhythm represented the most faithful Italian rendition of reggae released at that time. The fact that an established artist like Berté was inspired to record a song with such an idiosyncratic rhythm demonstrated the growing awareness of reggae in Italy as a consequence of the international popularity and exposure of artists such as Bob Marley, Peter Tosh, and Jimmy Cliff. It also spoke to the continued influence of the rock-reggae contaminations emanating from Britain, which, aside from punk, could also be heard in the work of new wave groups, such as The Police.

1980 proved to be a watershed year for reggae in Italy. The first book in Italian dedicated to the topic was published: *Reggae: Origini, storia e protagonisti della musica giamaicana*, by Gianfilippo Pedote and Lele Pinardi. More importantly, however, was the return tour of Peter Tosh, who this time played a total of five concerts throughout Italy, the most in any country by him that year. During the tour, Tosh performed "Mystic Man" on Rai 2's television programme *C'era due volte* (see valeriovda), a song in which he overtly declared his rejection of American fast food and hard drugs. During the entire performance on Italian television, Tosh held a burning "spliff" in his hand, a gesture of anti-institutional defiance. This episode provided another example of how the mass dissemination of reggae through the commercial media industries simultaneously facilitated its visibility *and* its transmission of counter-hegemonic messages.

---

[12] Puff Bong's only official recording is the almost impossible to find 12-inch single "Goin' On/One More" released in 1986 on Mail Records.

THE ROOTS AND ROUTES OF REGGAE FROM JAMAICA TO ITALY   41

Ultimately, as mentioned in the introduction, the growing awareness and popularity of reggae in Italy culminated in Bob Marley's historic performance in Milan, one of the first music concerts in Italy since the end of the abovementioned moratorium. The phenomenal crowd was a testament to the more open musical perspectives that had developed amongst young Italians by the start of the 1980s. Castaldo notes that an eclectic sensibility with "no barriers" had developed, and this meant that reggae could be appreciated by those who also listened to such genres as *canzone d'autore* or rock (in FusoElektronique 2011). The record attendance also demonstrated the significant inroads that reggae and its culture had begun to make in Italy, a fact which was further reinforced by extensive media coverage of the event. However, after the initial excitement caused by Marley's performances in 1980 had died down, the mainstream and commercial interest in reggae diminished considerably (Vito "War" Fiorentino in Bunna et al. 2011, p. 37).

Nonetheless, by the early 1980s, an autonomous and underground network of Italian reggae scenes had begun to emerge from the ashes of Italy's 1970s counter-culture. In 1981, the year of Marley's death, Africa United (later Africa Unite) was formed in the town of Pinerolo, in the south-west of Torino.[13] Taking their name from a famous Bob Marley song, Africa United were eventually to become Italy's most longevous reggae band. Also in 1981, Italy's first Rastafarian community appeared in the Sicilian town of Catania, giving rise to the roots reggae band, Jah Children Family, and later producing Italy's first fanzine dedicated to Rastafarian culture, *The Lion of Lions*, in 1985 (Bettini and Tosi 2009, pp. 231–32).[14] Also, in Milan a Vincentian reggae musician named Papa Winnie teamed up with local Italian musicians to form the pop-reggae band, Irie.[15] However, as we discuss in the following chapter, it was in the Apulian city of Bari, deep in the South of Italy, that the most political, multifaceted, and musically original of these early Italian reggae scenes emerged.

---

[13] For a detailed first-person account of Africa Unite's 30-year history, see Bunna et al., *Trent'anni in levare: Storia della storia di Africa Unite*. See also the exhaustive compilation *Biografica Unite* (Universal Music, 2008).

[14] Information about Jah Children Family is almost non-existent, and there are no existing recordings of their music. However, in 1999, two of the founding members of Catania's original Rastafarian community, Jahro' and Rad Dedo, became members of the Zu' Luciano Band, producing the album *Tutti Muti* (Everyone Silent, Terre Harse, 2000).

[15] While no recording of this early formation exists, as a solo artist, Papa Winnie released numerous studio productions between 1988 and 2003 and made appearances on Italian television.

42 S. SCARPARO AND M. S. STEVENSON

WORKS CITED

Barrow, Steve, and Peter Dalton. 2004. *The Rough Guide to Reggae*. London: Rough Guides. Print.

Bettini, Stefano, and Pier Tosi. 2009. *Paperback reggae: Origini, protagonisti, storia e storie della musica in levare*. Firenze: Editoriale Olimpia. Print.

Bunna, et al. 2011. *Trent'anni in levare: Storia della storia di Africa Unite*. Genova: Chinaski. Print.

Carrà, Raffaella. 1970. REGGAE RRR. https://www.youtube.com/watch?v=xMJB8iuepuQ. Accessed 9 Feb 2018.

Chang, Kevin O.B., and Wayne Chen. 1998. *Reggae Routes: The Story of Jamaican Music*. Philadelphia: Temple University Press. Print.

Connell, John, and Chris Gibson. 2004. World Music: Deterritorializing Place and Identity. *Progress in Human Geography* 28 (3): 342–361. Print.

Curtis, James M. 1987. *Rock Eras: Interpretations of Music and Society, 1954–1984*. Bowling Green Ohio: Bowling Green State University Popular Press. Print.

Dawson, Ashley. 2005. 'Love Music, Hate Racism': The Cultural Politics of the Rock Against Racism Campaigns, 1976–1981. *Postmodern Culture* 16 (1): 1–13. Print.

———. 2007. *Mongrel Nation: Diasporic Culture and the Making of Postcolonial Britain*. Ann Arbor: University Press of Michigan. Print.

Di Paola, Pietro. 2010. Popular Songs, Social Struggles and Conflictual Identities in Mestre-Marghera (1970s–1980s). In *Radical Cultures and Local Identities*, ed. Krista Cowman and Ian Packer, 111–127. Newcastle upon Tyne: Cambridge Scholars. Print.

Edmonds, Ennis. 1998. Dread 'I' In-a-Babylon: Ideological Resistance and Cultural Revitalization. In *Chanting Down Babylon: The Rastafari Reader*, ed. Nathaniel S. Murrell, William D. Spencer, and Adrian A. McFarlane, 23–35. Philadelphia: Temple University Press. Print.

Epifani, Mattia, dir. 2011. Rockman. Goodfellas. DVD.

Fabbri, Franco. 2007. Orchestral Manoeuvres in the 1970s: L'Orchestra Co-operative, 1974–1983. *Popular Music* 26 (3): 409–428. Print.

Fiori, Umberto. 1984. Rock Music and Politics in Italy. *Popular Music* 4: 261–277. Print.

Fischlin, Daniel. 2003. Take One/Rebel Musics: Human Rights, Resistant Sounds, and the Politics of Music Making. In *Rebel Musics: Human Rights, Resistant Sounds, and the Politics of Music Making*, ed. Ajay Heble and Daniel Fischlin, 10–43. Montréal: Black Rose Books. Print.

FusoElektronique. 2011. Stelle. Speciale Bob Marley—Parte 1. Rai. Documentary. *YouTube*, May 15. https://www.youtube.com/watch?v=w_7xgQqPtrw. Accessed 7 July 2011.

Ginsborg, Paul. 1990. *A History of Contemporary Italy: Society and Politics 1943–1980*. London: Penguin. Print.

Goodyer, Ian. 2009. *Crisis Music: The Cultural Politics of Rock Against Racism.* Manchester: Manchester University Press. Print.

Grispigni, Marco. 1996. Combattenti di strada. La nascita delle culture giovanili in Italia. In *Ragazzi senza tempo: Immagini, musica, conflitti delle culture giovanili,* ed. Massimo Canevacci et al., 17–64. Genova: Coast and Nolan. Print.

Guarnaccia, Matteo. 2010. *Re Nudo Pop & altri festival: Il sogno di Woodstock in Italia, 1968–1976.* Milano: Vololibero. Print.

Gunst, Laurie. 2003. *Born Fi' Dead.* Edinburgh: Canongate. Print.

Hebdige, Dick. 1979. *Subculture: The Meaning of Style.* London: Routledge. Print.

Henzell, Perry, dir. 1972. *The Harder They Come.* New World Pictures. Film.

Ho, Christine G.T., and Keith Nurse. 2005. *Globalisation, Diaspora and Caribbean Popular Culture.* Kingston: Ian Randle Publishers. Print.

Jones, Simon. 1988. *Black Culture White Youth: The Reggae Tradition from JA to UK.* London: Macmillan. Print.

Katsiaficas, Georgy. 1997. *The Subversion of Politics: European Autonomous Social Movements and the Decolonization of Everyday Life.* Oakland: AK Press. Print.

King, Stephen A. 2002. *Reggae, Rastafari and the Rhetoric of Social Control.* Jackson: University Press of Mississippi. Print.

Letts, Don, dir. 2016. *The Harder They Come.* BBC. Film.

Liperi, Felice. 1996. L'Italia s'è desta: Tecno-splatter e posse in rivolta. In *Ragazzi senza tempo: Immagini, musica, conflitti delle culture giovanili,* ed. Massimo Canevacci et al., 163–205. Genova: Coast and Nolan. Print.

Lipsitz, George. 1994. *Dangerous Crossroads: Popular Music, Postmodernism, and the Poetics of Place.* London: Verso. Print.

Lull, James. 2000. *Media, Communication, Culture: A Global Approach.* 2nd ed. Cambridge: Polity Press. Print.

Lumley, Robert. 1991. *States of Emergency: Cultures of Revolt in Italy from 1968 to 1978.* London and New York: Verso Books. Print.

Manfredi, Tommaso. 2008. *Dai Caraibi al Salento: Nascita, evoluzione e identità del reggae in Puglia.* Lecce: AGM. Print.

Manuel, Peter, and Wayne Marshall. 2006. The Riddim Method: Aesthetics, Practice, and Ownership in Jamaican Dancehall. *Popular Music* 25 (3): 447–470. Print.

Manuel, Peter, Kenneth Bilby, and Michael Largey. 1995. *Caribbean Currents. Caribbean Music from Rumba to Reggae.* Philadelphia: Temple University Press. Print.

Marshall, Wayne, and Ronald Radano. 2013. Musical Antinomies of Race and Empire. In *The Cambridge History of World Music,* ed. Philip V. Bohlman, 726–743. Cambridge University Press. Print.

O'Connor, Alan. 2008. *Punk Record Labels and the Struggle for Autonomy: The Emergence of DIY.* Lanham, MD: Lexington Books. Print.

Pedote, Gianfilippo, and Lele Pinardi. 1980. *Reggae: Origini, storia e protagonisti della musica giamaicana*. Milano: Gammalibri. Print.

Potter, Russell A. 1995. *Spectacular Vernaculars: Hip Hop and the Politics of Postmodernism*. Albany: State University of New York Press. Print.

Stolzoff, Norman. 2000. *Wake the Town and Tell the People: Dancehall Culture in Jamaica*. London: Duke University Press. Print.

Thomas, Deborah A. 2004. *Modern Blackness: Nationalism, Globalization, and the Politics of Culture in Jamaica*. Durham, NC: Duke University Press. Print.

Valcarenghi, Andrea. 2007. *Underground: A Pugno Chiuso!* Rimini: NdA Press. Print.

valeriovda. 1980. Peter Tosh—Mystic Man @ 'C'era due volte' 1980. https:// youtu.be/llWCjIPkiSM. Accessed 4 Dec 2013.

Veal, Michael E. 2007. *Dub: Soundscapes and Shattered Songs in Jamaican Reggae*. Middletown: Wesleyan University Press. Print.

Discography

Africa Unite. 2008. *Biografica Unite*. Universal Music. 2CD/DVD.

Small, Millie. 1964. My Boy Lollipop. *My Boy Lollipop*. Fontana. EP.

Symarip. 1970. *Skinhead Moonstomp*. Trojan Records. LP.

The Wailers. 1973. *Catch a Fire*. Island Records. LP.

CHAPTER 3

"Inna Different Stylee": The Renaissance of Youth Culture and Politics in Bari

Bari's pioneering reggae scene of the early to mid-1980s provides an emblematic example of how the local synthesis of reggae culture in Italy transcended the strictly musical realm. The scene was established through the Italian roots/dub/world fusion band, Different Stylee, which was formed in 1982.[1] Bari's scene also proved to be a crucial factor in the considerable growth of reggae in the neighbouring Apulian subregion of Salento. Moreover, due to their explicitly political approach, characterized by the adoption of the autonomous cultural practices of *autoproduzione* (self-production) and *autogestione* (self-management), Different Stylee were a forerunner to the so-called posses (to which we will return later) which spread reggae and hip hop throughout the Italian peninsula in the early 1990s.

Andy Bennett and Richard Peterson's definition of the notion of the music scene is useful for our discussion of Bari's reggae scene. According to Bennett and Peterson, the music scene incorporates specific dress and behaviour, through which fans "forge collective expressions of 'underground' or 'alternative' identity" and "identify their cultural distinctiveness from the 'mainstream'" (2004, p. 2). In addition, these music scenes

---

[1] Different Stylee was Enrico Trillò—drums; Antonella Di Domenico—bass, lead vocal; Gianluca Iodice—keyboards, guitar, bass, melodica; Mimmo Pizzutilo—rhythm guitar; Sandro Biallo—keyboards, percussion; Nico Caldarulo—percussion; Michele Tataranni—trumpet; Lello Monaco—trombone; Terry Vallarella—backup vocals.

© The Author(s) 2018   45
S. Scarparo, M. S. Stevenson, *Reggae and Hip Hop in Southern Italy*, Pop Music, Culture and Identity,
https://doi.org/10.1007/978-3-319-96505-5_3

are largely DIY and rely on small collectives, entrepreneurial fans, and volunteers (Bennett and Peterson 2004, p. 5). Bennett and Peterson's distinction between *local* and *translocal* music scenes is also helpful to our discussion of the initial phase of reggae's expansion in Italy. They describe a local scene as

> [a] focused social activity that takes place in a delimited space and over a specific span of time in which clusters of producers, musicians, and fans realize their common musical taste, collectively distinguishing themselves from others by using music and cultural signs often appropriated from other places, but recombined and developed in ways that come to represent the local scene. (2004, p. 8)

In doing the above, emergent local scenes "use music appropriated via global flows and networks to construct particular narratives of the local" (Bennett and Peterson 2004, p. 7). *Translocal scenes*, on the other hand, are "widely scattered local scenes" that "interact with each other through the exchange of recordings, bands, fans, and fanzines" (Bennett and Peterson 2004, pp. 6, 8). We adopt the term "translocal" in order to refer to the interconnected network of local scenes and contexts that emerged *within* Italy from around 1984. We distinguish the term *translocal* from *glocal* and *transnational*, which we interpret as denoting means of articulating connections which transcend national borders.

A conceptualization of the local music scene also requires a specific definition of the term "local." As Bennett explains, there have been primarily two ways in which the term "local" has been applied in relation to popular music. In some instances, it has been interchangeable with "national," as opposed to "international" or "global" aspects of popular music consumption. In other instances, "local" is used as a means of understanding processes of musical production and consumption "in the context of specific urban and rural settings" (2000, p. 52). According to Bennett, although both uses of the term have helped to understand the significance of music in everyday life, their articulation of the local as an "uncontested" and "fixed" space is problematic. Since "different social groups appropriate and mark out social spaces within a particular place," the local becomes "a highly contested territory that is crossed by different forms of collective life" (Bennett 2000, pp. 52–53). The pre-eminence of location is also central to theories of subcultures, which, in their conquering of physical and cultural "space" for the young, "cluster around particular locations" and explore "a set of social rituals which underpin ... collective identity" (Clarke et al. 1993, pp. 45, 47). Thus, by using the term "local scenes," we refer to specific urban (or rural) settings that incorporate both physical and cultural space, are informed by socioculturally unique characteristics, and which articulate specific collective identities.

Equally important to our understanding of Italy's first local reggae scenes is the way in which the forces of globalization influence sociocultural space. The generative interplay between the global and the local creates a dialectic that resonates with Roland Robertson's concept of "glocalization," which explains the process of globalization by which imported social categories and practices assume a local flavour or character in their new setting (1995, pp. 25–44). In this respect, the processes of globalization interact with local structures and traditions to create a "local-global problematic" that in turn produces new networks that generate "a space of flows" (Roudometof 2015, p. 776). Such space restructures local (often urban) contexts but "does not replace the traditional space; rather, by selectively connecting places with each other, it changes the functional logic and social dynamics" (Roudometof 2015, p. 777).

This understanding of the relationship between the global and the local foregrounds the processes of hybridization and synthesis involved in the spread of cultural forms such as reggae and hip hop, which are adapted to privilege the sociocultural issues and priorities of their new cultural environment. James Lull maintains that "[t]he foundations of cultural territory—ways of life, artefacts, symbols, and contexts—are all open to new interpretations and understandings .... Because culture is constructed and mobile, it is also synthetic and multiple" (1995, pp. 160–61). A consideration of the multiple natures of culture and its capacity to create new chains of meaning in various locations is central to our understanding of reggae's rhizomatic transculturation in locations such as Bari, where its symbolism and idioms were recontextualized and reinterpreted within a pre-existing youth subculture of the Left.

This syncretic and global process occurring in Bari led to the creation of a musical (sub)culture which resisted the hegemonic cultural and political forces of the 1980s in both symbolic and tangible ways. Our emphasis on location and symbolic resistance is indebted to subcultural theory, which posited British punks, Rastafarians, and rude boys as collective counter-hegemonic responses to the conditions of class (see Hebdige 1979; Clarke et al. 1993). Bari's scene demonstrates how the symbolic

48   S. SCARPARO AND M. S. STEVENSON

counter-hegemonic aspects of marginal musical cultures (i.e., reggae and punk) are able to generate locally specific meanings and relevance when they venture into new cultural and geographic territories.

Together with the anarcho-punk movement of the 1980s with which it engaged, Bari's reggae scene laid the foundations for the socially and politically conscious "posses" that emerged within the *centri sociali organizzati autogestiti* (organized self-managed social centres or CSOAs) at the beginning of the 1990s. Through its reworking of public spaces, by means of physical occupation, and the dissemination of counter-information, through independent media forms such as free radios and fanzines, Bari's scene produced what Bennett refers to as "new urban narratives" (2000, p. 66). Such narratives enable young people "to view the local in particular ways and apply their own solutions to the specific problems or shortcomings that they identify with their surroundings and the policies and practices that shape these surroundings" (Bennett 2000, pp. 66–67). Hence, Bari's early reggae scene provides an important historical and narrative bridge between the era of youth-led collective action of the late 1970s and the increasingly atomized 1980s, thus providing a key example of reggae's role in renewing and continuing counter-cultural youth politics and resisting the hegemonic *riflusso*.[2]

REGGAE'S ARRIVAL IN BARI AND THE RENEWAL OF YOUTH POLITICS

A key agent in the history of Bari's reggae scene is Mimmo (Superbass) Pizzutilo, who played rhythm guitar in Different Stylee and founded the pioneering fanzine, *Rebel Soul*.[3] Like many of Italian reggae's early

---

[2] Due to its marginal and underground quality, there have been limited studies dedicated to Bari's scene. Nevertheless, two works have shed light upon this fundamental yet obscure context. Published in 2008, Tommaso Manfredi's book, *Dai Caraibi al Salento*, collates interviews and other primary and secondary sources to form a narrative of the evolution of the Apulian reggae scene. In 2011, Mattia Epifani's documentary film, *Rockman*, developed and enriched key aspects of Manfredi's text. As well as exploring the formation of Different Stylee and their cultural activities at *la Giungla* through new interviews and rare footage, the film focuses on the enigmatic figure of Militant P (Piero Longo) and his transportation of reggae from Bari to the neighbouring province of Salento.

[3] Pizzutilo is still active in the (southern) Italian reggae scene through his work with the Bass Culture booking agency and his involvement with one of Italy's many self-constructed sound systems: I&I Project Sound System from Altamura.

"INNA DIFFERENT STYLEE": THE RENAISSANCE OF YOUTH CULTURE... 49

protagonists, his personal journey began in the late 1970s during the era of the politicized youth movement. The assimilation of *la musica in levare* (as it is often referred to in Italy)[4] by politicized youth on the Left, from the late 1970s, must be understood in relation to the changing relationship between culture, politics, and new forms of communication that developed between 1975 and 1981. The personal narrative of Pizzutilo's encounter with reggae music provides an emblematic example of these paradigmatic shifts.[5]

Pizzutilo links his first musical experiences to his early political and cultural activities in Bari from approximately 1977, when he joined the Italian Communist Youth Federation. While at senior high school, Pizzutilo came into contact with the political and cultural ferment of the *movimento* (the student movement). The various components of the *movimento* were particularly hostile towards the traditional and institutional Left, and, as already mentioned in our previous chapter, they asserted a "youth identity" based on marginality and difference. Georgy Katsiaficas stresses that it was a movement of Italy's "second society": unemployed and marginally employed people, youth, minorities, and women (1997, p. 14).

Pizzutilo explains that, while it was very similar to what was happening elsewhere in Italy, Bari's movement took place in a more "provincial" dimension where what had first happened in the North and Rome was experienced much later. The student movement brought Pizzutilo into contact for the first time with the organizations of the extreme Left, whose young members would meet and socialize in the street.[6] Primarily, they sought to carry out creative autonomy through cultural and political initiatives which were separate from organizational structures (Personal interview).

One of the most important examples of this creative autonomy was the publication of a magazine or fanzine. Pizzutilo outlines that the artisanal

---

[4] *In levare* can be translated as "upbeat" and emphasizes the characteristic offbeat or upbeat rhythmic pattern of Jamaican popular music.

[5] The majority of his account is taken from edited segments of a personal interview conducted with him in August 2012. In the interest of readability, we provide only our English translation of the edited segments included in this account.

[6] As in other parts of Italy, leftist youth politics in Bari were firmly ideological and divided between sectarian organizations such as the Trotskyites, Stalinists, anarchists, or *Lotta Continua*. *Lotta Continua* ("Continuous Struggle") was a far Left extra-parliamentary group which published an eponymous newspaper.

and collaborative process behind its production involved approximately three months of discussions, writing, and graphic design. Importantly, music formed a key element of the magazine's cultural discussion: "We would listen to rock, folk music, certain examples of Italian jazz-rock (Area, Perigeo), and then the Canterbury scene (Robert Wyatt, Soft Machines, Gong). We were outside the political organizations. In these contexts, I met the majority of the people with whom I shared the reggae experience" (Personal interview).

As discussed in the previous chapter, the transnational influence of record labels such as Island and Virgin had contributed to the internationalization and crossover success of reggae during the mid- to late 1970s, and from 1977 onwards, Dischi Ricordi published Island Records' entire catalogue, launching the Bob Marley phenomenon in Italy. As a consequence, many records began to arrive in the import stores and some titles were printed in Italy. It was Pizzutilo's initial exposure to the music of Bob Marley during this period (when he was 16 years of age) that led to his new obsession for reggae. Reggae's limited media exposure forced Pizzutilo to seek out records and information by visiting every single record store in Bari. He explains that collecting records became a personal "obsession" (*mania*) (in Manfredi 2008, p. 27), and the artisanal laboriousness and maniacal intensity of his early record collecting is significant. Not only does it demonstrate the obsessive passion of Italy's early reggae fans, but it also highlights the fundamental difference between the more passive consumption of mainstream musical genres and the active, independent, and critical approach required by connoisseurs of such marginal music genres before the internet made access to such music much easier.

This active and critical approach has the potential to stimulate a deeper level of understanding and knowledge which can then be shared with others, a key factor in the development of a local music scene. Through this process, Pizzutilo helped to create an initial nucleus of reggae aficionados in Bari who soon began the challenging and lengthy process of teaching themselves to play reggae (Personal interview).[7] This same nucleus hitchhiked to Milan for the Bob Marley concert, which they interpreted as an encouraging sign that the counter-culture continued on in new forms.

---

[7] Pizzutilo's friend and fellow member of Different Stylee, Rosapaeda, confirms that her own passion for reggae started with Bob Marley but was facilitated by "Mimmo Superbass" (Pizzutilo) who shared with friends his record collection and organized for them to get together to listen to this music (Email interview).

"INNA DIFFERENT STYLEE": THE RENAISSANCE OF YOUTH CULTURE... 51

Reinforcing this point further, Pizzutilo states that the "tens of thousands of people" who surrounded him at the concert represented a "new cross-section of society" which seemed to have "rediscovered itself" around Bob Marley after the abrupt end of the movement of the 1970s. Hence, the cultural politics associated with reggae offered an alternative to the long-established leftist critique used to understand society and to formulate strategic opposition that, according to Katsiaficas, was partially responsible for the collapse of the movement (1997, p. 56).

Moreover, reggae's outward rejection of violence contrasted with the brutality of the politically motivated terrorism of the *anni di piombo* (Years of Lead, c.1969–1983) which, according to historians such as Paul Ginsborg, "bore a great deal of responsibility for the abandonment of collective goals and the triumph of the *riflusso*" (Ginsborg 1990, p. 401).[8] Indeed, Ginsborg argues that the terrorist activities carried out during the Years of Lead "deprived social protest of any political space, making the choice between the status quo and the armed bands the only one available" (Ginsborg 1990, p. 401). Hence, the early 1980s were increasingly characterized by arrests, mass sackings, and the fracturing of social solidarities. Furthermore, the urban landscape changed dramatically as a consequence of economic restructuring which gave rise to post-industrial cities and caused the banishment of the weak and marginalized into ever-expanding grey peripheries (Solaro 1993, pp. 17–18). The growth of a new generation of underemployed and unprotected youth, many of whom were working in the black economy and lived in impoverished peripheries, was a direct consequence of this increased economic restructuring and political repression (Ginsborg 2001, pp. 54, 58). As urban life became increasingly difficult and inequitable, an acute sense of social unease culminated in a heroin epidemic that produced more than 200,000 young addicts (Solaro 1993, p. 19).[9]

While the retreat into the private seemed "to nail inherited politics to an increasingly narrow horizon," characterized by narcissism and "a cul-

---

[8] The *anni di piombo* (Years of Lead) refers to a period from 1969 to the early 1980s in which political and social unrest in Italy led to more than 14,000 acts of politically motivated violence. During this time, there were approximately 567 right-wing and left-wing terrorist groups active in Italy, killing 362 and injuring 4500 people. For a detailed discussion of the social and political context of the *anni di piombo*, see Lumley 1991, pp. 279–312; Ginsborg 1990, pp. 348–405; Bull and Giorgio 2006; Vecchio 2007; and Voglino et al. 1999.

[9] For a confronting cinematic depiction of this epidemic, see Claudio Cagliari's film, *Amore Tossico* (Toxic Love, 1983).

de-sac of perpetual mourning" (Chambers and Curti 1982, p. 28), the adaptation of reggae culture in Italy, and specifically in Bari, instead represented a crucial example of the creative and expressive renewal of collective cultural politics in the 1980s. Although many disenfranchised youths retreated from politics, there was also a flowering of new creative modes of oppositional practice. In fact, Tommaso Tozzi asserts that the material and theoretical link between the new counter-cultural forms of the 1980s and those of the 1960s and 1970s undermines the "official" historical narrative of the 1980s as a time of collective apathy and narcissism (2008, pp. 7–54).

Pizzutilo confirms that reggae played an active role in these processes of rupture and continuity with the ideologies and practices of the 1970s. Although Pizzutilo explains that the early 1980s was a period of epochal change, defined by ideological uncertainty, disillusionment, and confusion, reggae provided:

> a new certainty, a new reason to burn inside about something. And, in a certain sense, I saw continuity with the beautiful essence of the things that I had experienced, such as the sense of justice, the aspiration for something better or more just. The music was tightly intertwined with politics, in a very spontaneous and vital manner. (Personal interview)

Evoking Pizzutilo's understanding of the role that reggae music played in his life, in *Music in Everyday Life*, Tia DeNora claims that "music is a powerful medium of social order" capable of creating relationships between "the polis, the citizen and the configuration of consciousness" and of articulating identities and emotions that empower people (2000, 163). Nuancing DeNora's argument, John Street questions the relationship between music and politics, arguing that "if musical pleasure and choice are purely private matters of personal consequence, they are not political" (2012, p. 6). Instead, for Street "music *embodies* political values and experiences, and *organizes* our response to society as political thought and action. Music does not just provide a vehicle of political expression, it *is* that expression" (p. 1, emphasis in original). Similarly, Simon Frith writes that music is an aesthetic practice which "articulates *in itself* an understanding of both group relations and individuality, on the basis of which ethical codes and social ideologies are understood" (2007, p. 295). Since social groups only get to know themselves as groups through cultural activity and aesthetic judgement, making music "isn't a way of expressing ideas; it is a way of living them" (2007, p. 296). Thus, musical identification provides an "ethical agreement" that offers "a way of being in the world, a way of making sense of it" (Frith 1996, p. 272). Pizzutilo's recollections confirm this understanding of music as articulated by DeNora, Street, and Frith. In this respect, reggae (and later reggae-inflected hip hop) provided marginalized Italian youth with a music that helped them to articulate a way of being in the world: a music that embodied political values, constituted identities, and elicited emotions that had the potential to create communities and empower beyond the pleasure of listening to music for entertainment. Indeed, Reggae's critique of the exploitation and injustice of the "Babylonian" system, and its Rastafarian spirituality incorporating vegetarianism, a reverence for nature, messages of peace and love, and the exaltation of marijuana, resonated with socially conscious Italian youth seeking a non-institutional everyday political practice. Pizzutilo expands further upon this notion of an ethical politics grounded in daily attitudes and practice:

> Seeking to live in a different way to that proposed by the system and, therefore, seeking liberation; not necessarily the revolution that changes the economic system, but a different daily practice. Thus, having cleaner, simpler relations with people and taking care of one's body. An example of living which also seeks to give a positive example to others, but without abandoning the social debate. (Personal interview)

This post-political practice is emblematic of the "decolonization of everyday life" carried out by autonomous social movements (Katsiaficas 1997, p. 6). As Katsiaficas argues, by shifting "the sites of the contestation of power" from politics to everyday life, this process stands in opposition to the ever-increasing pervasiveness of commodification (1997, p. 6). In Italy, however, the post-political practices developed during the 1980s in relation to reggae, an imported "black" dance-oriented musical form, were nothing less than paradigm shifting. As discussed in the previous chapter, in fact, throughout the 1960s and 1970s, imported forms of black music were interpreted by the *movimento* largely as examples of commercial hegemonization. Whilst in the US and the UK the choice to listen to black music might have been considered oppositional, in Italy it was widely seen to represent mental and cultural colonization.[10] Significantly, the reggae,

---

[10] The politically and ideologically fraught relationship between youth belonging to the movement and black music is confirmed by Florentine reggae veteran, Stefano "il Generale" Bettini, who participated in the free music movement of the late 1970s and explains that

54   S. SCARPARO AND M. S. STEVENSON

and later hip hop culture, that emerged in the 1980s reversed the attitude of the preceding two decades of youth political thinking in relation to popular music.

The reworking of pre-existing political practices within the framework of a new reggae culture was embodied in what Pizzutilo refers to as the "guerrilla culture" (*guerriglia culturale*) of Bari's Reggae Diffusion collective, which initiated spontaneous and autonomous activities from around 1980. Different Stylee's bassist and lead singer, Antonella Di Domenico, aka Rosapaeda, explains that following their shared experience in left-wing groups during 1976 and 1977, the Reggae Diffusion project "became a necessity" for those involved because what they perceived to be the "revolutionary" philosophy of reggae provided them with a more effective language in which to express their "resistance and militancy" (Email interview). As Rosapaeda recounts: "We lived the rhythm of reggae, we found the meaning of our rebellion through practicing a compassionate lifestyle. We became vegetarians and naturists, and we produced a fanzine in which we attempted to articulate another way in which to live life" (Email interview).

The concept of a guerrilla culture provides a direct alternative to the violent guerrilla tactics of the left-wing terrorists that had hijacked the movement and expedited its repression and disintegration. In the words of Pizzutilo, the concept of Reggae Diffusion was

> [a] legacy of the years in which we practiced militant politics. The first thing we wanted to do when we developed a passion for reggae was to share it (we still didn't know how to DJ, etc.). The first thing that came spontaneously was to do a sort of agitprop, and therefore make stencils for spray art, or write things on walls, or make stickers, or produce fanzines. And so, we began precisely to employ this "know-how" to make it known to others. Because we saw it precisely as a form of political propaganda; music wasn't a business. This was Reggae Diffusion, a form of musical propaganda not for business. (Personal interview)

Thus, a process of transculturation was underway through which the non-institutional and anti-capitalist practices of the collective movement were adapted to establish and disseminate a new musical (sub)culture, and

reggae, funk, and early rap were seen in a bad light because they were heard in the discos and therefore associated with political apathy (Personal interview). Pizzutilo also explains that at that time there was an emphasis on "cerebral" progressive rock and jazz-rock.

Pizzutilo's philosophy of a guerrilla culture, which provides cultural resistance from below, was coherent with reggae's counter-hegemonic roots in the sound system cultures of Kingston and London.

New Connective Marginalities: Reggae and Punk from Bari to London

Because of its Jamaican origins, reggae resonated with Italian youth opposed to the power structures they associated with the Anglo-American cultural hegemony. This correlation of reggae with a minority culture was especially significant for youths from Italy's South, who experienced entrenched and widespread socioeconomic inequalities in comparison with their northern compatriots. For example, in contrast with the rest of the nation, during the 1980s the active workforce in the South remained a declining percentage of the population, and women's employment was stagnant. Furthermore, the majority of irregular, non-protected workers not covered by social insurance and pension schemes (known as *non-garantiti*) were to be found in the South (Ginsborg 1990, p. 410). These structural inequalities also ran deep into the music industry itself, with opportunities and managerial professionalism almost entirely confined to Rome and Milan (Pizzutilo, Personal interview).

Historically, southerners have been discriminated against by what Schneider terms the "neo-Orientalist" discourse that followed Italian unification (1998, p. 3). Prior to and after unification, which many view as "annexation of territory" on behalf of Northern interests (Verdicchio 1997, pp. 22–23; Gramsci 1997, p. 71), northern Italians considered the South as "a type of *terra incognita*" (Pugliese 2008, p. 3) that needed to be "disciplined" (Gramsci 1997, p. 94). Through this process, northerners turned to the metaphor of Africa as a way to define the South, often using the terms *terroni* and *africani* (Africans) interchangeably in reference to southern Italians (Pell 2010, p. 179). As Joseph Pugliese argues:

> The deployment of the loaded signifier "Africa," as the lens through which the South was rendered intelligible for Northerners, marks how the question of Italy was, from the very moment of unification, already racialised by a geopolitical fault line that split the peninsula and its islands along a black/white axis. From the beginning, then, the so-called *questione meridionale* (southern question) encoded a set of racialised presuppositions in which the whiteness of the North operated as an a priori, in contradistinction to the

problematic racialised status of the South, with its dubious African and Oriental histories and cultures. (2008, p. 3)

This practice of othering generated a "lingering sense of 'interior estrangement' that has positioned and marked Southerners as *in* Italy, but not *of* Italy" (Scarpino 2005, p. 161; cited in Pugliese 2008, p. 6, emphasis in original). Hence, since southerners were configured as the Africans of Italy, the identification of southern Italian youth with black music coming from another context marked by the violence of colonialism and imperialism is not surprising. This duality of identification and difference speaks to Stuart Hall's advocacy of a politics "which works with and through difference, which is able to build those forms of solidarity and identification which make common struggle and resistance possible but without suppressing the real heterogeneity of interests and identities" (1996, p. 445). Evoking this complex duality of identification and difference, Pizzutilo states that they were proud to be *terroni* (Personal interview). The appropriation of a pejorative term, roughly translated as "dirty peasant", that is often used by northern Italians to describe southerners, illustrates the problematic and conflicted process of social, political, and cultural colonialism that has marked Italy since its unification.

It must also be recognized that the cultural provincialism and conservatism of southern Italian locations, such as Bari, rendered life even more difficult for those who deviated from accepted norms and identified with counter-cultural forms such as reggae. Additionally, within the southern Italian context, reggae was still perceived in terms of its exotic difference from dominant Western cultural paradigms. In the words of Pizzutilo, "I was truly captured by this mix of Third Worldism, rebellion, but also exoticism, sensuality, a rhythm that was completely new, absorbing, and hard" (in Epifani 2011). This impression of exoticism was intensified due to the fact that, unlike in Britain or France, reggae culture was not introduced and mediated by an immigrant and diasporic community since in Italy and, above all, in Bari in the South, there weren't many immigrants at that time.

Thus, not only did their identification with reggae's inherent marginality draw on a parallel or horizontal marginality, but it was rooted in the expressive power of an exotic "Other" which diverged from the racial, cultural, and historical experiences of its southern Italian adherents. Yet this foregrounding of the "Other" subsequently fed into the creation of a new, self-reflexive, and hybrid youth identity based on an inherent sense of *difference* from the cultural hegemony and a sense of solidarity and affinity with other oppressed peoples.

Consequently, although the dynamic of Italian reggae's early connective marginalities tended to essentialize "blackness" as a marker of "Otherness" or difference, this tendency also intersected with the legacy of Italy's colonial past and its involvement in the exploitation of Eastern African countries such as Ethiopia. It had in fact been Mussolini's invasion of Ethiopia in 1935 that had helped to crystallize Rastafari's ideology of Ethiopianism and its equation of modern-day Italy (and the Vatican) with ancient Rome (Chevannes 1994, pp. 42–43). Therefore, while official Italian history and culture tended to suppress the historical memory of Italy's brutal colonial legacies at home and abroad, reggae helped to bring these suppressed histories to light by establishing both intranational *and* international connections, along with non-official cultural alliances. In so doing, it challenged the colonial foundations of the Italian nation which marginalized the South, as well as the prominent ideologies of Catholicism and Fascism.

Thus, the adoption of reggae and its Rastafari-inspired anti-colonialism by marginalized Italians assumed extra significance in the South of Italy where the musical style of reggae became intertwined with social identity. This confirms Simon Frith's argument that music is able to engage with the politics of identity because its formative flows mirror those of identity. As he writes, "identity is *mobile*, a process not a thing, a becoming not a being," and "our experience of music—of music making and music listening—is best understood as an experience of this *self-in-process*" (Frith 2007, p. 294, emphases in original). Music, then, is socially and existentially interlinked with identity through the ethics of taste in that "our sense of identity and difference is established *in the process of discrimination*" and, through our choice of popular music, we create a particular social identity (Frith 1996, p. 18). Further, this musically connected social identity is "also a production of non-identity—it is a process of inclusion and exclusion" (Frith 2007, p. 264). This active creation of identity and non-identity is especially strong in relation to reggae music, which appealed to marginalized and self-marginalized Italians who consciously rejected Italy's hegemonic culture. Within the connective marginality paradigm, reggae's "blackness," therefore, has become both a global signifier of marginalization and a conscious declaration of *difference* from the cultural mainstream.

This construction of a marginal youth identity based on an aesthetic of cultural difference also helped Bari's reggae nucleus to forge connections with other peripheral youth subcultures, such as the punks.[11] While punk was initially misinterpreted within Italy's counter-cultural movement due to its ambiguous anarchism and confrontational aesthetic and iconography, it was firmly established in Italian youth culture by the early 1980s (Donadio and Giannotti 1996, pp. 124–25, 129). Punk had arrived through a gradual stream of records and television images, but more direct contact through trips to London and other Northern European capitals soon followed.

The local recontextualization of punk involved the synthesis and cultural translation of foreign sources within local political contexts and traditions (De Sario 2009, p. 45). Punk rapidly developed ties to the autonomous youth contexts and provided the *centri sociali organizzati autogestiti* (organized self-managed social centres) movement with its cultural identity. However, punk was founded on an apocalyptic vision of the death of ideologies (Solaro 1993, p. 23) and adopted the slogan "no future" as an affirmation of its lack of faith in society and in the concept of progress. Consequently, anarchism was the only political ideology compatible with punk (Solaro 1993, p. 22). The influence of British punk bands, particularly The Clash, helped to spread both a passion for political song lyrics and for fusion with other sounds, reggae in particular. This worked to bring a part of the Italian punk audience closer to reggae music, both directly and indirectly (Bettini and Tosi 2009, p. 230).

Although the *movimento* originally rejected punk and reggae, paradoxically, the foundation for the eventual adoption of these two foreign forms was laid by the movement itself. In fact, the movement of the 1970s was based on the search for new languages and the appropriation of marginal identities. Consequently, towards the end of the decade, there was a proliferation of terms within the movement which were used to highlight and describe collective identity, social position, and social conflict: marginals (*emarginati*), proletarian youth (*giovani proletari*), minorities (*minoranze*), the unprotected (*non garantiti*), and the precarious (*precari*) (Lumley 1991, p. 341). Punk, the product of intercultural dialogue between white and black working class London youth, and reggae, a Jamaican music disseminated in London through an immigrant and diasporic subculture, fed

---

[11] Hebdige argues that the uncompromising and subversive "blackness" of reggae resonated with the "anarchic values" of punk (1979, p. 64). The evolution of these connective marginalities between punk and reggae perhaps reached its apex with the emergence of the black Rastafarian punk band, Bad Brains, in Washington, DC in the late 1970s.

into these new political processes of collective identity formation in Italy, providing an idiosyncratic cultural voice for those "children of the movement of 1977" who refused to be swept up into the resignation and individualism of the *riflusso*. Thus, more than being a consequence of shared musical tastes, Pizzutilo stresses that the bond between Bari's reggae aficionados and punks was based on their disidentification with the mainstream and their shared cultural, socioeconomic, political, and spatial marginality (Personal interview).[12]

For many young Italians, London's cultural and musical melting pot provided direct access to an underground and subversive urban reggae culture and, in particular, the vibrant and grassroots culture of the sound system. In 1982, the nucleus of the band Different Stylee made its first road trip to London in order to experience first-hand the reggae culture of its Afro-Caribbean community. These trips exposed Pizzutilo and his companions, who squatted in a disused building in Ladbroke Grove, to London's Notting Hill Carnival, its reggae subculture, and the "guerrilla" dissemination of reggae music through radio stations and sound systems. This direct cultural contact with a grassroots local reggae (sub)culture was to change permanently their conceptualization of reggae. As Pizzutilo recounts:

> The most important thing was learning what a sound system was; then we saw these people alternating on the microphone and they were practising deejay style. Also understanding the difference between us and them. We really felt this difference because we discovered we had kind of made reggae ours; we practically merged it with our own experiences and we imagined it in a different way. (Personal interview)

The other crucial component of London's guerrilla reggae culture that resonated with Bari's Reggae Diffusion collective was West London's pirate radio station, DBC (Dread Broadcasting Corporation), or Rebel Radio. Simon Jones explains that "by mixing music with cultural and political issues, and presenting it in the language, style and idioms of the dancehall," reggae-oriented stations like the DBC "managed to dissemi-

---

[12] Pizzitulo explains, "We associated with the punks in Bari, but not because we liked the same music. We understood them better because they were fanatics like us. They were also quite politically rebellious. We weren't rich kids. We didn't have money to go to clubs and we met on the street. We had the example of punk-reggae in London, we knew about these things. We all liked The Clash" (Personal interview).

60 S. SCARPARO AND M. S. STEVENSON

nate undiluted black musical traditions to white listeners in a manner unprecedented in the history of British broadcasting" (1988, p. 85). DBC was Britain's first black music radio station and, due to its illegality, it was forced to constantly change frequency in a situation that reflected the racial and cultural marginalization of Afro-Caribbean communities in Thatcher's Britain. Pizzutilo recalls that they would find flyers indicating the new frequency while walking on the street in Ladbroke Grove and later make their own pirate recordings of the broadcast on cassettes (Personal interview). These London experiences resonated with the Italian non-institutional political subculture characterized by the *centri sociali* and *radio libere*, influencing the manner of reggae's transculturation and glocalization in Bari.

THE RECLAMATION OF SPACE AND THE MUSIC POLITICS OF *LA GIUNGLA*

Further demonstrating the synthesis of reggae with the cultural and political contexts and practices of the 1970s, the Reggae Diffusion cooperative and Different Stylee formed what was arguably the first *centro sociale organizzato autogestito* (organized self-managed social centre) in Italy's South, *la Giungla*. The spread of musical *centri sociali* in the 1980s was another lasting development of the youth movement of the 1970s that was to directly influence the evolution of punk and reggae in Italy. By 1976, there had been a wave of approximately 1500 public housing building occupations, particularly in Milan. Many of these occupations were converted into what were to be the precursors of the *centri sociali*, the *circoli del proletariato giovanile* (proletarian youth associations). A fundamental objective of these squats was the creation of an alternative and autonomous culture and sociability emphasizing the collective ideals of "being together" (*stare insieme*) (Lumley 1991, p. 300). The political themes dealt with by the *circoli* were strictly tied to daily problems and centred on the issue of relationships in the world of work, the occupation of spaces for self-management, and the fight against heroin (Bertante 2005, p. 145).

The *circoli del proletariato giovanile* undertook a poignant critique of the failings of the counter-culture's ideals in the face of an increasing sense of social, economic, and political powerlessness. Many of the youth behind these new forms of aggregation came from the extreme peripheries of the city and/or formed part of the growing mass of students without prospects, the unemployed, or the underpaid and temporarily employed

(Solaro 1993, pp. 15–16). Bertante explains that this autonomous movement emerged as a moment of resistance against capitalist restructuring and as a refusal to conform to the new technologies organizing work (2005, p. 155). This practice of taking over disused buildings spread to premises suitable for transformation into political and cultural centres, the most emblematic of these early occupations of disused buildings being *Leoncavallo*, which was established in a large abandoned factory in 1975.

According to Alba Solaro, the *centri sociali* that developed from the *circoli del proletariato giovanile* in the early 1980s were a response to the chronic lack of social services and stood in opposition to a society that privileged standardization of behaviour and of belief systems (1993, p. 13). Alberto Campo describes them as derelict urban spaces "liberated" and transformed into places of "alternative" sociability where marginality becomes central (1995, pp. 25–26). Relocating and remerging in a nomadic and decentralized manner, these centres provided "viable alternatives to traditional institutionalized versions of opposition," and, "by aiding in the establishment of social and political spaces that might function as sites of resistance," they manifested instances "of collaborative agency on the part of disenfranchised groups" (Verdicchio 1997, p. 161).

In the early 1980s, the anarchic and antagonistic Italian punks represented the recomposition of those fragments of social opposition resistant to the widespread political apathy, individualism, and heroin addiction of the *riflusso* (Campo 1995, p. 25). As a "disturbing ensemble of signs and languages," punk represented the "perfect post-political code" for the *centri sociali* (Campo 1995, p. 26). Campo explains that their anarchism was characterized by anti-militarism and environmentalism, and, in terms of artistic production, they chose to situate themselves outside the official market and independently produce and distribute materials, such as records, videos, counter-informational documents, and fanzines (1995, p. 26). Carrying on the tradition of the 1970s, the anarcho-punk movement refused to consider culture as a commodity and therefore practised *autoproduzione* (self-production) and *autogestione* (self-management).[13]

As had happened in London, in a number of Italian contexts, this confrontational urban punk sensibility merged with the culture and militant rhythms of reggae. The most groundbreaking of these contexts was precisely Bari's pioneering *centro sociale*, *la Giungla*, which had been inspired

---

[13] The first examples of self-production in the anarcho-punk movement date back to the foundation of Bologna's Attack Punk label in 1981.

by a lack of social spaces in the city and the new wave of anarcho-punk social centre occupations taking place throughout Italy in the early 1980s. Pizzutilo explains that the example at a national level came from Milan's *Virus* or Tuscany's *Il Grande Ducato Hardcore* (in Epifani 2011).[14] *Virus* was an occupied house, not far from the centre of Milan, which was the "temple" of the anarcho-punk movement (Solaro 1993, p. 24). As well as exhibiting live bands, it produced a punkzine called *Anti Utopia*. Besides publishing *Anti Utopia*, one of the main objectives of *Virus* was to fight against "the logic of heroin" and it disseminated counter-information through two radio programmes, *Popolare* and *Blackout* (Solaro 1993, p. 24).

The story of *la Giungla* bears many similarities to that of *Virus*. There was a lack of autonomous social spaces in Bari, and Enzo Mansueto, who was one of Bari's first punks and a protagonist in the occupation, declares that Bari was a "desert" without a future for the youth (2006, pp. 93–94).[15] Along with the Reggae Diffusion/Different Stylee collective, the founding members of *la Giungla* were various punk groups, members of the extreme Left group *Democrazia Proletaria* (Proletarian Democracy), and anarchists (see Epifani 2011). The collective process behind the occupation was tenaciously long; after meetings and discussions to plan for the occupation, there were two failed attempts which were immediately cleared out by the authorities. Following this resistance from above, Bari's reggae-punk alliance staged various demonstrations outside the city council offices.

Finally, in November 1983, a successful occupation was realized in the extremely peripheral industrial zone of Stanic, which was named after the large petroleum factory that once employed people from the area. As Pizzutilo explains, the neighbourhood comprised housing projects for the factory workers and their families, and the site of the occupation was a former *dopolavoro* (afterwork club), an abandoned and derelict theatre and sport complex that had been used for the social activities of the work-

---

[14] *Il Grande Ducato Hardcore* refers to the Tuscan anarcho-punk movement, which had its base at Pisa's *Victor Charlie* and produced a fanzine called *Nuove dal Fronte*, in which there was a section dedicated to reggae.

[15] The origins of Bari's anarcho-punk scene date back to 1979, a couple of years after the phenomenon reached Italian shores, with a raucous concert at the university's Faculty of Languages by a group named Wogs. This was the beginning of a series of concerts involving, amongst others, Massimo Lala, who was to become "an icon of Bari's punk scene" (Mansueto 2006, p. 89) and Different Stylee's first vocalist. Bari's punk scene expanded with the emergence of groups like Bloody Riot, Undernoise, Lobotomy, Last Call, Rem, and Skizo.

ers' families before the factory closed down (Personal interview). Adding to the symbolic significance of the occupation is the fact that the *dopolav-oro* clubs were initially established during Mussolini's regime. Consequently, this reclamation of space might be understood as a reaction against, and an attempt to make sense of, the alienating urban degradation of 1980s deindustrialization as well as forms of institutional repression more generally.

As previously mentioned in this chapter, the rise of post-industrial cities also enacted a process of spatial marginalization, and the establishment of *la Giungla* is to be understood as a direct form of resistance to these forces and as a means of reshaping the "centre-margin" dialectic. This fact is reinforced by Pizzutilo's description of the location as "really a miserable place, abandoned by everyone. Because it was not even really the ghetto. It was nothing at all" (in Epifani 2011). Yet, despite its layers of symbolic significance, *la Giungla* was occupied primarily for practical reasons: to establish an autonomous space in which to conduct cultural activities based around music.

Stock footage available on Pizzutilo's YouTube channel (djsuperbass) provides a clearer picture of the period of occupation. The footage captures the colourful demonstrations involving Bari's first sound systems, which were held in the street outside Bari's council and prefecture offices between the initial failed occupations and the final successful one. The footage shows a small white Renault parked with two speakers on the roof playing a UK release of the song "Young Rebel" (Top Notch, 1983), by the Jamaican singer Johnny Clarke. The idea to transform the car into a portable discotheque was inspired by the concept of the Jamaican-style sound system, which they had experienced first-hand in London. The dub flavour of the music is reinforced by a close-up of the steering wheel, which shows "DUB" and the letters LKJ, the initials of the highly political UK-based dub poet, Linton Kwesi Johnson, in stencilled lettering.[16]

The footage then cuts to one of Different Stylee's early live performances, during which the band covers the "Young Rebel" *riddim* that was

---

[16] Linton Kwesi Johnson is a crucial figure in the history of British reggae and black British cultural identity. He is renowned for the militant nature of his poetry, largely written during the racially charged Thatcher era of the late 1970s and early 1980s. For an analysis of Linton Kwesi Johnson's dub music and reggae poetry, see Chap. 4 of Dawson's *Mongrel Nation*. Concerning the practice of stencilled lettering, Pizzutilo explains that, following the example of the punks, they would reproduce logos and lettering on clothing and their cars (Personal interview).

64 S. SCARPARO AND M. S. STEVENSON

heard on the street through their improvised sound system. As the band plays the heavy drum and bass-driven rhythm, Massimo Lala, who was Bari's historic punk vocalist and the first vocalist of Different Stylee, chants *"Giungla"* to rally support from the crowd. Through their playing techniques, the musicians simulate the studio-mixed effects of dub reggae.[17] Indeed, Jamaican dub and British reggae and punk were central to the group's early aesthetic, and as a musical style, dub in particular proved to be an ideal expression of the *centri sociali*'s ethics of cultural autonomy and difference. As Michael Veal stresses, in fact, dub's "low-fi, densely textured aesthetic and self-consciously crude production values marked it as an 'authentic' and exotic pop music to Western ears" (2007, p. 57). Furthermore, dub's inherently non-verbal and fragmented quality was ideal for Italian youth seeking to find new languages and forms of expression that went beyond logocentric and totalizing ideologies.[18]

Also in the stock footage, there are several scenes of the youth from *la Giungla*, the majority of whom are styled as punks, campaigning in the street. Rather than chanting political slogans, as was the norm in the 1960s and 1970s, the youth dance, hop, and blow whistles to Anthony Johnson's 1982 Jamaican-produced single, "Gun Shot" (Midnight Rock), which emanates from the Renault-generated sound system. The lyrics—"Every day is a gunshot and another one get drop / … Love your brother and your sister / And things will be much better, yeah / If you live by the sword, you die by it"—give voice to the non-violent ethics of these punk-reggae youth, thus demonstrating their break with the ideological extremism of the *anni di piombo* (the Years of Lead).

Later in the video footage, The Clash's seminal punk-reggae cover of "Police and Thieves" (CBS, 1977), originally sung by Junior Murvin and produced by Lee Perry in 1976 (Island Records), becomes the soundtrack to the collective demonstration. The song's lyrics—"Police and thieves in the streets / Oh yeah! / Scaring the nation with their guns and ammuni-

---

[17] As explained in the previous chapter, dub is the remixed version of a record, with the vocal either entirely or partly removed. On the remaining rhythm track, the bass and drums are brought to the foreground, and the other instruments are fragmented and distorted through sound effects, such as echo and delay, along with other mixing techniques.

[18] Veal explains that dub was able to articulate post-modern subjective and cultural experiences through aesthetic fragmentation by using music "as a way of using art to break down the power of excess wordage…. Fragmentation can also be seen as inevitable in an age in which cultural codes of all kinds are being deconstructed, reconstructed, and recombined at an unprecedented rate" (2007, p. 259).

tion"—originally dealt with political violence, gang warfare, and police brutality in Jamaica, before being used by The Clash to comment on London's phase of violent social upheaval beginning with the race riots at the Notting Hill Carnival of 1976. However, semantically recontextualized within early 1980s Italy, the lyrics can be understood to provide a stark commentary on the institutional, political, and criminal violence of the *anni di piombo* and the related *strategia della tensione* (strategy of tension),[19] as well as the savage state repression of the collective movements and the expanding activity of southern Italy's various criminal organizations.

In other fragments of archival footage, which are inserted into the documentary *Rockman*, there are examples of *la Giungla*'s opposition to the heroin epidemic that was afflicting the nation's youth. The struggle against heroin's destructive impact was a central point of the *centri sociali*'s counter-informational and political activities, aiming to provide marginalized youth with a place in which to reclaim control of their own lives (Solaro 1993, p. 19). Bertante explains that Italy's counter-cultural tradition considered heroin to be a murderous and repressive drug which stood in opposition to the liberating potential of marijuana or LSD (2005, p. 144). Fittingly, the Rastafarian reggae tradition also stood firmly in opposition to "Babylonian" drugs such as heroin and cocaine, whilst exalting the medicinal and spiritual properties of marijuana. In the footage from *Rockman*, a member of *la Giungla* claims that heroin is being used by institutional forces to prevent political struggle, and, on another occasion, a shot of the social centre's external wall displays the words, "No to heroin," sprayed in black graffiti.

The statement about heroin being used as a form of control is representative of the theory developed within the *centri sociali* that the highly addictive drug was being used as an instrument of social neutralization. After 1978, the wide availability of heroin was primarily blamed on the Mafia and the CIA (Katsiaficas 1997, pp. 39–40). This interpretation by the *centri sociali* had its roots in the previously discussed *circoli del proletariato giovanile*, which viewed heroin's atomizing consequences as evidence of the drug's convenience to "bourgeois society" (Bertante 2005, p. 147). While the *centri sociali* responded to the epidemic through

---

[19] The "strategy of tension" refers to a series of right-wing terrorist attacks that were linked to institutional forces and aimed to create the pre-conditions for an authoritarian regime. The strategy is discussed in further detail in Chap. 5.

research, counter-information, and rehabilitation, the official institutions refused to dismantle the economic interests supporting the market and instead tended towards the criminalization and repressive control of the addict (Solaro 1993, p. 32).[20]

Dissemination Through Alternative Media: "Ganja University" and *Rebel Soul*

While Italy's autonomous youth cultures fought against the fragmenting forces of deindustrialization, they also profited from the concomitant rise of the information society and its spread of new technologies. The most important example of this was the rapid spread of *radio libere* (free radios), from 1976, in the wake of the constitutional court's ruling against the state's monopoly of the airwaves. Marco Grispigni singles out the *radio libere* as the movement's most definitive and important new mode of cultural expression (1996, p. 55), and this new technology replaced "the vertical, hierarchical structure and one-way flow of messages with egalitarian organization and horizontal and multiple flows" (Lumley 1991, p. 304). Bologna's legendary Radio Alice provided a key example of the significance of using a live and uncensored listener phone-in.[21]

In a guerrilla fashion, the *radio libere* subverted the hegemonic communicative infrastructure. As well as rendering mass communication more democratic, new types of foreign music began to reach the airwaves. As Concetto Vecchio explains, it was Radio Alice that broadcast Led Zeppelin, Frank Zappa, Patti Smith, and The Who for the first time (2007, p. 65). Unfortunately, many of these pioneering free radios, including Radio Alice, were shut down by police or forced into closure through financial difficulty (Lumley 1991, p. 305). Furthermore, Radio Alice aside, the free radio stations were often rigidly politicized and lacking in an autonomous cultural identity. Thus, rather than being a generative force in their own right, imported musical elements were integrated much later (Lumley

---

[20] A particularly effective strategy was the imposition of an exclusion policy for those under the influence of the drug, which was combined with the incentive of only being permitted entry to the *centri sociali* when sober. The provision of a choice between access to the *centri sociali* and heroin consumption facilitated rehabilitation.

[21] For a detailed discussion of the pioneering practices of Radio Alice, see Bifo and Gomma 2001; Vecchio 2007, pp. 65–107. For a cinematic account of the impact of Radio Alice on youth politics in Bologna, see Guido Chiesa's 2004 film, *Lavorare con lentezza* (Working Slowly, Radio Alice).

"INNA DIFFERENT STYLEE": THE RENAISSANCE OF YOUTH CULTURE... 67

1991, pp. 305–06). Nevertheless, this tradition of independent radio programming was subsequently appropriated within the autonomous musical culture of the 1980s and was fundamental to reggae's dissemination in Italy.

The Reggae Diffusion collective conducted a programme called "Ganja University" on the local free radio station, *Progetto Radio*. The programme's title conveyed the intention to provide an oppositional cultural education, which would have also been influenced by the group's first-hand observations of the abovementioned pirate reggae radio station, DBC, in London. Rosapaeda explains that the reggae broadcast was accompanied by a discussion of the social and cultural activities of *la Giungla* (in Epifani 2011). Pizzutilo also stresses the way in which the radio established a progressive politics of the everyday and became a way of making music a total part of life (in Epifani 2011).

According to John Downing, such examples of radical alternative media aim to express "opposition vertically from subordinate quarters directly at the power structure and against its behaviour" through horizontal networks of support and solidarity (2001, p. xi). Such rhizomatic forms of radical alternative media, and their capacity to form these counter-hegemonic alliances, assume particular importance in Italy, where the freedom and diversity of the mainstream media have been traditionally weak.[22] Along with the use of free radio, the artisanal publication of *Rebel Soul*, one of Italy's very first reggae fanzines, between 1984 and 1985 by Pizzutilo, the Reggae Diffusion collective, and its cooperatives (Frontline/M.O.L.E.), was another vital component of their guerrilla use of radical alternative media. The underground publication of *Rebel Soul* served to expand the frontiers of Italy's reggae culture by opening up communicative networks between the Bari scene and other local Italian scenes, thus leading to a *translocal* phase. In fact, late in 1985 *Rebel Soul* merged with the other foundational reggae fanzine, *Ital Reggae*, which was founded in May 1983 as the product of another vibrant scene in the north-eastern Ligurian town of Savona, to form *Ital Soul*.[23]

---

[22] A few examples being: Mussolini's Fascist regime; the pre-1976 state monopoly of radio; the surreptitious taking over of Italy's leading newspaper, *Corriere della Sera*, by the anti-democratic Masonic lodge P2 in 1977 (see Ginsborg 2001, p. 147); the concentration of media ownership in the hands of a single man: Silvio Berlusconi (see Stille 1995).

[23] *Ital Reggae* was overseen by Gianni "Asher" Galli, one of the first music journalists to specialize in reggae in a magazine with a national circulation: *Rockerilla*. Digitized versions of *Ital Reggae* have recently been made available through the *Liguria Reggae* website.

Pizzutilo was *Rebel Soul*'s editor and graphic layout artist, and he articulates the fanzine's raison d'être as follows:

> I had gathered a lot of knowledge, records and experiences, and I felt the need to share them along with our whole alternative vision of life: vegetarianism, anti-nuclearism, etcetera. It was a very militant initiative. The example came from the world of English and Italian punk-rock fanzines; something similar for reggae was missing and information about reggae in general was lacking. (Personal interview)

The fanzine's production utilized handwriting, typewriter, transferable characters, and radiograph (amongst other graphic techniques of the epoch), creating a handmade bricolage-like visual effect. The magazines were distributed at market stalls and record stores or by post through contacts and distribution points in various Italian cities. The content of the fanzine was rich and varied, including translations of selected songs and book extracts, reviews, promotion of concert dates, new musical releases, information about Italy's two specialized reggae distributors (Concerko in Belluno and Good Stuff in Rome), counter-information about Rastafari, cannabis, the consumption of organic foods, the mainstream music industry and media, and comic strips.

The opening page of the first edition of *Rebel Soul* (April 1984) combines images of Bob Marley and of Massimo Lala next to Reggae Diffusion's white Renault. A critique of the shallow commercial exploitation of music by the mainstream culture industry is contrasted with the autonomous, collaborative, and oppositional identity and project of the Reggae Diffusion collective within *la Giungla* and its adoption of the counter-hegemonic model of the Jamaican sound system. The same edition publicizes an up-and-coming "Tribute to Bob Marley" concert at the Teatro Tendastrisce, to be held on May 11, 1984.[24] Organized by Marco Provvedi's Roman cooperative, *Gli avventurieri del*

Selected pages of the five issues of *Rebel Soul*, the three issues of *Ital Soul*, and the sole issue of *Ritmo Vitale* were digitized by Mimmo Pizzutilo and posted through his Facebook page in September 2012.

[24] Founded in 1977, Teatro Tendastrisce is a historically significant open-air concert venue which can hold up to around 4000 spectators. Marco Provvedi, nicknamed "Daddy Reggae" due to his pioneering role in organizing some of Italy's very first reggae events, was a musician and concert organizer/promoter. In 1986, he established the record distribution network, Good Stuff, specializing in reggae and other black music.

deserto di mattoni, this concert was to incorporate four of the historic first wave of Italian reggae bands: Different Stylee, Irie (Milano), Jah Children Family (Catania), and Puff Bong (Venezia). This was an event of historic significance, since it was Italy's first-ever reggae festival and the first national meeting of the peninsula's diverse local nuclei.[25] Different Stylee was invited at the last minute by Provvedi on the advice of Giorgio Battaglia, who wrote about reggae for the magazine, *Rockstar*. This festival helped to launch Different Stylee outside of Bari, while also bringing into relief their less conventional and dub-inspired stylistic approach. As Pizzutilo comments, "we had a deeper reggae culture than the others, more unrestrained; we had moved beyond Bob Marley" (Personal interview).

This encounter also proved to be a watershed moment for the translocalization of the various Italian reggae scenes. In the subsequent summer 1984 edition of *Rebel Soul*, Pizzutilo gave an account of the importance that the festival had in demonstrating the connective, transcultural potential of reggae. Furthermore, he stressed the importance of creating a movement in opposition to the mainstream music industry:

> For the groups that played there, it was both a point of arrival (a comparison with the others non-existent up until now) and departure. It confirmed that, despite the inaccurate way in which reggae was promoted in Italy (everything intended to highlight only Bob, the "Star" of the situation), there are people who have adopted this music in a sincere way. These four bands in Rome demonstrated that playing reggae is right and normal for Italians, without racial barriers. I would like this concert to serve as a stimulus to all the Italian dreads to begin playing, to come out into the open and communicate the human and subversive vibrations of reggae to all, to live fully this music and create self-managed channels of diffusion. Because we can't put our faith in the moral poverty and the stupidity of the music business. (n.pag.)

The increasing interconnectedness of Italy's local reggae scenes of the period is further confirmed by a list of contacts, including Marco Provvedi and his cooperative in Rome, Gianni Galli and the fanzine *Ital Reggae* in Savona, the new distributor of reggae and African music in Belluno called Concerko, and Reggae Diffusion's own Frontline cooperative (later to become M.O.L.E.) in Bari. The impression of a national scene constitut-

---

[25] Pinerolo's Africa United being the only notable absentee.

ing various interconnected localities solidifies throughout the subsequent three editions of *Rebel Soul*, the three editions of *Ital Soul*, and the single edition of its final incarnation, *Ritmo Vitale*, between summer 1985 and autumn 1986. An array of groups, "posses" (taken from the Jamaican street slang for gang and often mistakenly spelt in the singular as "possee"), and individuals from throughout the peninsula are cited: Africa United (Pinerolo), Human Rights (Crotone), Wadada and Struggle (Bari), Dread Nesta Lion (Arezzo), Radical Roots and Vito "War" Fiorentino (Milan), Gela (Caltanisetta), Salerno Possee (Salerno), Briggy Bronson and Savona Posse (Savona), Niù Tennici (Verona) Capannole Possee, Cesena Posse (Cesena), Fiumicino Posse (Fiumicino), Via Merulana Possee (Rome). Such a list provides evidence that, by the middle of the decade, a self-managed and self-produced roots reggae circuit had emerged which paralleled that of the hardcore punk scene (Bettini and Tosi 2009, p. 232).

An article in the second edition of *Rebel Soul* explicitly demonstrates how concepts imported through reggae culture were being locally synthesized to reimagine and rearticulate the counter-cultural youth politics and practices of Italy's extra-parliamentary Left. The article in question discusses the political implications of consuming organic food as a means of "decolonizing" dietary habits from the unsustainable, polluting, and speculative forces of "Babylon":

> It is necessary to learn to select food with coherence ... because we have the right to be healthy and defend ourselves from the culture of Babylon.... [I]t is necessary to eliminate all that isn't natural and which responds only to the demands of profit.... [T]he search for personal balance is the antithesis of the logic of those who pollute our air, destroy our land, package fake and carcinogenic food ..., rendering us simply objects of speculation and profit. (n.pag.)

In the light of contemporary debates about environmental sustainability, endemic obesity, the ethics of factory farming and hormone use by the meat industry, and the invention and patenting of GM seeds by multinationals like Monsanto, this promotion of an ethical process of dietary resistance appears thoroughly progressive.

Significant here is the symbolic appropriation of the previously mentioned Rastafarian concept of Babylon. Adopted from biblical scriptures, in Rastafarian discourse and symbolism Babylon has an array of connotations and nuances, constituting a "symbolic delegitimation of those Western values and institutions that historically have exercised control over the masses of the African diaspora" (Edmonds 1998, p. 24). In a global context, "Babylon is that worldly state of affairs in which the struggle for power and possessions takes precedence over the cultivation of human freedom and the concern for human dignity" (Edmonds 1998, pp. 24–25). As the symbolic concept of Babylon was assimilated and disseminated within the Italian context, it assumed new cultural nuances and informed changing political practices. Together with the extension of the concept of Babylon to Fascism or the ethics of food production and consumption, in the editorial to the June 1983 edition of Savona's *Ital Reggae*, Asher Galli had denounced Italy's corrupt political class as supporters of "Babylonian power."

The Closure of *La Giungla* and the Evolution of Different Stylee's Musical Practice

In addition to staging concerts and theatre performances via their cooperative, *la Giungla* implemented their grassroots politics through a diverse range of initiatives designed to engage with the marginalized community of the peripheral and degraded Stanic area. Such community initiatives were typical of the *centri sociali*, which sought to give new life to "dead" spaces and provide services that the local governments had failed to provide. Stanic was plagued by widespread heroin abuse, extreme marginality, and violence (Pizzutilo, Personal interview). Despite attempts by the members of *la Giungla* to bring something positive to this neglected neighbourhood, their striking visual and cultural difference led to misunderstanding and violent rejection by segments of the area's lumpenproletariat youth.

As Solaro emphasizes, life for the *centri sociali* was more difficult in Italy's South than elsewhere, since they not only clashed with the institutions but "also with organized crime and with the general situation of backwardness and unemployment" (1993, p. 47). Indeed, *la Giungla* was forced to contend with the Stanic area's omnipresent organized crime, which exploited the already-disadvantaged community through drugs and an illegal housing racket. Disturbed by the more regular police presence that had accompanied the founding of the *la Giungla*, these criminal elements violently intimidated the centre's members.

Despite such open threats, *la Giungla* continued to provide community programmes with the support of local residents. But eventually the area's criminal elements forced the youth to willingly abandon their hard-fought occupation. Pizzutilo explains that they were compelled to abandon the occupation due to a lack of protection from the local authorities. The inability or unwillingness to nourish and protect the neglected area's only community initiatives from organized crime was another poignant reminder of the failure of Italy's institutions, especially with regard to those refusing to assimilate to the dominant culture.

In spite of the dissolution of *la Giungla*, Different Stylee's musical activity continued unabated through further translocal collaborations and supporting performances for a number of touring Jamaican and British reggae artists, predominantly in Rome. Following the release of their first self-produced demo tape in 1984, which collated both live and studio recordings, they released their first EP/LP, *Mini Album Dubwize* (Mole Reggae Diffusion), in 1986.[26] *Mini Album Dubwize* comprised six dub/instrumental tracks and one vocal track. The recording was self-produced by Amedeo Vox, an autodidact sound engineer belonging to the collective, and the sleeve's graphic art was produced in-house by Pizzutilo. The EP was recorded in Rome at Wonderland Studio and mixed in London by the British-Jamaican sound engineer and dub specialist, Bertie Stammer.[27]

The economically disadvantaged reality of Italy's South had prevented Different Stylee from recording earlier, since in Bari there was no recording industry (Pizzutilo, Personal interview). Hence, the self-production of their EP without industry support was a significant achievement for these practitioners of a marginal genre who were also from a marginal territory. As mentioned above, the practice of *autogestione* (self-management) was inextricably and ideologically tied to that of *autoproduzione* (self-production) and was an active criticism of the commercialization of culture and a rejection of the market and the productive system (Solaro 1993, pp. 26–28). This ethical and aesthetic framework is mirrored in the lyrics

---

[26] 1986 also witnessed the release of Puff Bong's first and only recording, a 12-inch disco mix containing the tracks "Goin' On" and "One More," and Africa United's first self-produced and self-distributed LP, *Mjekrari*.

[27] Pizzutilo explains that Different Stylee had played at a large reggae festival in Rome in July 1985 boasting renowned Jamaican and British artists, such as Barrington Levy, Gregory Isaacs, Sly and Robbie, Militant Barry, and Jah Woosh. Bertie Stammer was the sound engineer on that day, and he was so impressed by Different Stylee's sound that he invited them to his studio in London.

and music of the EP's lead and only vocal track, "Mr Babylon," which provides the most emblematic example of the group's musically mediated reinvention of left-wing politics and their recontextualization of reggae's idioms and metaphors.

"Mr Babylon"'s critique of the increasing voracity of 1980s consumer capitalism must be understood in relation to its contemporary context. Paul Ginsborg points out that, during the 1980s (and 1990s), "Italy was very much part of that quarter of the world's population which consumed three-quarters of its resources each year and produced the greater part of its pollution and waste" (2001, p. 28). Furthermore, the reconciliation of ecological, political, and economic necessities was "dispiritingly" low on the nation's agenda: "enrichment was still everything, and longer-term considerations had barely begun to penetrate the collective consciousness" (2001, p. 28).

"Mr Babylon" was sung in Patois-shaded English by Rosapaeda, with an Italian translation of the lyrics appearing on the sleeve's reverse. The choice of English or Jamaican Patois by Italian aficionados-cum-artists was inevitable, since it was the only example of reggae that they had, and the rhythmic metre and melody of reggae's lyrics were tied to these languages. Pizzutilo explains that everything that they had listened to up until that point was in English, and it therefore seemed very difficult to sing in Italian (Personal interview). Rosapaeda also confirms that at that time she preferred English to Italian as she found the former to be more "musically expressive" (Email interview). Moreover, Patois expressions in combination with Rastafarian metaphors were also inseparable from the group's conscious identification with a marginal and subaltern culture and language.

As discussed in the previous chapter, ever since the days of slavery, Jamaican Patois had been a vernacular of resistance. Russell Potter argues that there are two general classes of vernacular languages corresponding to the active and passive experiences of colonialism (1995, p. 57). These two classes are hegemonic vernaculars and subversive "resistance vernaculars," which make "inroads against the established power-lines of speech" (1995, pp. 57–58). In Britain, Jamaican Patois became not only a resistance vernacular amongst black youth, as an expression of an oppositional and collective cultural identity, but it was adopted into the vocabulary of the young white Brits as part of their white rude boy style and identity.

Thus, Different Stylee's use of Patois and appropriation of the Babylon metaphor was fundamental to their own rejection of hegemonic ideologies, as it created a symbolic connection between the marginality of black

Jamaicans/Britons and the marginality of Bari's oppositional youth. Equally as important as these language-based elements of "Mr Babylon" are its formal elements. These are most powerfully manifest in the song's use of a rockers-style beat and moody instrumentation. An emphasis on beat 3 is in all reggae drumbeats, but with the rockers beat (pioneered by Sly Dunbar), the emphasis is also on beat 1, usually played on the bass drum. The rockers beat provides a more militant and foreboding edge, and variations of it were prevalent in UK reggae and dub during the early to mid-1980s through artists such as Aswad and Jah Shaka. The instrumental opening to the track is particularly suggestive, gradually layering and interlinking a heartbeat-like drum pattern, lilting and melancholic flute, sparse bass and rhythm guitar, electric organ, percussive bells, and snatches of piano. This process of progressive layering reaches a crescendo that ushers in Rosapaeda's falsetto vocals and the driving rockers groove, which is embellished further only by synthesized horns.

As well as building tension and setting the dramatic tone of the song, the purpose of this extended and rather atypical intro is to lend gravitas and depth to the hauntingly chanted minor-key vocals which follow.[28] Unconventionally, the song consists of a first verse (repeated three times) and a chorus (repeated eight times). This unusually sparse and repetitive vocal pattern leaves space for its evocative, dub-inspired rhythmic variations, whilst also exalting the simple yet solemn message:

> Stop your big hands,
> Mi seh change your style, Mr Babylon,
> You destroy the land,
> Progress you bring is a real Armagideon,
> You must understand.

The first three lines incorporate two imperative sentences and one declarative sentence directed at "Mr Babylon," who might be understood as the subject and object of the song. The title "Mr" initiates a process of personification whereby the hegemonic and patriarchal political and economic system is transformed into a male subject/object, a process which is rendered more poignant by the female gender of the interlocutor. The imperative sentence—"Stop your big hands"—provides a denunciation of,

---

[28] The tonal quality of Rosapaeda's vocals is comparable to that of Puma Jones, who sang with the internationally acclaimed Jamaican reggae outfit, Black Uhuru, during the late 1970s and early 1980s.

"INNA DIFFERENT STYLEE": THE RENAISSANCE OF YOUTH CULTURE... 75

and a plea to end, the insatiable greed and consumerism of the 1980s, along with its associated ecological destruction.

The Patois expression, *mi seh* (of the second imperative sentence, "Mi seh change your style") is frequently used to reinforce a statement or, in this case, the command directed at Mr Babylon: "change your style." "Change your style," which might be translated as "change your ways" or "change your attitude," is an idiomatic Jamaican expression used to convey disapproval towards unsavoury actions and behaviour, in this case Mr Babylon's destruction of "the land." Besides its reference to the environmental degradation caused by the profit-driven exploitation of natural resources and urban development, the following line—"The progress you bring is a real Armagideon"—hints at the apocalyptic global threat created by nuclear arms and nuclear energy.[29] As Pizzutilo recalls, "while we were recording in the studio the Chernobyl incident occurred. At the time, the anti-nuclear theme was very strong. It was one of the rare experiences of large-scale movements in which we felt involved, after the Seventies" (Personal interview).

The nuclear disaster in Chernobyl, Ukraine, contaminated vast portions of the globe, with associated deaths worldwide estimated to be as high as 824,000 (Yablokov et al. 2009, p. 322). The implicit link between "Mr Babylon" and the Chernobyl crisis is rendered explicit in an alternative dub version of the song, "Chernobyl Dub (Mr Babylon Heavy Mix)," which appears on the mini album. Pertinently, Veal argues that dub can be interpreted as an expression of historical trauma where "the privileging of rupture ... comes to symbolize the disruptions in cultural memory and the historical shattering of existential peace" created by the transatlantic slave trade (2007, p. 205).

Engineered by Bertie Stammer in London, "Chernobyl Dub (Mr Babylon Heavy Mix)" strips down "Mr Babylon" to its stark drum and bass core. Only fleeting snatches of rhythmic guitar and piano are present, serving to reinforce the underlying sense of disruption and loss. The total absence of the original vocals hints at the apocalyptic annihilation unleashed by the radioactive explosion. The deeply destabilizing and fragmented overall quality of the track is reinforced by sound effects that jarringly and repeatedly interfere like mini explosions or radioactive crackles.

---

[29] "Armageddon" is pronounced in the Rastafarian manner as *Armagideon*, which conflates the name of this apocalyptic battle with the biblical character of Gideon, a warrior and man of God whose name means "destroyer."

The dub version thus provides a profoundly expressive critique of the fall-out from the disaster. It might be understood also as a highly innovative meditation on the trauma that such a tragedy would inevitably manifest in the future, and it may also be interpreted as a warning against future tragedies, such as the Fukushima disaster of 2011.

Returning to the original vocal version, the four punchy and blunt declarative sentences which constitute the chorus underpin the inherent ethical critique of the song.

> Life that you live is a wicked trap,
> Thinking of money, you just can't stop,
> Fooling around like an idiot,
> And every day you need a lot.

The first two lines comment on what is perceived to be the unethical or "wicked" face of Italian politics and consumer capitalism of the 1980s. The dramatic changes in Italian society and political culture during the 1980s can be largely attributed to Bettino Craxi's government (1983–1987). According to Ginsborg, the Craxi years "saw a radical divorce between politics on the one hand, and morality and the law on the other" (2001, p. 150). During this period, "modern trends of entrepreneurship, of consumption and individual liberty were to be celebrated as such, without being submitted to any reflexive filters" (2001, p. 151). The period's role in restoring and concentrating wealth and power, whilst dismantling trade-union representation and employees' rights, was characteristic of wider neoliberal economic trends which had become the new "common sense" in Reagan's US and Thatcher's Britain (see Harvey 2005, pp. 39–63).[30] In Italy, the 1980s were also characterized by "an unusually strong elision of economic and political power" (Ginsborg 2001, p. 40), as demonstrated by the bond between Craxi and Silvio Berlusconi.[31]

---

[30] David Harvey explains how the break with deeply embedded Keynesian economic principles and the penetration of egocentric values of self-enrichment into the Western popular consciousness "required the prior construction of political consent" (2005, p. 39). He contends that the Gramscian notion of "common sense" (defined as "the sense held in common") typically grounds consent. Harvey states that "common sense" is typically constructed "through the corporations, the media, and the numerous institutions that constitute civil society" (2005, p. 40).

[31] Craxi was the godfather to one of Berlusconi's children and a witness at his wedding. In 1984, Craxi quashed judicial opposition to Berlusconi's push to establish a national television monopoly.

Alexander Stille asserts that Berlusconi's introduction of commercial television in Italy "was perhaps the greatest agent" of the rise of a neoliberal consumer economy in which a "new set of values based on personal wealth and success reigned" (2006, p. 7). The Americanization of Italian culture via Berlusconi's wholesale importation of hundreds of American films and mini-series was concomitant with an advertising assault that worked to promote and normalize the new overtly consumerist culture of the 1980s (see Jones 2003, p. 125). Berlusconi's commercial television was also irreverently sexist, parading semi-naked women at every opportunity. Thus, the final two lines of the chorus—"Fooling around like an idiot / And every day you need a lot"—might be understood as a critique of the new hegemonic "common sense" created by Berlusconi's commercial television culture.

In contrast to the purely roots-dub quality of "Mr Babylon," the remaining tracks on *Mini Album Dubwize* hint at the beginnings of a stylistic openness that was to characterize Different Stylee's approach for the remainder of the 1980s and until their dissolution in 1992. The band's live repertoire was extensive, varied, and highly original, moving beyond the strict boundaries of reggae and dub to what can be classified as "reggae world fusion." In large part retaining the drum and bass fundamentals of reggae, an array of stylistic influences, ranging from traditional southern Italian through to African, Latin, and rap, increasingly characterized their work. The group had already begun to develop a passion for African and other music from around the world, while also drawing on the Italian traditions that they had been exposed to from a very early age, such as Neapolitan music.

This coexistence of diverse influences is evident in a live recording from 1988.[32] One of the pieces, "Rap 'n' Dance," incorporates funk and rap elements, while another, "Rockers," merges an up-tempo reggae rhythm with African drumming and the European folk sound of the *fisarmonica* (piano accordion). Of particular note is the groundbreaking incorporation of traditional southern Italian elements, as demonstrated by the experimental renditions of two classics of Neapolitan *tarantella*: "Canto delle Lavandaie del Vomero" (Song of the Laundrywomen from Vomero) and "Tamurriata Nera" (Black Dance).[33] The fact that Different Stylee were

---

[32] These recordings can be listened to and downloaded from Mimmo Superbass' *SoundCloud* account (see Discography).

[33] The term *tarantella* is used generically to refer to a range of southern Italian folk dances. The specific dance name varies with every region, for example: *tammuriata* in Campania and *pizzica* in the Salento subregion of Apulia.

performing songs in Neapolitan rather than standard Italian is significant and can be attributed to a range of factors. Firstly, Rosapaeda's family originated from Naples and the singer grew up listening to Neapolitan music, to the extent that she has described this music as the "soundtrack" of her childhood (Email interview). Secondly, the prevalence of Neapolitan musical traditions in the South stemmed from Naples' hegemony during the Kingdom of the Two Sicilies, which lasted from 1815 to 1861 and included the southern regions of mainland Italy and the island of Sicily. Thirdly, the work of the *Nuova Compagnia di Canto Popolare* (New Folk Song Company) during the 1970s, which aimed to rediscover and promote the traditions of the people of Campania, provided a pre-existing model for Different Stylee's adoption of Neapolitan folk elements.

The originality of Different Stylee's musical syntheses, however, stemmed from their symbolic connective marginalities. The combination of African drumming and percussion with the dialectal "Canto delle Lavandaie" provides a metaphor for the meeting of the two "Global Souths" of Apulia and Africa, while in "Tammurriata Nera" this intercultural encounter reaches its narrative conclusion through the account of a Neapolitan woman giving birth to the child of an African-American soldier at the end of the Second World War. This metaphor of interracial mixing, which was grounded in historical reality, was to assume an even greater level of significance in examples of Neapolitan reggae from the early 1990s. In addition to establishing symbolic connections through their brand of reggae world fusion, Different Stylee opened up practical levels of intercultural dialogue and horizontal solidarity through musically mediated friendships with some of Bari's first African immigrants. The most important of these was with a Senegalese musician named Ibu M'Boye, who had stumbled upon a Different Stylee street concert and begun to improvise vocally on stage with the band. After this street encounter, M'Boye became a regular member of the band's line-up for a couple of years (Pizzutilo, Personal interview).[34]

Different Stylee's second and final studio release was a self-produced 12-inch containing two tracks, recorded in Bari and mixed by Amedeo Vox: "Serenata" (Serenade) and "Spread Your Love" (Mole Records, 1988). The rhythmically experimental "Spread Your Love," composed and arranged by Iodice and sung in English by Rosapaeda, expands

---

[34] Footage of M'Boye performing the song "Day by Day" with the band can be viewed on YouTube at the channel of *amed ox*.

upon the themes raised in "Mr Babylon" by explicitly referring to "big men," who are "killing humanity for money" and "don't want a flower to grow" in their "world full of material gain" where "vanity is the game." Particularly interesting is the song's substitution of the gender-imbalanced collective appeal "my brothers" with "my sisters." Not only does this linguistic choice reflect the vocalist's gender, but it posits women as the potential future agents of a progressive and socially grounded politics based on love and empathy, which stands in opposition to the destructive greed of male power.

Also composed and arranged by Iodice, "Serenata" is Different Stylee's first Italian language song, its lyrics written, with great difficulty, by Rosapaeda and Sandro Biallo. According to Pizzutilo, the cumbersome prosody of the Italian language rendered the composition of Italian lyrics "laborious," and it came more spontaneously for Rosapaeda to experiment in Neapolitan (Personal interview). Furthermore, as opposed to Neapolitan, the Italian language did not have strong cultural roots in the South and there were no local musical traditions in the Italian language to act as inspiration. Pizzutilo explains further that the Latin and Flamenco influences of the song led to the new definition of "Mediterranean reggae" (*reggae mediterraneo*) by music critics. Plastino maintains that "Mediterraneanness" "often represents the element fundamental to the development of a local musical identity, *glocal* and sometimes global" (2003, p. 28). The nebulous and broad nature of the definition "Mediterranean" therefore lends itself well to the open-ended and culturally inclusive musical identity of Different Stylee.

Along with its Mediterranean suggestions, "Serenata" also incorporates band elements inspired by the street theatre experiences of the Teatro Origine, the experimental theatre company which cohabited within the same cooperative as the band. This theatrical aspect was an integral part of Different Stylee's live repertoire and can be seen in the unconventional television performance of "Serenata" on the programme *Jeans 2*.[35] Rather than mime the playing of instruments with verisimilitude, members of the band draw attention to the artifice of their performance with self-reflexive theatricality. Perhaps Different Stylee's crowning achievement, however, was the inclusion of "Serenata" on a globally distributed various artists compilation, *Reggae From Around the World*. Released in 1988 on the

---

[35] *Jeans 2* was a programme promoting emerging music groups; footage of this performance is included in the documentary, *Rockman*.

reputable US-based reggae label, RAS, this compilation was the first attempt to document reggae music at a global level (Pizzutilo in Manfredi 2008), and it comprised the internationally renowned reggae artists Alpha Blondy (Ivory Coast) and Peter Broggs (Jamaica). Hence, Different Stylee were consecrated as foundational protagonists in an expanding global reggae community. And, although the group disbanded in the early 1990s, many of its members continued to be influential in the years to come, both within and outside Italy's reggae circles. Significantly, through the syncretic fusions they pioneered, Different Stylee not only reinforced the glocal and transcultural qualities of reggae, but they also paved the way for the future processes of indigenization and hybridization of reggae and reggae-inflected hip hop that will be discussed in subsequent chapters.

WORKS CITED

Bennett, Andy. 2000. *Popular Music and Youth Culture: Music, Identity and Place.* London: Macmillan Press. Print.

Bennett, Andy, and Richard A. Peterson. 2004. Introducing Music Scenes. In *Music Scenes: Local, Translocal and Virtual,* ed. Andy Bennett and Richard A. Peterson, 1–15. Nashville: Vanderbilt University Press. Print.

Bertante, Alessandro. 2005. *Re nudo. Underground e rivoluzione nelle pagine di una rivista.* Rimini: NdA Press. Print.

Bettini, Stefano. 2012. Personal Interview. September 6.

Bettini, Stefano, and Pier Tosi. 2009. *Paperback reggae: Origini, protagonisti, storia e storie della musica in levare.* Firenze: Editoriale Olimpia. Print.

Bifo and Gomma, eds. 2001. *Alice è il diavolo: Storia di una radio sovversiva.* Milano: Shake Edizioni Underground. Print.

Bull, Anna Cento, and Adalgisa Giorgio, eds. 2006. *Speaking Out and Silencing: Culture, Society and Politics in Italy in the 1970s.* London: Legenda. Print.

Cagliari, Claudio, dir. 1983. *Amore Tossico.* Gaumont. DVD.

Campo, Alberto. 1995. *Nuovo? Rock?! Italiano!* Firenze: Giunti. Print.

Chambers, Ian, and Lidia Curti. 1982. Silent Frontiers. *Screen Education,* 36–47. London: Society for Education in Film and Television. Print.

Chevannes, Barry. 1994. *Rastafari: Roots and Ideology.* New York: Syracuse University Press. Print.

Chiesa, Guido, dir. 2004. *Lavorare con lentezza.* CG Entertainment. DVD.

Clarke, John, Stuart Hall, Tony Jefferson, and Brian Roberts. 1993. Subcultures, Cultures and Class: A Theoretical Overview. In *Resistance Through Rituals: Youth Subcultures in Post-war Britain,* ed. John Clarke and Stuart Hall, 9–74. London: Routledge. Print.

Dawson, Ashley. 2007. *Mongrel Nation: Diasporic Culture and the Making of Postcolonial Britain.* Ann Arbor: University Press of Michigan. Print.

"INNA DIFFERENT STYLEE": THE RENAISSANCE OF YOUTH CULTURE... 81

De Sario, Beppe. 2009. *Resistenze innaturali: Attivismo radicale nell'Italia degli anni '80*. Milano: Agenzia X. Print.

DeNora, Tia. 2000. *Music in Everyday Life*. Cambridge: Cambridge University Press. Print.

Donadio, Francesco, and Marcello Giannotti. 1996. *Teddy-boys, rockettari e cyberpunk: Tipi mode e manie del teenager italiano dagli anni Cinquanta a oggi*. Roma: Riuniti. Print.

Downing, John D.H. 2001. *Radical Media: Rebellious Communication and Social Movements*. Thousand Oaks: Sage Publications. Print.

Edmonds, Ennis. 1998. Dread 'I' In-a-Babylon: Ideological Resistance and Cultural Revitalization. In *Chanting Down Babylon: The Rastafari Reader*, ed. Nathaniel S. Murrell, William D. Spencer, and Adrian A. McFarlane. Philadelphia: Temple University Press. Print.

Epifani, Mattia, dir. 2011. *Rockman*. Goodfellas. DVD.

Frith, Simon. 1996. *Performing Rites*. Cambridge, MA: Harvard University Press. Print.

———. 2007. *Taking Popular Music Seriously: Selected Essays*. Aldershot, Hampshire: Ashgate. Print.

Galli, Gianni, ed. 1983. Ital Reggae 2: n. pag. Print.

Ginsborg, Paul. 1990. *A History of Contemporary Italy: Society and Politics 1943–1980*. London: Penguin. Print.

———. 2001. *Italy and Its Discontents: Family, Civil Society, State 1980–2001*. London: Penguin. Print.

Gramsci, Antonio. 1997. *Selections from the Prison Notebooks of Antonio Gramsci*. Ed. and Trans. Quentin Hoare and Geoffrey Nowell Smith. New York: International Publishers. Print.

Grispigni, Marco. 1996. Combattenti di strada. La nascita delle culture giovanili in Italia. In *Ragazzi senza tempo: Immagini, musica, conflitti delle culture giovanili*, ed. Massimo Canevacci et al., 17–64. Genova: Coast and Nolan. Print.

Hall, Stuart. 1996. New Ethnicities. In *Stuart Hall: Critical Dialogues in Cultural Studies*, ed. Stuart Hall, David Morley, and Kuan-Hsing Chen, 441–449. London: Routledge. Print.

Harvey, David. 2005. *A Brief History of Neoliberalism*. New York: Oxford University Press. Print.

Hebdige, Dick. 1979. *Subculture: The Meaning of Style*. London: Routledge. Print.

Jones, Simon. 1988. *Black Culture White Youth: The Reggae Tradition from JA to UK*. London: Macmillan. Print.

Jones, Tobias. 2003. *The Dark Heart of Italy*. London: Faber and Faber. Print.

Katsiaficas, Georgy. 1997. *The Subversion of Politics: European Autonomous Social Movements and the Decolonization of Everyday Life*. Oakland: AK Press. Print.

82 S. SCARPARO AND M. S. STEVENSON

Lull, James. 1995. *Media, Communication, Culture: A Global Approach.* Cambridge: Polity Press. Print.

Lumley, Robert. 1991. *States of Emergency: Cultures of Revolt in Italy from 1968 to 1978.* London and New York: Verso Books. Print.

Manfredi, Tommaso. 2008. *Dai Caraibi al Salento: Nascita, evoluzione e identità del reggae in Puglia.* Lecce: AGM. Print.

Mansueto, Enzo. 2006. Dai wogs alla Giungla (1979–1984). *Lumi di punk: La scena italiana raccontata dai protagonisti*, 83–102. Milano: Agenzia X. http://www.agenziax.it/wp-content/uploads/2013/03/lumi-di-punk.pdf. Accessed 8 Feb 2018.

Pell, Gregory. 2010. 'Terroni di mezzo': Dangerous Physiognomies. In *From Terrone to Extracomunitario: New Manifestations of Racism in Contemporary Italian Cinema*, ed. Grace Russo Bullaro, 178–218. Leicester: Toubador. Print.

Pizzutilo, Mimmo, ed. 1984a. *Rebel Soul* 0: n.pag. https://www.dropbox.com/s/l0eucpnpw7ft132/IL_MEGLIO_DI_REBELSOUL.pdf. Accessed 10 Sep 2012.

———, ed. 1984b. *Rebel Soul* 1: n.pag. https://www.dropbox.com/s/l0eucpnpw7ft132/IL_MEGLIO_DI_REBELSOUL.pdf. Accessed 10 Sep 2012.

———, ed. 1984c. *Rebel Soul* 2: n.pag. https://www.dropbox.com/s/l0eucpnpw7ft132/IL_MEGLIO_DI_REBELSOUL.pdf. Accessed 10 Sep 2012.

———, ed. 1984d. *Rebel Soul* 3: n.pag. https://www.dropbox.com/s/l0eucpnpw7ft132/IL_MEGLIO_DI_REBELSOUL.pdf. Accessed 10 Sep 2012.

———, ed. 1985. *Rebel Soul* 4: n.pag. https://www.dropbox.com/s/l0eucpnpw7ft132/IL_MEGLIO_DI_REBELSOUL.pdf. Accessed 10 Sep 2012.

———. 2012. Personal Interview. August 13.

Plastino, Goffredo. 2003. Inventing Ethnic Music: Fabrizio De André's *Crueza de mä* and the Creation of *Musica Mediterranea*. In *Mediterranean . Mosaic: Popular Music and Global Sounds*, ed. Goffredo Plastino, 267–286. New York: Routledge. Print.

Potter, Russell A. 1995. *Spectacular Vernaculars: Hip Hop and the Politics of Postmodernism.* Albany: State University of New York Press. Print.

Pugliese, Joseph. 2008. Whiteness and the Blackening of Italy: *La Guerra Cafona, Extracomunitari* and Provisional Street Justice. *Portal: Journal of Multidisciplinary International Studies* 5 (2): 1–35. http://epress.lib.uts.edu.au/journals/index.php/portal/article/view/702. Accessed 20 Jan 2017.

Robertson, Roland. 1995. Glocalization: Time-Space and Homogeneity-Heterogeneity. In *Global Modernities*, ed. Mike Featherstone, Scott Lash, and Roland Robertson, 25–44. London: Sage Publications. Print.

Rosapaeda. 2017. Email Interview. October 20.

Roudometof, Victor. 2015. The Glocal and Global Studies. *Globalizations* 12 (5): 774–787. Print.

Schneider, Jane. 1998. Introduction: The Dynamics of Neo-Orientalism in Italy (1848–1995). In *Italy's Southern Question: Orientalism in One Country*, ed. Jane Schneider, 1–23. Oxford: Berg. Print.

Solaro, Alba. 1993. Il cerchio e la saetta: Centri sociali occupati in Italia. In *Posse italiane: Centri sociali, underground musicale e cultura giovanile degli anni '90 in Italia*, ed. Carlo Branzaglia, Pierfrancesco Pacoda, and Alba Solaro, 11–70. Firenze: Editoriale Tosca. Print.

Stille, Alexander. 1995. *Excellent Cadavers: The Mafia and the Death of the First Italian Republic.* New York: Pantheon Books. Print.

———. 2006. *The Sack of Rome: Media + Money + Celebrity = Power = Silvio Berlusconi.* London: Penguin. Print.

Street, John. 2012. *Music and Politics.* Cambridge: Polity Press. Print.

Tozzi, Tommaso, ed. 2008. *Arte di opposizione: Stili di vita, situazioni e documenti degli anni Ottanta.* Milano: Shake. Print.

Veal, Michael E. 2007. *Dub: Soundscapes and Shattered Songs in Jamaican Reggae.* Middletown: Wesleyan University Press. Print.

Vecchio, Concetto. 2007. *Ali Di Piombo.* Milano: Rizzoli. Print.

Verdicchio, Pasquale. 1997. *Bound by Distance: Rethinking Nationalism through the Italian Diaspora.* Madison, NJ: Fairleigh Dickinson University Press. Print.

Voglino, Alex, et al. 1999. *Miserabili quegli anni: Dalla contestazione al terrorismo: Analisi critica degli anni Settanta.* Firenze: Tarab. Print.

Yablokov, Alexey V., Vassily B. Nesterenko, and Alexey V. Nesterenko. 2009. *Chernobyl: Consequences of the Catastrophe for People and the Environment.* Boston: Blackwell Publishing. Print.

Discography

Different Stylee. 1986a. Chernobyl Dub (Mr Babylon Heavy Mix). *Mini Album Dubwize.* Mole Reggae Diffusion. EP.

———. 1986b. Mr Babylon. *Mini Album Dubwize.* Mole Reggae Diffusion. EP.

———. 1988a. Serenata. *Serenata.* Mole Records. 12-inch.

———. 1988b. Spread Your Love. *Serenata.* Mole Records. 12-inch.

Johnson, Anthony. 1982. Gun Shot. *Gun Shot.* Midnight Rock. LP.

CHAPTER 4

Sud Sound System and the Revival of Salentine Language, Culture, and Identity

Bari's reggae scene proved to be the catalyst for an even more intense process of transculturation in the neighbouring Apulian subregion of Salento, which was initiated by the pioneering raggamuffin/reggae posse, Sud Sound System (SSS).[1] Founded in 1987/1988, and active to the present day (albeit with only some of its original members), SSS can rightfully stake their claim as *the* most accomplished and influential protagonists in Italy's diversified national reggae milieu.[2] Through their debut singles, "Fuecu" (Fire) and "T'à Sciuta Bona" (It Went Well for You), which were produced in 1991 on the independent reggae/rap record label from Bologna, Century Vox Records, SSS were at the vanguard of a revolutionary period in underground music production in Italy, commonly referred to as the "posse era." SSS has since released and produced more than ten albums and compilations, collaborated with an array of local and international

---

[1] *Il Salento* (in dialect *lu Salentu*), also known as *Terra d'Otranto*, refers to the southeastern heel-like extremity of the region of *Puglia* (Apulia in English).

[2] The founding members of SSS are Militant P (Piero Longo), DJ War (Antonio Conte), Treble, aka Lu Professore (Antonio Petrachi), Papa Gianni (Giovanni Rollo), GgD (Pierluigi De Pascali), and Don Rico (Federico Vaglio). Nandu Popu (Fernando Blasi) and Terron Fabio (Fabio Miglietta) joined in the early 1990s. SSS has undergone numerous changes in formation: the founding members Militant P and DJ War left the crew in 1992 and 1994, respectively; Treble also departed in order to begin a solo career in 2005; Gopher D (Dario Troso) was a member between 1994 and 1998. Currently the crew consists of Don Rico, Nandu Popu, Terron Fabio, Papa Gianni, and GgD.

© The Author(s) 2018
S. Scarparo, M. S. Stevenson, *Reggae and Hip Hop in Southern Italy*, Pop Music, Culture and Identity,
https://doi.org/10.1007/978-3-319-96505-5_4

86 S. SCARPARO AND M. S. STEVENSON

reggae artists, and were even invited to Australia in 2010.[3] They gained a considerable level of cultural legitimacy in Italy and abroad and played a crucial role in pioneering the evolution of locally distinct versions of reggae (and hip hop) in Salento and throughout Italy. SSS has in fact been responsible for the commonplace understanding of Salento as "Italy's Jamaica" (Pacoda 2011, p. 8; Campo 1995, p. 81; Militant 1997, p. 57) and have been credited with instigating a "Salentine renaissance" (Pacoda 2011, pp. 7–10, 25–31, 81–98).

Through their synthesis of imported musical idioms with local perspectives and dialect, SSS's reinvention and promotion of a specific Salentine cultural identity inspired youth to reconnect with their history and traditions. This bottom-up process of neoculturation attempted to articulate a locally rooted yet broadly inclusive consciousness, which provided a new model of resistance to Italy's homogenizing cultural structures, narratives, and identities. As such, this use of reggae engages meaningfully with many of the issues that have been at the heart of the *questione meridionale* (southern question) since Italy's unification.

As Pasquale Verdicchio points out, the South is perceived as a "dissonant national subject," which continues to be scarred by the colonial project of Italian unification and its ensuing political, cultural, and economic hegemony (1997, pp. 21–51). Conversely, the "Southern Italian population has been integrated into a nationalist program incapable of, to a certain extent unwilling to, fully include it in its orchestration" (Verdicchio 1997, p. 22). The peasant bands or resistance groups, which formed after unification in opposition to continued exclusion from land ownership, demonstrated the fact that Garibaldi's unifying Savoyard forces from the North were viewed as yet another instance of foreign occupation (Verdicchio 1997, p. 25; Pugliese 2008, pp. 3–7). Yet, as Joseph Pugliese points out, the southern anti-unification insurgents were cast "in terms of bands of savage and petty criminals, thereby depoliticizing their struggle against the violent process of unification" (2008, pp. 1–2). Hence, since unification, the process of creating an imagined community (Anderson 1983) has been characterized by disavowal and erasure.

The imperative to create and impose a coherent national culture, in fact, demanded "the erasure or exclusion of a large part of the peninsula's cultural identity" (Verdicchio 1997, p. 57). Crucial to the invention and

---

[3] Footage of their Melbourne concert can be found on Mathias Stevenson's YouTube channel, irie2012.

imposition of a coherent cultural model was the selection of a national language that could claim both literary and political prestige. Thus, debates in support of the cultural and linguistic unity of Italy have long privileged the prestige of the Florentine Renaissance, embodied by literary figures such as Dante, Boccaccio, and Petrarch, over the cultural production of other groups on the Italian peninsula. Hence, the Florentine language became "a powerful symbol of the modern unity of national Italy," and, by association, "the prestige or dominance accorded to the industrialized, city life of northern Italy" (Ives 2004, p. 84). The pre-eminence of the Florentine model was central to this process of forming "the fictions of a common culture stable within the borders of the nation" (Verdicchio 1997, p. 32). The disregard for local diversity and the suppression of local languages and dialects have marked the history of the Italian state, most conspicuously during the Fascist period but also continuing into the present.[4]

Within this ongoing context of cultural oppression and survival, SSS challenged the fiction of a homogeneous Italian cultural identity by foregrounding diversity through the synthesis of the imported musical idioms of reggae and reggae-inflected hip hop with local cultural and historical counter-narratives, local languages, and folk elements. Although they were not the first musicians to use *il salentino* (Salentine dialect) in their music, what made the musical activity of SSS revolutionary was their creation of what local ethnomusicologist, Federico Capone, labels a *dialetto tecnologico* (technological dialect), which involved an active process of linguistic modernization and recontextualization (2003, p. 52). By recontextualizing *il salentino* through reggae, and through its diffusion outside regional confines by way of live performances and studio recordings, SSS invested their local dialect with an unprecedented degree of legitimacy and prestige.

The question of language is a key element in Gramsci's writings on hegemony. Specifically, he argues that the imposition of a national language, or written normative grammar, seeks to "create a unitary national linguistic conformism" and is therefore "always an act of national-cultural politics" (2000, p. 355). Given that language is intricately connected to the way in which we think about and make sense of the world, both

---

[4] Debates around the *questione della lingua* (the language question) pre-date the unification of Italy. For accounts and analyses, see Richardson 2001, pp. 63–80. For accounts of language policies prior to and during fascism, see Klein 1986 and Simonini 1978.

88 S. SCARPARO AND M. S. STEVENSON

collectively and individually (Gramsci 2000, pp. 326–27), the southern languages which were marginalized within Italy's national cultural hegemony, such as *il salentino*, came to represent a peripheral or subaltern subjectivity.[5] Interpreting Gramsci's notion of the subaltern, Gayatri Spivak declares that "everything that has limited or no access to the cultural imperialism is subaltern—a space of difference" (in de Kock 1992, p. 45), and, consequently, subaltern groups are posited socially, politically, and geographically outside of the colonial power structure. The binary categories dominant/subordinate and official/subaltern are embedded within the structures of Italian nationhood (Verdicchio 1997, p. 67), in which subalternity has traditionally been personified as southern (Verdicchio 2005, pp. 1–13). Consequently, like other subaltern groups across the world, southern Italians have been "denied their own history in official historical narratives" and in "the constitutive history" of their nation (Harindranath 2006, p. 54).

Russell Potter's notion of the "resistance vernacular" provides a useful conceptual tool for understanding SSS's use of the Salentine dialect in conjunction with raggamuffin reggae to create a counter-hegemonic voice and counter-narrative for the subaltern South (1995, pp. 56–76).[6] Alongside the strictly linguistic usage of the term "vernacular" to denote non-official languages, such as Patois and dialect, Potter also refers to subaltern idioms, such as African-American rap and Jamaican raggamuffin, as "black vernaculars", thus conflating the distinction between language, culture, and identity. Potter argues that the resistance vernacular "deform[s] and reposition[s] the rules of 'intelligibility,'" becoming "by its very existence, an act of resistance to the 'standard'" (1995, p. 68). Resistance vernaculars work subversively to make "inroads against the established power-lines of speech," while "hegemonic vernaculars," such as Dante's

---

[5] Gramsci used the term "subaltern" when referring to the hegemony of a social group over a "series of subordinate groups" (1997, p. 182). The "subaltern" for Gramsci is a social group "which has not yet gained consciousness of its strength [and] its possibilities, [and] of how it is to develop ... beyond the economic-corporate stage and [how to rise] to the phase of ethical-political hegemony in civil society, and of domination in the State" (1997, pp. 159–60).

[6] Mitchell has also previously adopted Potter's notion of the resistance vernacular in his analysis of the use of indigenous languages in global hip hop music (see Mitchell 2000). He also argues that the use of dialects alongside other foreign musical traditions, such as reggae and hip hop, undermines the hegemonic culture through the creation of a "new culture," which reinforces a personal connection to regional roots and reconciles the contemporary culture with traditional associations (1996, p. 166).

SUD SOUND SYSTEM AND THE REVIVAL OF SALENTINE LANGUAGE...   89

vernacular, secure "the fiction of the 'unified' state" and lead to cultural erasure and appropriation by dominant forces (Potter 1995, pp. 57–58). Rather than completely overthrowing the status quo, resistance vernaculars enact multiple and unpredictable "guerrilla incursions" (Potter 1995, p. 76), serving to disrupt the illusion of consent and pose oppositional and subaltern world views. This understanding of the acentred and guerrilla nature of resistance vernaculars, such as Patois, dialect, raggamuffin, and hip hop, speaks directly to the concept of the rhizome: an "acentered and nonhierarchical system" characterized by "alliance" and a "guerrilla logic point of view" (Deleuze and Guattari 1987, pp. 17, 21, 45). In fact, Deleuze and Guattari assert that "there is no language in itself, nor are there any linguistic universals, only a throng of dialects, patois, slangs, and specialized languages," and "there is no mother tongue, only a power take-over by a dominant language within a political multiplicity" (1987, p. 7).

Originating in Jamaica during the mid-1980s, raggamuffin (or ragga) is an up-tempo form of reggae in which the instrumentation is primarily electronic and the vocals are "chatted" or "toasted" in the everyday Patois of the deejay (in the US and the UK: MC).[7] Strong affinities exist between raggamuffin and hip hop; hip hop evolved at least partly as a consequence of Jamaican-born DJ Clive "Kool Herc" Campbell's transportation of the sound system to the Bronx, and both hip hop/rap and raggamuffin evolved as expressions of the black underclass. Furthermore, both genres involve a rhyming spoken-word style of vocal delivery in vernacular language over technologically produced instrumental backing. During live performances, this instrumental backing is reproduced using record players and a sound system.

Due to their stylistic similarities and exchanges through cultural flows and immigration, there has been considerable crossover between the two expressive forms, and, as will be discussed in the present and subsequent chapters, the mixing of raggamuffin and rap was prevalent in Italy during the early 1990s. SSS's synthesis of raggamuffin and rap with dialect became a particularly powerful method of resisting cultural fragmentation and subalternity. Assuming its own level of cultural prestige, Salentine reggae

---

[7] The term "raggamuffin" is an intentional misspelling of "ragamuffin," and the genre identified itself as the voice of Jamaica's ghetto youths and rude boys. The term "dancehall" is often used synonymously with raggamuffin/ragga, especially since the late 1990s. Raggamuffin represents the evolution of the deejay style originated by such artists as Count Machuki and King Stitt mentioned in Chap. 2.

in turn became a means to critique Salentine (and southern) marginality and a testament to the living presence of non-official cultural diversity within the official national culture.

MILITANT P AND STRUGGLE: REGGAE'S BRIDGE BETWEEN BARI AND SALENTO

In spite of the considerable achievements and strong contemporary following of SSS throughout Italy, particularly amongst a youth audience, the important story of their foundation remains largely unknown. Central to this little-known story is Piero Longo (Militant P), who acted as reggae's bridge between Bari and Salento and was more recently the main subject of the documentary film, *Rockman* (2011).

Longo's first in-depth contact with reggae music occurred during the free radio transmissions of "Ganja University," conducted by Bari's Reggae Diffusion collective (Longo in *Ritmo Vitale*) and discussed in the previous chapter. Longo's association with Mimmo Pizzutilo and Different Stylee was also crucial in the early stages of his reggae education (in Manfredi 2008, p. 33), when he was involved with the respected reggae group, Struggle. The group, in fact, was directly inspired by and linked to *la Giungla* and Different Stylee, with a few members, such as percussionist, Nico "Different" Caldarulo, forming a part of both groups, and their heavy brand of rockers-style roots and dub was reflective of this association. In the eyes of his friend and founding SSS member, Antonio "Treble" Petrachi, Struggle achieved a stylistic and technical level that has remained unparalleled in the history of Italian reggae. Further, Petrachi stresses that the potency of the group was enhanced by the hypnotic expressiveness of Longo's vocal delivery (Personal interview).

In 1987, not long after the release of Different Stylee's previously discussed EP, *Mini Album Dubwize*, Struggle put out their first and only official recording: a self-produced demo tape titled *Struggle to Live*, which contained eight vocal and dub tracks. The lyrics were written and performed in English, with Italian translations provided on the cassette's sleeve. The A-side was recorded live at Bari's Snoopy Club and the B-side was recorded in Different Stylee's Mole Studio by Amedeo Vox. In a 1986 interview appearing in the only edition of the fanzine, *Ritmo Vitale* (*Ital Soul* with a new name), Struggle listed their primary musical influences as English reggae, such as Dennis Bovell and Jah Shaka, dub, roots reggae,

Burning Spear, and Different Stylee.[8] Whilst Different Stylee evolved from a roots-dub sound into what we have termed reggae world fusion, Struggle did not deviate from a richly textured, drum and bass heavy, rockers-style roots-dub that would not have sounded out of place on the sound systems of London or Kingston.

Along with the stylistic parallels between Different Stylee and Struggle, there is also a clear thematic continuity stemming from their shared politics and collaborations. For example, Struggle's composition, "Nuclear City," is an ominous critique of the grave risks of atomic energy that parallels Different Stylee's "Chernobyl Dub (Mr Babylon Heavy Mix)." Similar to Different Stylee's track, "Nuclear City" was released soon after the Chernobyl crisis, and both bands used music as a direct form of advocacy by organizing concerts and benefits in support of the anti-nuclear movement. In contrast to the entirely instrumental "Chernobyl Dub," however, "Nuclear City" conveys its message through the gravity of Militant P's deep vocal tones and repeated verses, which are complemented by a heavily textured yet melancholic *one drop* rhythm.[9]

As for all of their songs, the lyrics to "Nuclear City" are in English, highlighting the fact that Italian reggae was still in its early phase of transculturation and that the process of musical identification was still largely projected outwards, towards a foreign "Other."

> Nuclear city,
> What a dreary city, for me …
> Murder city,
> … You're killing, you're killing me,
> … True love, where have you gone?
> True love, where are you from?
> Murder Babylon,
> Murder Babylon,
> … You're killing, you're killing true love.

The association of nuclear or atomic energy with a murderous, dehumanizing, and destructive urban Babylon can be read as an intertextual

---

[8] Dennis Bovell is a Barbadian-born British reggae musician and producer best known for his collaborations with the dub poet Linton Kwesi Johnson; Jah Shaka is a London-based sound system operator and dub reggae producer; Burning Spear is a celebrated Rastafarian Jamaican roots reggae singer.

[9] One drop is considered the foundational reggae beat, where the main emphasis falls on the third beat of the bar.

extension of the discourse initiated by "Mr Babylon," which, as discussed in the previous chapter, appropriated Rastafarian metaphors to critique modern society and technological advancement. Militant P's gruff and lamenting vocal style complements and reinforces the inherent foreboding of the message, and the symbiosis between form and meaning is elaborated further by the sombre and heavy instrumentation, which foregrounds the rhythm section whilst leaving space for moody percussion, hypnotic horns, jagged guitar riffs, and frequent echo and reverb.

The EP's title track, "Struggle to Live," blends rhythmical and lyrical elements to focus the field of political struggle on the everyday, existential realm, and can therefore be understood as the group's musical manifesto. The rhythmic backing to "Struggle to Live" is densely layered and clearly influenced by British sound system reggae. Also reminiscent of "Mr Babylon" is an extended atmospheric intro, with poignant pan-pipe synth guiding in a driving rockers beat. The drum and bass are again foregrounded and adorned by soulful guitar riffs, the accentuation of the rhythm by the horn section further enhances the marching quality of the rockers sound, and the incorporation of bongos increases its underlying sense of exoticism while complementing the lyrical subtext of alienation and "Otherness." This rhythmic backing complements the core thematic summarized by the Patois-inflected chorus:

> Live! Struggle to live,
> Love! Struggle to love,
> You must be crazy,
> To think that it's so easy,
> Living ina Babylon.

The opening imperatives of the first two lines equate love with life. However, as expressed in the lyrics to "Nuclear City," Babylon is responsible for the death of love, and so the quest to find or maintain love, and in turn life, becomes a struggle that has the potential to erode an individual's emotional, psychological, and spiritual wellbeing: "I'm tired of fighting every day / I'm so depressed, for this." Yet, the central idea is that resistance is intertwined with determination and positivity: "But I'm going on with my fight / Master of the game / Faith is still the same / Yes my trust is living." Thus, faith and trust are put forth as essential to overcoming the daily pressures and injustices of the Babylonian system.

As discussed in Chap. 3, Pizzutilo spoke of the need to make politics a practical element in everyday life and of how the language of reggae facilitated this shift in emphasis away from institutional politics. Indeed, the everyday struggle that both gives the group its name and is dealt with by the song not only assumes existential, affective, and psychological significance, but is also inherently political, insofar as it stands in opposition to the hegemonic state of affairs. As Laurie Langbauer asserts, "[p]olitics can also mean contestation, the fight not to nullify but to assert disagreement, the struggle to be heard rather than silenced" (1992, p. 48).

From an early stage, Longo was attracted to deejay style reggae and began emulating this vocal style in pseudo Patois. His attraction to deejay style, or toasting, was particularly rare in Italy at this time. The generic description, deejay style, refers to this style of toasted reggae between the 1970s and early to mid-1980s, also sometimes called rub-a-dub style, while from the late 1980s through to the 1990s onwards, it was typically referred to as raggamuffin/ragga or dancehall. For our purposes, we will refer to this reggae subgenre up until 1985 as deejay style and post-1985 as raggamuffin.

Although it can be understood as the Jamaican equivalent to rapping, the tradition of toasting in fact pre-dates rap. Toasting is also stylistically different, with a greater emphasis on melodic intonation, non-semantic vocalization, and repeated end rhymes, which lend it a more rhythmic, chant-like quality. Whereas in hip hop the rapper is referred to as an MC and the person who lays down the beats as the DJ, in reggae the toaster is referred to as the deejay and the person who provides the musical backing is the selector.[10] Apart from Militant P, the only other Italians toasting during this early phase (around 1984) were three youngsters from the Savona Posse in Liguria: Papa Retz, Ranking Sinyx, and Briggy Bronson.[11] Militant P's first toasting experiments took place with Bari's sound system,

[10] To avoid confusion, when referring to someone who plays records for a crowd of people, we will either use the Jamaican expression "selector" or the initials "DJ."

[11] The three deejays from Savona commenced their stylistic experiments in Jamaican Patois through their association with the radio programme, *Trouble*, on the free radio, *Radio Vecchia Savona*. Theirs was the first Italian deejay style, and Diego Pievino (Briggy Bronson) earned the epithet "the Originator" (see Bettini and Tosi 2009, p. 232). Little is known about these enigmatic figures, but a limited number of musical documents remain. In 1984 they self-produced and distributed a cassette entitled *DJ Connection*, and in 1987 Bronson produced a solo cassette entitled *Bubbler*, both of which were recorded entirely in Patois. Regardless of their failure to have a long-term or widespread influence, Briggy Bronson and the rest of the Savona Posse must be acknowledged as pioneers and inspirations for Militant P.

94   S. SCARPARO AND M. S. STEVENSON

Reggae Diffusion (see Chap. 3), with which he toured some of Italy, including the neighbouring Salento (Pizzutilo, Personal interview).

SOUTHERN CONNECTIVE MARGINALITIES

Longo's association with *la Giungla*, Different Stylee, and Reggae Diffusion led him to identify with the Africanist aesthetic of musical forms, such as Afrobeat and reggae, which he then transported to his friends in San Foca, Salento, where he would spend the summer months. As Petrachi explains, "he told us that there was a different type of music to what we listened to and which could be relevant for us and the way we wanted to be. At the beginning he called it *la musica delli niuri* [Salentine dialect for 'black music']" (in Manfredi 2008, p. 33). Not only did this identification with a cultural and racial "Other" appropriate "blackness" as a symbol of exclusion and difference from Italy's dominant culture, but it reflected the connective marginality that Longo, as an Apulian youth, felt towards black Jamaicans through the conduit of reggae: "he always said to us: 'let's listen to this music because it speaks about people that are suffering, who have left Africa, ... There are parallels with us.' ... It was as if he felt like a black, insofar as he was a Southerner ... and so he also felt the need to speak about his rights and reclaim his culture" (Petrachi in "La musica").

These resonances felt by Longo in relation to the subaltern black experience speak to the racist foundations of Italian unification. Through the positivist theorists of race, southern inferiority became an unquestioned scientific fact and was used to justify socioeconomic disadvantage. A key protagonist in the advancement of such theories was Alfredo Niceforo, who traced the inferiority of southerners to their supposed African descent. Jane Schneider asserts that the codification of differences between the North and the South has occurred within a "symbolic geography" of a "neo-Orientalist" discourse that continues to this day within a wider hegemonic context (1998, pp. 1–3). With the rise of the Lega Nord (Northern League) in the 1980s and early 1990s, which will be discussed in more detail in the following chapter, racial stereotyping of southern Italians and their discursive framing as Africans continued to have considerable currency.

Seen in this light, whiteness has been "absolutely constitutive in the formation of hegemonic Italian identity, politics and culture" (Pugliese 2008, p. 32). Consequently, the identification with and adoption of the "black" Afro-Caribbean musical form of reggae by Longo and his friends, through the connective marginality dynamic, offered them the means through which (as was the case with Different Stylee) they could articulate an alternative to dominant understandings of Italian cultural identity and nationhood, along with the apparatuses of power that these understandings supported.

The intercultural dialogue and exchange, already opened up by the transnational punk-reggae association, reinforced the connective marginality that Salentine youth felt towards reggae. As Petrachi explains, although groups like The Clash were whites, "they played reggae songs, even if it seemed like a hard, white brand of reggae, and we found this fascinating" (Personal interview). Furthermore, Petrachi claims that the formal qualities of reggae reminded them of Salentine music: "the accent on that beat seemed a bit strange to us and reminded us of something familiar. I'm convinced that it also sounded like something of ours; folk music has those sorts of accents. And so, unconsciously, it was already natural for us" (Petrachi, Personal interview).

During this period, Salento's rich cultural and linguistic traditions were in sharp decline. When asked if there was a sense of cultural pride at this time, Petrachi declared:

> There was nothing. The word Salento, therefore the idea of Salento, was no longer used by anyone. It was really removed from the collective imagination and dialect was considered a product of cultural backwardness. Perhaps only in university environments some professors were able to understand that something profound existed from a historical and cultural perspective. (Personal interview)

This lack of cultural consciousness also bore witness to the neglect of Salento's rich musical traditions. As Petrachi recounts: "when we began to do reggae, *la pizzica* no longer existed and the musical styles you could hear at local festivals were mainly Flamenco, Tango, and Mazurka" (Personal interview).[12]

The neglect and decline of Salento's rich cultural traditions reflected a widening social and existential malaise afflicting the region's youth which resulted in an array of issues, such as heroin addiction, unemployment,

---

[12] *Pizzica* (translatable as "bite"), also known as *pizzica pizzica* or *pizzica tarantata*, is an Italian folk dance (part of the *tarantella* family of dances) originating in the Salento peninsula and brought to light by the research of Italian anthropologist, folklorist, and historian of religions, Ernesto De Martino, in his 1961 work, *La terra del rimorso* (The Land of Remorse, 1961).

96 S. SCARPARO AND M. S. STEVENSON

exploitation, and organized crime. For vulnerable youth with limited economic opportunities, the local Mafia (*Sacra Corona Unita*)[13] represented a particularly serious risk and, for Petrachi and his friends, reggae music provided a means to resist its influence:

> At the time, the entire Salento was Mafia. And it was something that sort of divided the youth in two: those that were fortunate enough to stay out of it, and those, on the other hand, that fell into it just like a funnel. In that respect, reggae also kind of helped us to get away from it. There was exploitation, as of course there is now. But at the time it was really heavy. There were clashes in the town; people murdered on the doorstep of the bar. Young men whose heads were cut off because they were dealing heroin. We experienced all these things but the power of reggae music's message helped us to see music as a weapon of resistance; at least to resist within ourselves. (Petrachi, Personal interview)

Thus, for the young nucleus of SSS, reggae music provided a focus, outlet, and purpose which steered them clear of crime and heroin abuse, and the group of friends formed a sort of extended family that was referred to as the Salento Posse (Petrachi, Personal interview).

Transculturation from Below: Dialect, Roots and Culture, and Edutainment

From around 1986 to 1987, the posse would hold reggae parties at Papa Gianni's place by the sea during the summer holiday months. Here they began vocally experimenting and improvising over the B-side instrumental versions, or *riddims*, of DJ War's seven-inch records imported from London. As Giovanni "Papa Gianni" Rollo recalls: "After a dinner between friends, we would pick up the microphones and begin to tell our stories in rhyme. There, between twenty friends this land's new 'era' began" (in Pacoda 2011, pp. 94–95). This practice of setting up one or two turntables, an amplifier, microphone, and speakers was a small-scale recontextualization of the sound system practices originating in Kingston, which had given rise to deejay style in the late 1960s and to New York's hip hop scene in the early 1970s.

---

[13] Although the noun "Mafia" originated in Sicily, it is typically used to refer to the various criminal organizations that afflict the southern Italian regions: Sicily (*Cosa Nostra* or *Mafia*), Campania (*Camorra*), Calabria ('*Ndrangheta*), Apulia (*Sacra Corona Unita*). See John Dickie's *Mafia Brotherhoods*.

Papa Gianni's parties thus marked the beginnings of reggae's next and most profound phase of transculturation in Apulia and Italy. The unplanned parties in the countryside were held far away from the circuits and spaces of Italy's commercial culture industry. Realizing that the prosody of local dialect adapted very well to reggae's dilated rhythms, the young reggae aficionados soon began carrying out their own vocal improvisations in Salentine dialect (Rollo in Pacoda 2011, p. 94). They initially began by experimenting with assonances between words and expressions in the two minor languages of *il salentino* and Jamaican Patois. *Hear mi nuh* (listen to me now) became *sienti moi* (listen now); *come in nuh* (come in now) became *camina moi* (move now); and *ah bwoy* (oh boy) became *ahi li guai* (what sorrow problems cause). Petrachi explains this process in more detail:

> For example, at the time they [Jamaicans] said "*ah bwoy*," and Gianni transformed it into "*ahi li guai*" (what sorrow problems cause), because the Mafia controls all of us, understand? But from that process the use of the Salentine dialect was born. Looking for assonance with Jamaican Patois [became] a way of reflecting on the condition of the youth in Salento at the time. (Personal interview)

Hence, through homophonic and semantic interplay between Jamaican Patois and dialect, an act of experimentation over imported reggae *riddims* developed into a process of cultural and linguistic synthesis. This process subsequently facilitated a philosophical and existential reflection on the perilous circumstances and lack of cultural identity for Salentine youth. This reflection was in turn inspired by an understanding of the marginalized condition of black Jamaicans, and marked the initial stages of Sud Sound System's counter-hegemonic resistance vernacular.

By forming an intercultural and interlinguistic dialogue with their Afro-Caribbean and Afro-American counterparts, SSS thus undertook a self-appropriation of the racial "Other" as a form of opposition. For example, as a means of simultaneously stating pride in their cultural identity and their position of "Otherness," the adoption and semantic alteration of the derogatory term "*terrone*" by SSS's Terron Fabio for his stage name are comparable to the reappropriation of the term "nigger" by black

Jamaicans, black Americans, and black British.[14] A parallel Jamaican example would be the singer/deejay Nigger Kojak. Rollo confirms that it was "a historic moment.... An embrace between two worlds that were very different but also very close. At that time, the stories of what was happening in the ghetto of Kingston weren't too far removed from the style of life in many towns in our region" (in Pacoda 2011, p. 94).

Petrachi stresses further that a new consciousness was inspired by the local resonance of reggae's emphasis on roots and culture as a symbol, "a banner," which for them "really related to everything" (Personal interview). Reinforcing this connective marginality was the following statement from the group: "we realized that in the Jamaican songs there was an infinite southerness. The same attachment to one's roots, the desire to sing about love and sentimentalism, the intolerance for oppression" (in Pacoda 1993, p. 97). By bringing together two seemingly distant cultures, this process of neoculturation soon developed into something of wider significance. As Petrachi explains, through this process of cultural-linguistic evolution, raggamuffin became a vehicle for biting social critique:

> [W]e began to recount things in *salentino*. Papa Gianni was one of the first improvisers. He would improvise about problems related to the lack of work, about the corrupt employment process, about the mess of election time. And a song was born that went: *Brizzino Brizzino*[15] *don't screw it up, free up the wage, employ the kid.* Of course, it was a big hit and perhaps that was [our] first socially engaged song. (In Manfredi 2008, p. 51)

Since the mass of people attending the parties at Papa Gianni's house had grown too large, SSS began organizing autonomous dancehalls in outdoor spaces. The fact that the parties were organized outside institutional processes, official communicative channels, and mainstream cultural spaces demonstrated the group's unwillingness to surrender to Italy's homogenizing culture industry, which was defined by commercial television and mega-pop concerts. Furthermore, these rural dancehalls were fundamentally democratic, being guided by an open microphone policy and the conflation of the distance between performer and audience. These points have been reinforced by SSS in their own words:

[14] As discussed in the previous chapter, the derogatory term *terrone* (roughly translated as dirty peasant) is used by northern Italians to describe southerners.

[15] Brizzino was a powerful Christian Democrat from Calimera. According to Petrachi, he was a type of employment baron (Personal interview).

SUD SOUND SYSTEM AND THE REVIVAL OF SALENTINE LANGUAGE... 99

All we needed was a generator, a beaten-up sound system and records ... moving around in semi-illegality, without printing invitations or flyers, the news traveled by word of mouth. Everyone did everything: those who wanted to use the microphone did so, and the same thing applied for the backing music, those who had it brought it.... It's not as if we were thinking about becoming singers, forming a group and then making records at the time: everything came to be spontaneously, from the pleasure of telling our stories, about our real or imaginary lives. (In Campo 1995, p. 83)

SSS's pirate dancehalls struck a balance between hedonistic enjoyment and social critique. Petrachi explains the centrality of this relationship between entertainment and education, stating that dancehalls were joyful occasions but were also used to comment on the two major problems afflicting Salentine youth at that time: Mafia and heroin (Personal interview). According to the noted Salentine filmmaker, Edoardo Winspeare, these parties awakened a sense of "rebellion" and "consciousness" (in Pacoda 2011, p. 48). This ability to celebrate free time, while also demonstrating opposition and raising awareness through social and cultural messages, is particularly relevant to reggae's deejay and raggamuffin styles. As Simon Jones explains, the role of the Jamaican reggae lyricist is not only to "articulate the collective consciousness of their audience, but also to organise and politicise it" (1988, p. 27). Accordingly, "reggae can be seen to continue within the most fundamental of African musical traditions by functioning as a vehicle of learning and education as much as a source of entertainment" (Jones 1988, pp. 27–28).[16]

This didactic oral tradition originating in Africa was also prominent in hip hop and, most explicitly, through KRS-One's concept of music as "edutainment," or a blend of education and entertainment.[17] As Petrachi explains: "We really believed in what KRS-One said, that is: 'edutainment'; education and entertainment. There's dancing, there's the idea of freeing oneself from something, but not for *nothing*, freeing yourself for *something*" (Personal interview).

Lacking complete confidence in the use of dialect outside their local context, however, the young vocalists continued to use predominantly Jamaican Patois and English. Nonetheless, a significant event in Holland

---

[16] Of course, this is not always the case, and the prominence of so-called slackness lyrics (celebrating sex and guns) in the 1980s provides a counterpoint to the "cultural" lyrics with which reggae was associated in Italy and throughout the world.

[17] Formalized in 1990 with his release of the album, *Edutainment* (Jive).

shifted their perspective. Petrachi explains that he, Longo (aka Militant P), and the Roman reggae selector, Lampa Dread,[18] were conducting a small tour of Europe when one evening they found themselves in a club near the border with Germany:

> We were still singing in English (imagine what English it was) and during one gig a group of German-Jamaican Rastas almost insulted us, because what we were saying was incomprehensible. The leader of the crew took us into a corner and said to us: "Why don't you try singing in your own language? At least you know what you're saying." And so, Militant did one of his pieces in *barese* [dialect of bari], which spoke about a time when he had been beaten up just for wanting to sing reggae. (Personal interview)

Longo's piece in the dialect of Bari was the defiantly ironic "M'e Sciut Bon" (It Went Well for Me), which was based on assonance between this dialectal expression and the Patois words/expressions "mash it, bun" (destroy it, burn), typically used to affirm a sense of potency. After performing the song, the German-Jamaican Rasta said: "'Yes, now I don't understand, but I like the rhythm of it and I know you're saying something meaningful in your language. Now you're real!'" (Petrachi, Personal interview).

Sud Sound System's increasing use of dialect directly countered the dominant tendencies of the time, which discouraged its use amongst youth and tended towards cultural and historical erasure:

> When we began our Jamaican-Salentine dances, dialect was prohibited. It was something for the elderly, incomprehensible and useless for the youngsters who were encouraged to express themselves "well" at home and at school, wiping out the history of their parents and grandparents in the name of "good Italian." (Rollo in Pacoda 2011, pp. 91–92)

Nonetheless, Sud Sound System showed that *il salentino* could be combined with raggamuffin to establish a syncretic resistance vernacular, which both articulated a self-conscious identity grounded in the "Other" and rejected society's dominant cultural tendencies. As Fernando "Nandu Popu" Blasi recounts:

> Probably it was a moment in which people wanted to speak dialect to demonstrate a little anti-conformism .... Hence our choice to listen to

---

[18] Lampa Dread was to later form Italy's historic posse and sound system One Love Hi Powa.

raggamuffin, which means: "ragged," "unkempt" ..., we associated ourselves with this term, we made it ours. "Trendiness" was starting to arrive, it was the era of the "*paninari*" and, at the time, singing in dialect meant rejecting the Italian language, which was utilized for musical styles that really didn't attract us at the time. (In Manfredi 2008, p. 42)

The term *paninari* refers to the middle to upper class northern youth scene of the 1980s, which originated in Milan and was known for its association with designer clothes, fast food, Americanization, and apolitical consumption. As Francesco Donadio and Marcello Giannotti explain, the *paninari* were the symbol of the wave of *riflusso* and apathy of the 1980s (1996, pp. 188–89). Thus, the musical and linguistic choices of raggamuffin and dialect were made in opposition to the hegemonic and homogenizing consumerist ideals and culture promoted during the neoliberal 1980s, and which rode the wave of Berlusconi's commercial television revolution.

Tarantamuffin and the Connection with Local Traditions

SSS's first direct encounters with Salento's neglected musical traditions, at the local taverns, or *putee*, were also fundamental to their transculturation of reggae and development of a consciousness-raising musical practice. Rollo recounts that the extended posse would arrive in a large group and take over the taverns to rehearse, and on one such occasion a group of elderly *pizzica* musicians spontaneously accompanied them with their instruments: "there lay, I believe, the origins of the *neopizzica salentina*, not just as a musical phenomenon but as a social phenomenon relating to the 'rediscovery' of a territory" (in Pacoda 2011, p. 95). This proved to be but the first of many such encounters, with veteran folk musicians, such as the Li Ucci and Luigi Stifani, beginning to attend and perform at the dancehalls organized by SSS. Winspeare stresses that this cultural revival initiated through SSS's dancehalls was to develop into a vital form of resistance against the influence of organized crime: "A Mafia model of criminality could have permanently asserted itself and was avoided due to a popular reaction through a profound love for traditions. Otherwise Salento would have become a desperate South like the others" (in Pacoda 2011, p. 48).

Before long, such encounters and affinities began to be formally studied and theorized by the French anthropologist and ethnomusicologist, Georges Lapassade, and Italian sociologist, Pietro Fumarola. They argued that the "therapeutic" use of music by SSS displayed continuities with the function of the traditional Salentine folk music form of *la pizzica* and could accordingly be understood as its contemporary equivalent. *Pizzica* was the product of the religious cult of *il tarantismo*, where through an "extended erotic dance cycle," specialized musicians perform a ritualistic and therapeutic exorcism of the shock-like ill-effects of the venom of a "supernaturally charged tarantula bite" (Saunders 1993, p. 884). Federico Capone maintains that *il tarantismo* was not a physical suffering resulting from the bite of the spider but was primarily a cathartic means for expressing one's malaise and for escaping daily rural life, particularly for women (2003, p. 40).

Fusing the term *tarantella*, generically used to refer to southern folk dances, with *raggamuffin*, Lapassade coined the neologism, *tarantamuffin*. He used this term to describe the confluence of innovation, tradition, global, and local that was taking place in Salento at that time. According to William Anselmi, this "particular form of hybridization conveys tradition and otherness in terms of their similarity as a means to re-appropriate one's anthropological culture", and creates "correspondences with other exploited, subjugated cultures expressed through one's own local reality (in terms of language and history)" (2002, p. 40). Similarly, Salvatore Colazzo has claimed that the music of SSS involves the search for and discovery of "new alliances" (1994, pp. 171–72). The evolution of such a *glocal* form of music, which brings together distant, minor, and peripheral cultures, provides a key example of reggae's powerful connective marginalities in Italy's South.

Attention from the academic world inspired Sud Sound System's revolutionary project to reconfigure the "southern question" and establish a community resistant to fragmentation and exploitation. Petrachi explains in further detail:

> We had frequent contact with university professors from Lecce, who were the only ones that understood our discourse. They explained to us that while Rome was being founded ..., here in Roca, and in the entire Salento, an advanced civilization existed: the Messapians. As a student of agricultural studies, I saw that in the historical period up until 1860, the South was the richest part of Italy. So, I convinced my friends that Salento, for its history,

culture and artistic sensibility, was advanced and not underdeveloped. In a certain sense, the musical evolution that was carried out in Salento was precisely this: give music the revolutionary value to reconstruct an identity, which, in its absence, had allowed the Mafia to exploit the fragmentation of the community. And so little by little we constructed this word "Salento," because for us it signified "Jamaica." (Personal interview)

Reggae's capacity to establish new chains of meaning, and syncretic cultural identities celebrating roots, tradition, exchange, and otherness, was further confirmed through the parallel activity of Massilia Sound System (MSS). MSS was formed during the mid-1980s in Marseille, France, as a reaction to social and economic crisis and the rise of the racist National Front. As founding member Papet Yali recalls: "We began Massilia Sound System ... because Marseille was in crisis. It was very down, economically, socially and so on. The National Front with M. Le Pen came up strongly in Marseille, 28 per cent in the local polls, which was shameful to us, and we reacted to that by singing" (in "Massilia Sound System Interview" 2006). MSS developed a Provençal hybrid version of reggae and raggamuffin, which itself inspired the use of the neologism, *trobamuffin* (combining the Occitan word *trobador* with raggamuffin). By incorporating musical elements from the local tradition and adopting the endangered language of Occitan, their music reawakened a positive local identity amongst the youth in that region and in the South of France generally. Furthermore, they used their musical and linguistic fusions to promote cultural exchange. These resonances between the projects of SSS and MSS were made explicit in the early 1990s, when Petrachi met Papet Yali for the first time. This meeting gave Petrachi the inspiration to create something similar in Salento to what MSS were doing in Marseille.

Such parallels were not lost on Lapassade, who, after conducting fieldwork on *il tarantismo* in Salento in the early 1980s, returned to Lecce in 1991 to study Sud Sound System. Lapassade considered SSS and MSS as the best examples of synthesis between the Caribbean and the Mediterranean, and he maintained that the local dialectal project of SSS was even more systematic and well-defined than that of MSS (Lapassade and Rousselot 2009, p. 178). Both Lapassade and Fumarola were moved to study, with a certain dedication, the perceived continuities and affinities between Salento's folk music traditions and SSS's local version of raggamuffin. They even gave the burgeoning Salentine reggae scene an unprecedented degree of cultural legitimacy by setting up seminars and

104   S. SCARPARO AND M. S. STEVENSON

jam sessions at Lecce's university, which brought together the members of SSS, MSS, and traditional Salentine musicians.

Due to the largely unplanned way in which their musical narrative had developed, the members of SSS initially felt overwhelmed by such expansive claims of cultural continuity, which were conveyed through the concept of *tarantamuffin*. As Rollo explains:

> When the phenomenon of the dancehalls commenced, we would never have imagined that we would immediately have been "identified" as the new harbingers of *la pizzica*. *Tarantamuffin* wasn't a part of our plan, but everything moved chaotically and rapidly. Researchers and academics joined up with the old guys and us ..., we began to be invited to seminars at the universities, first in Bologna, then around Italy. (In Pacoda 2011, p. 96)

Petrachi suggests that from the very beginning they had "unconsciously" perceived a layer of continuity between the old and the new. To this end, he underlines that reggae also has an "ancestral" quality and, like *la pizzica*, uses the rhythm "as catharsis." Furthermore, he explains that the use of triplet rhythms, both in Salentine folk music and in reggae, also drew these forms together (Personal interview). Fittingly, in 1989 Petrachi composed a song named "Taranta Internazionale" (International Tarantula),[19] in which he toasted a classic folk music chorus in Salentine dialect—"M'a pezzecatu, m'a pezzecatu / La taranta m'a pezzecatu" (It bit me, It bit me / The tarantula bit me)—over an up-tempo reggae rhythm played by the Sicilian band, Calura. Mimmo Pizzutilo similarly reinforces the fact that both reggae and Apulian folk music have "ancestral roots" and that their hypnotic rhythms provide the basis for creating a "collective and liberating ritual" (in Manfredi 2008, p. 69). Moreover, according to Lapassade, the intense conviviality between SSS and their Salentine audiences reflected the common foundation between their reggae parties and the area's local folk traditions (Lapassade and Rousselot 2009, p. 178).

Further underlining the latent connective marginalities between the Salentine folk tradition and the black diasporic form of reggae, Rollo maintains that they both evolved as means of alleviating suffering caused by oppression. Members of his own family worked as tobacco farmers, in what Rollo refers to as conditions of "semi-slavery," and he recounts that

---

[19] This piece was never officially released, but a brief studio demo has been uploaded on YouTube under Petrachi's channel, "Treblestudio" (see Works Cited list).

the women would sing as a way to stay awake and finish the labour (in Pacoda 2011, p. 90). This story of female exploitation found voice in his music through his unofficial raggamuffin rendition of the female protest work song, "Fimmine Fimmine" (Women Women), in the early 1990s.

Despite such links, Capone criticizes the use of the term *tarantamuffin* to signify a direct union between *la pizzica* and reggae. According to Capone, just because some artists use dialect or elements of *pizzica* does not mean that one can refer to that type of music as *pizzica*. Rather, for Capone, the "folk-like quality" of the music owes to the fact that it originates and spreads "'from below'" (2004, p. 35). Echoing this statement, Antonio "DJ War" Conte claims that Salentine reggae can consider itself a type of folk music (*musica popolare*) because it is broad and sprouts "'from below'" (in Capone 2004, p. 71). Capone maintains further that, rather than an overt reinvention of the folk music traditions of Salento, the "international" reggae-hip hop of SSS demonstrates a desire, on behalf of the artists, to not distance themselves entirely from their roots (pp. 34–35).

In their desire to get in touch with their roots, Sud Sound System not only drew from rural Salentine folk music but also from the urban folk music of Lecce, which is another integral part of the local musical tradition (Capone 2003, p. 36). In his book, *Lecce che suona*, Capone traces the continuities in Salentine music from the distant past to the contemporary age, identifying Lecce's urban folk music of the 1970s and 1980s as "the ideal *trait d'union*" between traditional music—*la pizzica* and *la tarantella*—and contemporary music—reggae and hip hop (2003, p. 39). He also explains that these connections between Salento's rural and urban folk music and reggae-hip hop can be found both in unofficial recordings, predominantly in moments of vocal improvisation or "freestyle," and in official recordings (Capone 2009, p. 14). In our view, therefore, such intertextual connections and citations can be interpreted as a key component of reggae's (g)localization and transculturation in Salento.

Another fundamental link between rural and urban Salentine folk music and reggae is their mutual grounding in oral traditions. Capone argues, in fact, that in all forms of Salentine music, from the past to the present, oral improvisation has been a constant, whether through *stornelli* or freestyle (*Lecce* 11–12).[20] Some members of SSS compare the troubadours of Sicily and Apulia with the Jamaican sound system deejays and single out the

---

[20] *Stornelli* are a form of rhyming folk song relying on improvisation, which, similarly to freestyle, often took the form of "battles" between two people and involved double or hidden meanings.

efficacy of the use of dialect with reggae as evidence of this oral connection (Petrachi, Personal interview). Thus, the characteristic orality of Salentine reggae can also be understood as the product of the rhizomatic resonance between local and imported minor vernacular traditions, both of which were rooted in resistance.

BEYOND SALENTO: *ISOLA NEL KANTIERE*, THE REGGAE-HIP HOP CONNECTION

Crucial to the development of SSS's autonomous musical practice, and the Salentine posse's first official recordings, were the parallel experiences of its members outside Salento during the mid- to late 1980s. Both Antonio Conte (DJ War) and Antonio Petrachi (Treble) had moved to Bologna in 1983 to attend university, returning home to Salento every summer.[21] Also joining Treble and DJ War in Bologna were Pierluigi De Pascali (GgD) and Dario Troso (Gopher D), while Piero Longo (Militant P) would make frequent visits from Bari. Bologna was renowned for its experimental and underground youth culture, which, through the activity of Radio Alice, had been particularly important during the student movement of the late 1970s. DJ War, who was SSS's founding selector, played punk, reggae, and rap at Radio Alice's second incarnation, Radio Underdog.

From the summer of 1988, the hub of Bologna's rich musical underground was the CSOA, *Isola nel Kantiere* (*INK*), which was established in the closed wing of a theatre in the centre of town. *INK* was initially associated with Bologna's punk scene, but, at the beginning of the 1990s, the black musical forms of reggae and hip hop soon became *the* dominant soundscape for the socially and politically active youth gravitating towards the centre. Consequently, *INK* was characterized by an unprecedented climate of improvisation and experimentation (Pacoda 2000, p. 18).

This rare openness towards new musical influences also stemmed from the fact that *INK* was based on a less ideological and more practical cultural politics than the vast majority of other *centri sociali* in the 1980s (Pacoda 2000, p. 18). Another important feature of *INK* was its cultural, ethnic, and social diversity, which resulted in a rich exchange of influences and styles (Capone 2004, p. 19). The interregional connection fostered by

---

[21] Born in 1962, Antonio Conte was approximately four years older than Piero Longo (1966) and one year older than Antonio Petrachi (1963). Conte is recognized as one of the founders of Italian reggae, hip hop, and jungle music.

INK was especially significant considering the paucity of *centri sociali* in the South and their total absence in Salento.

Around the time of *INK*'s foundation, in 1988, DJ War and Gopher D had begun collaborating with each other through a group named Subnoise, which played punk and dub reggae, while Treble and GgD teamed up with the Sicilian-born hip hop DJ, Renato Amata (DJ R), to form the experimental formation, Mustafà MCs and DJ R, which blended hip hop with heavy metal and raggamuffin. This influx of musically gifted southern Italians at *INK* contributed to punk being gradually overtaken by reggae, particularly raggamuffin, and rap. This coincided with the increasing hybridization of these musical idioms in New York, following a new wave of Jamaican immigration during the mid- to late 1980s.[22] Bronx artist KRS-One's fusion of rap and reggae on the album, *Criminal Minded* (B-Boy Records, 1987), which was produced with his collective, Boogie Down Productions, was particularly influential in this new phase of increasing hybridity.

Criminal Minded was groundbreaking because it demonstrated for the first time "that blackness in the Bronx could be tied to Jamaicanness" and that Jamaicanness no longer carried the same stigma as it had done when Kool Herc first synthesized the Jamaican sound system with black American forms, such as funk and soul, in the 1970s (Marshall 2005, p. 8). *Criminal Minded*, in turn, directly inspired the UK's first raggamuffin-hip hop hybrid, Asher D and Daddy Freddy's *Raggamuffin Hip-Hop* (Music of Life, 1988). These examples demonstrated a merging of Jamaican with African-American "blackness," which further reinforced the transnational notion of "blackness" that was to mediate the transculturation of reggae and hip hop in Italy.

The fact that the transatlantic connective marginality between reggae and hip hop resonated in the very different sociocultural setting of Bologna reinforces the capacity of these two musical forms to create multilayered connections from below. However, the recontextualization of this connection was also mediated by a translocal process of cultural exchange specific to *INK*. The Salentines had brought their passion for reggae from the South of Italy to Bologna, and soon after helping to occupy and set up the centre, they initiated its first reggae-hip hop fusions (Petrachi, Personal

---

[22] In 1985, there had been two seminal reggae/raggamuffin-hip hop releases in New York: "Hard Core Reggae" (Sutra) by the Fat Boys and the collaboration between Jamaican deejay sensation, Yellowman, and Run-DMC, "Roots Rap Reggae" (Profile).

interview). Significantly, this south-to-north cultural flow inverted the usual north-to-south trajectory that had characterized Italian youth politics to date.

INK began to hold sporadic reggae-hip hop parties named "Ghetto Blaster", which led to the formation of the historic reggae-inflected hip hop crew, the Isola Posse All Stars. The crew, amongst others, included Treble, Papa Ricky, Gopher D, and DJ War. The use of the collective noun, "posse," was significant in itself. As mentioned in the previous chapter, the various local reggae scenes of the mid-1980s had already adopted the term from Jamaican slang to denote their collective nature. The international prominence of the term in the late 1980s reflected the increasing intercultural exchange between Jamaicans and African-Americans in New York. The Jamaican drug gangs that were dominant in New York during the 1980s had adopted the term from their favoured cinematic genre, the Western, and KRS-One had underscored his personal Caribbean connection by referring to his musical collective as the "BDP Posse." Through these rhizomatic chains of meaning, the term gained prominence in Italy at the end of the 1980s and beginning of the 1990s, where it was used not only to denote a group's musical affiliation with reggae and rap but also to indicate their connection to a specific autonomous or geographical context.

Contributing to *INK*'s cultural and stylistic melting pot was a range of other young musicians, such as Neffa from the southern region of Campania, who was originally a punk drummer with the band Negation, and the Sardinian-born hip hop DJ, Gruff.[23] Reinforcing *INK*'s transcultural connections, the black Barbadian-born MC/DJ and dancer, Soul Boy, who had migrated from England, is credited as being *INK*'s cultural authority and the person who instructed the young Italians in the parallel arts of rapping and toasting (Gopher in Capone 2004, p. 65).

In spite of Bologna's relative cultural and ethnic diversity, youth arriving from the South still experienced a degree of discrimination. Petrachi claims that, due to their cultural and linguistic differences, the young Salentines experienced their new environment as "Others," and this

---

[23] Neffa later formed part of the historic Italian rap collective, Sangue Misto, before beginning a commercially successful solo career combining pop and R&B/soul. DJ Gruff was one of the pioneers of Italian hip hop, recording as early as 1989. His most celebrated work was carried out with Sangue Misto, but he also produced the track "Passaparola" (Word of Mouth, Century Vox Records, 1992) by the Isola Posse All Stars.

sense of marginalization further reinforced the post-colonial and diasporic resonances of reggae and underscored the relevance of their musical project:

> When renting a house your dialect and accent impeded you. When you reflected on it you then said: "why am I here?" Actually, then you developed the idea of returning, which then encouraged a return to our roots. It always brought us back to Jamaican concepts. You've left the place you came from, but not because you've abandoned it; on the contrary, you live with that territory every day, because you are basing your musical project on it. (Personal interview)

Although their experiences in Bologna and elsewhere in Italy brought SSS closer to hip hop, to the extent that journalists and scholars commonly describe them as practitioners of hip hop, reggae music remained their genre of choice. As Petrachi explains:

> Hip hop is urban. We didn't come *from* the *centro sociale*, we came *into* the *centro sociale*. Sud Sound System came from the sea and the countryside; of course, also from the town and its troubles; the Mafia. We lived those things. That's what we always represented: Salento and Jamaica. In essence, we saw ourselves as being from a ghetto in the same way that reggae came out of the ghetto. It's true that hip hop is also from the ghetto, but it's still an urban ghetto; for us it was different. (Personal interview)

Hence, the young southerners' affective, existential, and ideological identification with reggae can be linked to an inherent and reasoned feeling of detachment and difference rooted in Salento's perception as a geographic, cultural, and economic rural periphery. Whereas the urban setting of the North was associated with Italy's cultural and economic centre, the rural setting of the South was implicitly tied to exclusion and marginality. Further confirming Petrachi's understanding of hip hop and reggae in terms of the city (centre) and the countryside (periphery), respectively, was the fact that hip hop was inextricably tied to New York and America's cultural and economic hegemony, while reggae was a cultural product of the marginal Jamaica. Through this symbolic geography, the rural periphery of Jamaica's ghettos was metaphorically linked with Salento, demonstrating how these ghettos became a transnational and transcultural metaphor for the world's "Global Souths."

The Translocal Breakout and Early Recordings of Sud Sound System

On January 21, 1989, SSS made their official debut outside Salento by performing live at Milan's historic *centro sociale*, *Leoncavallo*. They were invited by the centre's resident Lion Horse Posse, which at the time contained one of Italian reggae's first specialized radio DJs, Vito "War" Fiorentino. Fiorentino and the Lion Horse Posse promoted the concert, which proved to be a resounding success, through their contact with Militant P. The venue was packed, and the concert marked the beginning of a new national phase in SSS's activity, as they started to perform more regularly throughout Italy's underground network of *centri sociali* and worked towards their first studio recordings. Their 1991 debut recordings, "T'à Sciuta Bona" (It Went Well for You) and "Fuecu" (Fire), sold 6000 copies within the first year of release (Solaro 1991, p. 19). Significantly, SSS's debut recordings were also the first productions of the label Century Vox Records, which was to become a pillar of the Italian reggae-hip hop movement of the early 1990s.

"T'à Sciuta Bona" deals with heroin abuse, organized crime, and political corruption. These issues are fleshed out through the song's intertextual citations and direct address of three subjects/objects: a heroin addict, the Mafia, and a corrupt politician. Through the tripartite nature of its discourse, the song establishes an interconnected chain of responsibility that transports the listener from the microcosmic daily life and death struggles of the heroin user to a macrocosmic denunciation of the criminal distributors and their corrupt political benefactors.

The up-tempo and percussive polyrhythmic musical backing reinforces the urgency of the message, whilst also lending the song a heightened danceability. The incorporation of an electronic bassline and beat alongside the folk-inspired concertina, which accents the reggae offbeat, provides a sonic metaphor for the encounter between innovation and tradition, the urban and the rural, and the local and the international. This synthesis is further embodied in the pattern of the bass drum; the odd bars are accented four times (*one, two, three, four*), while the even bars are accented five times (*one, two, one-two-three*). This latter pattern evokes a typical accent of the southern *tammorra*, which is used in Salentine folk music.

The chorus, two lines in refrain, is chanted by the entire posse, with interjections from Don Rico (in brackets). Sung in the informal second-person address, the chorus bluntly informs the heroin user about the risks of addiction, which is portrayed as a form of Russian roulette: "T'à sciuta bona, dicu, t'à sciuta bona (osce) / T'à sciuta bona, dicu, t'à sciuta bona (ma crai?)" (It went well for you, I say, it went well for you [today] / It went well for you, I say, it went well for you [but tomorrow?]). The first verse is shared between Treble, Don Rico, and Militant P, who toast the lines in alternation. The following is an edited extract:

> Ma sinti scemu? Pe picca nu 'nci lassi,
> Le corna storte ca tieni a 'ncapu,
> Comu faci cu te piace ca poi te sienti fiaccu?
> Te minti a vomitare te sienti tuttu scemu e dienti,
> Nu rimbambitu dienti nu rimbambitu.
> (Are you an idiot? You nearly died,
> Your head's messed up,
> How can you like it if it makes you feel sick?
> You vomit, feel dopey and become,
> Brain-dead you become brain-dead.)

The final declarative phrase is repeated four times, driving home the incontrovertible message.

After the second chorus, GgD conveys an anti-drug message in the imperative register. A metallic effect is placed on his voice, giving the impression of an official radio transmission, and again, the use of repetition reinforces the message: "Nu te bucare, lassa stare / Nu te bucare ca te faci male" (Don't shoot up, leave it alone / Don't shoot up because you'll harm yourself). The remainder of the second verse, predominantly performed by Treble, details the crippling physical effects of addiction, such as impotence, and informs the addict that his days are limited: "Quarche giurnu scoppi, dicu quarche giurnu scatti" ("Someday you're gonna kick the bucket, I say some day you're gonna die").

The start of the third verse, performed by Papa Gianni, begins to shift the focus onto the broader context, focusing on the supply chain. It commences with two rhetorical questions—"Ma tie la sai a ci dai li sordi toi? / Ma tie la sai ci mangia su de tie?" (Do you know who you're giving your money to? / Do you know who's feeding off you?)—followed with the damning response: "La Mafia ca te suca lu sangu / La Mafia ca cite, ca ruba, e ca cumanna" (The Mafia is sucking your blood / The Mafia is killing, stealing, and controlling). Following these four lines, GgD adapts a chorus from KRS-One's (Boogie Down Productions) ragga-inflected song,

"Illegal Business" (Jive, 1988): "Cocaine business controls America / Ganja business controls America / KRS-One come to start some hysteria / Illegal business controls America." Importantly, the narrative of "Illegal Business" draws a connection between the hard drug trade in New York's ghettos and police and government corruption. "Illegal Business" also highlights how the non-legalization of "soft" drugs, like marijuana, serves official power, a line of reasoning that was prominent within the autonomous political contexts of Italy's *centri sociali.*

As well as paying their dues to the influence of KRS-One on their brand of musical edutainment, the intertextual adaptation of the American rapper's words in "T'à Sciuta Bona" provides a creative recontextualization of the original field of reference:

> Mafia business controlla la Sicilia,
> Mafia business controlla lu Salentu,
> Mafia business controlla l'Italia,
> Mafia business controlla la miseria.
> (Mafia business controls Sicily,
> Mafia business controls Salento,
> Mafia business controls Italy,
> Mafia business controls poverty.)

This intertextual citation thus creatively ties organized crime in Italy's South to the entire nation and its hegemonic political system, a fact which is underscored by the use of the standard Italian verb, *controllare,* instead of the Salentine, *contrullare.* Furthermore, the citation hints at the parallels between exploited and disadvantaged black/Jamaican Americans and exploited and disadvantaged southern Italians. During this self-reflexive segment, the musical accompaniment of the *scacciapensieri,* a type of Jew's harp widely used in the rural South, also provides a symbolic auditory marker of organized crime's widespread control of the region.

Toasted by Treble, the song's final verse posits a crooked and self-serving politician as the addressee to denounce the link between organized crime and Italy's corrupt political system:

> E tie ca stai settatu a subbra lu parlamentu,
> Te piensi ca si drittu sulu perce' t'annu votatu,
> Tra nu miglione e n'auru, nu scandalu e nu futtimientu,
> ... Ca lu problema piaga nu bete lu tossicu,
> Ma stu sistema socio-economico-politico,

Copertu de parole, ripienu de dollaru,
Che de la malattia se face lu companaticu.
(And you there sitting in parliament,
You think you're slick just because they voted for you,
Between one million and another, scandal and thievery,
... Because the plague of a problem isn't the junkie,
But this political socio-economic system,
Coated with words, stuffed with dollars,
Which makes this disease into its bread and butter.)

Not only is the politician here portrayed as an insatiable money-grabbing fraud, but the entire political and socioeconomic system is identified as both the root cause and profiteer of heroin addiction. The subsequent three lines—"E cu na manu a quai e cu na manu a ddrhai / Cu na manu a destra e cu na manu a sinistra / Biancu, russu, o niuru nu centra chiui nu cazzu" (And with one hand here and another one there / With a hand to the right and a hand to the left / White, red, or black has fuck all to do with it)—indignantly allude to the extent of systematic corruption, which tainted all sides of the political spectrum and was only fully revealed in 1992, when the *Tangentopoli* (Bribesville) scandal exploded in Milan.[24]

The final part of verse three makes a statement about the therapeutic and oppositional power of music that was emblematic of Sud Sound System's musical project. Firstly, it poses an existential conundrum in the first person, with two unsatisfactorily nihilistic alternatives: either accept the corruption and decay outlined above (*me mangiu sta minescia*) or commit suicide (*me futtu de la finescia*). However, the focus then belligerently shifts back onto the politician at the root of the problem, who is commanded to throw *himself* out the window since the posse has been rescued by the power of reggae: "La dici tie, de la finescia futtite tie / La

---

[24] In the song, white stands for the Christian Democrats, red for the Communists, and black for the Fascists. Although political corruption had long been endemic in Italy, the 1980s witnessed "a new and organized rapacity on the part of politicians, a spoils system which extended throughout the peninsula" (Ginsborg 2001, p. 180). Local and federal politicians increasingly became business politicians that were "interested primarily in the use of office to accumulate capital and further their careers" (Ginsborg 2001, p. 181). The modus operandi of the business politician was the collection of kickbacks from local businessmen, and this system became widespread (Ginsborg 2001, pp. 181–82). In addition, corruption in Italian political culture was permeated by organized crime (see Ginsborg 2001, pp. 201–12; Stille 1995, pp. 202–05, 390–402).

dici tie, la musica me sarva a mie" (You're the one saying it, throw yourself out the window / You're the one saying it, the music is what saves me).

"Fuecu," the A-side song of their first record, merges dialect, standard Italian, reggae, hip hop, and folk elements. In so doing, it creates a translocal (interregional) and glocal (international) synthesis, which is emphasized by the title's translation of the Jamaican Patois term *fyah*, equating the power of reggae music with fire. The electronic instrumentation, which combines reggae and hip hop elements, is progressively layered with vocals to create an upbeat mood. The track opens with skipping electric bass drum accompanied by sparse snare, which is joined by rolling electric bass. Don Rico's voice then sets the celebratory tone of the song by crying out: "Fuecu intra sta casa, camenati ca la musica è lu more!" (Fire in the house, move because music is love!). Electronic guitar layers the accents of the bassline, and percussive hi-hat and triangle arrive to overlay this rhythmic core. The collectively chanted reprise, "Uuuuh Fuecu!," kicks in along with syncopated reggae keyboards and repeats itself for an extended sequence. During this protracted chorus, there are hip hop scratches by DJ War and the sample,[25] "Quanno camini," taken from the classic Salentine folk song "Quanno Camini Tie" (When You're Walking, Fonit Cetra, 1977), provides an intertextual citation of local musical traditions. The implementation of these hip hop elements also anticipates the shift that takes place at the onset of the first verse, as the melodic raggamuffin rhythm makes way for a harder hip hop beat.

The introductory lines of verse one, toasted by Treble, combine declarative sentences, informing the listener about the unstoppable momentum of the crew, with imperative sentences exhorting the listeners to join in with the crew's musical movement. The use of first and second person plural verb conjugations, and verbs of movement, reinforces the collective, dynamic, and social nature of their project. Furthermore, the metrical use of dialect, in particular the rapid repetition of the imperative, "mena" (hurry), blends meaning with a rhythmic use of form to create a sense of physical urgency: "Ehi, nu ne fermamu moi / Sentitine e ballati dai / Nu ne fermamu moi / Eniti aquai mena, mena, mena moi!" (Hey, we're not stopping now / Listen to us and dance / We're not stopping now / Come here, hurry, hurry, hurry now!).

---

[25] A sample is a portion of one sound recording which has been taken and intertextually inserted into a different song or piece. The technique is common to hip hop (and raggamuffin).

This energetic opening anticipates Militant P's segment in Italian. Militant P adopts a gruff, Jamaican-style raggamuffin tone and uses authoritative declarative sentences, direct address, imperative verbs of movement in the second person, and repetition, to exalt and convey the liberating corporeal and cerebral power of the rhythm and implore the listener to become active. Alongside Treble's opening lines and the rhythmic and percussive properties of the instrumental backing, Militant P's vocals demonstrate how music forms a "dynamic relation with social life" and helps to invoke collective and individual "parameters of agency" (DeNora 2000, pp. 16–17).

> Fondamentale, il ritmo, fondamentale!
> Fondamentale, ti dico, fondamentale!
> Seguilo con la mente, ti dico, non ti fermare!
> Seguilo! Seguilo! Seguilo! Non ti stancare!
> Quello che ti dico è liberati,
> Quello che ti dico è muoviti,
> Ritmo del Sud raggamuffin locale,
> Salta mentre il ritmo della musica incalza.
> (Fundamental, the rhythm, fundamental,
> Fundamental, I say, fundamental,
> Follow it with your mind, I say, don't stop!
> Follow it! Follow it! Follow it! Don't slow down!
> I'm telling you to free yourself,
> I'm telling you to move,
> Rhythm from the South, local raggamuffin,
> Jump while the rhythm's pumping.)

Significant here is the inherent juxtaposition between these lyrics in the national standard Italian and their reference to the local southern origins of SSS's raggamuffin in the penultimate line of the segment. This not only serves to frame SSS's subaltern musical voice as a liberating force within the nation's hegemonic framework, but also confirms the underlying process of transculturation at play.

The stylistic and textual references to raggamuffin in the first two segments of the verse are followed by hip hop rhythms and GgD's rapping in a hybrid of Italian and dialect. The alternation between Italian and *il salentino* provides a linguistic model for SSS's transcultural resistance to standardizing forces from above:

Fuecu! Arriva dal sole,
Colpisce l'accento sulle parole,
S doppia S muove lo spirito
Dentro a ddhru l'anima ne atte,
Segue traduce emozioni per liriche e moi camina moi,
Te fuecu te amore e te guai,
Te sta parlu chiaru, chiaru, chiaru,
te osce e te crai.
(Fire! It arrives from the sun,
It strikes the accent on the words,
S double S moves the spirit,
And follows inside where my spirit vibrates,
Translating emotions into lyrics,
About fire, love and troubles,
I'm speaking clear, clear, clear to you,
About today and tomorrow.)

In the penultimate line, the dialectal use of first person present continuous and direct address, along with a repeated emphasis on communicative clarity, makes explicit the didactic register of the song and its claims to communicative immediacy and authenticity.

At the commencement of the second verse, the bassline is replaced by electronic guitar, leaving space for the entirely dialectal vocals of Treble and then Don Rico. Again, the lyrical composition uses collective first and second person plural verb forms and a combination of imperative and declarative sentences, to stress the need for collective resistance through resilience and a non-discriminatory sense of unity. Such use of *il salentino* deprovincializes and globalizes this language, underlining its broad expressive potential:

Zumpa te quai zumpa te ddhrai,
E se la vita te pare tosta nu rrenditi mai,
Nu bu litigati nu bu dividiti,
N'unicu sangu tutti belli uniti,
Ca stamu tutti subbra lu stessu munnu,
E nu putimu lassare cu bascia a funnu,
Ca ci ni rispettamu e bene ni ulimu,
Sempre chiu nnanzi dicu ne li sciamu.
(Jump here and there,
And if life seems tough don't ever give in,
No fighting, no divisions,
We're of one blood and must unite,

> Because we live in the same world,
> And we can't allow it to crumble,
> Because with respect and love,
> We can really progress.)

Subsequently, Papa Gianni reiterates the relationship between the group's reggae fusion and an open-minded philosophical consciousness— "Questo ritmo ti fa pensare / Senza farti schematizzare" (This rhythm makes you think / Without making you dogmatic)—before reinforcing in dialect that reggae has the potential to bring about profound change.

The reggae register then returns through rhythmic keyboard, as the entire posse chant a self-affirming statement about their territorial origins, their inclusive humanism, and their role as cultural producers:

> Te lu Salentu enimu,
> Cucummari mangiamu,
> E a dunca sciamu sciamu,
> Mentimu fuecu e mpezzecamu,
> ... Simu te lu Salentu e tenimu lu core ardente,
> Rispettamu sempre tutta quanta la gente,
> E nu te pensare ca sta sulu sciucamu,
> Ca intra stu modu cultura sta facimu.
> (We come from Salento,
> We eat watermelon,
> And wherever we go,
> We blaze fire and burn,
> ... We're from Salento and we have burning hearts,
> We always respect all people,
> And don't think we're playing,
> Because this is how we make culture.)

Further demonstrating their adaptation of popular dialectal language and expressions, Capone explains that the first four lines of the section above were taken from a local football stadium chant (2004, p. 28).

The debut 12-inch release from SSS provided a fundamental impetus for Italy's nascent posse movement of the early 1990s and the growth of the Century Vox Records label. Petrachi describes its success:

Salentine DJs fell in love with "Fuecu" because it was very danceable and original. They pumped it in the discos, so the people heard it there and then heard it on the radio, then saw interviews more or less everywhere. Prominent journalists became enamoured, stating: "the new *canzone popolare d'autore* is born." This made "Fuecu" a heavily promoted song by everyone. Hearing it on the radio was considered an honour for a Salentine and for Salentines around Italy. (Personal interview)

Consequently, *il salentino* went from being a form of expression linked to the most marginalized sections of the Salentine population, to common heritage across the Italian peninsula (Winspeare in Pacoda 2011, pp. 91, 85). As was the case with the legitimization and diffusion of Patois through Jamaican reggae artists, SSS invested the language of Salento with unprecedented levels of cultural prestige.

The release of the record was also followed by numerous concerts, including a national Century Vox Records showcase tour and a presentation of the mix in Salento with the well-known folk trio, Ucci, at the site of Aradeo's historic Tre Masserie. In 1991 and 1992, the group appeared on Rai 3's satirical television programme, *Avanzi*, performing "Fuecu." Following this performance, SSS were invited as guests on Rai's widely followed music radio programme, *RaiStereoNotte*. In early April 1992, they were included in Recanati's *Festival delle Nuove Tendenze d'Autore*, further confirming their growing cultural legitimacy. Demonstrating their expanding translocal connections, between April and May of 1992, they recorded their next series of singles for Century Vox Records at Madaski's Spliff a Dada Studio in Pinerolo, near Turin. One of these tracks, "Reggae Internazionale" (International Reggae), was Treble's ode to Salentine cultural pride and reggae's power and potential to establish local, transnational, and transcultural connections. Originally composed and performed in 1990 with Calura (see Discography), the official version of "Reggae Internazionale" was performed over a digital reworking of a classic Jamaican *riddim*, produced by Bunny Lee,[26] and it represents one of SSS's most melodic and emotionally powerful pieces. These qualities of the composition are manifest in its evocative chorus, transcribed below:

> Abbàsciu lu Salentu nui bruciamu cu llu reggae,
> Ca lu tenimu a 'ncapu e lu tenimu intra lu core,
> Abbàsciu lu Salentu nui bruciamu cu llu reggae,
> Ca lu tenimu a 'ncapu e lu tenimu a 'npiettu.

[26] The *riddim* accompanied Johnny Clarke's cover of Barbara Lynn's R&B classic, "If You Should Lose Me" (Clocktower Records, 1978).

> (Down in Salento we burn with reggae,
> Because we have it in our minds and hearts,
> Down in Salento we burn with reggae,
> Because we have it in our heads and chests.)

By using the preposition *abbàsciu* (down) with the first-person plural subject pronoun *nui* (we), the chorus establishes a southern point of view and a firm sense of community. As is the case with "Fuecu," the southern "we" is posited as a potent cultural agent, and this agency is tied to reggae's capacity to permeate the intellectual (*capu*) and the emotional (*core*) realms.

In the ensuing segment, transcribed below, Treble shifts the discursive register to the first person singular. He thus appropriates the sense of cultural agency referenced in the chorus through a "dialectalization" of the reggae rhythm that promotes his Salentine cultural roots and traditions. Consequently, the song's use of *il salentino* self-reflexively conflates the gap between form (aesthetics) and meaning (ethics) to establish a musically mediated identity:

> Ca lu ritmu intra lu core ma trasutu,
> E lu stile de la capu ma bbessutu,
> Ma la tradizione nu m'aggiu scerratu,
> E cu llu dialettu l'aggiu coloratu,
> Ca de la cultura tegnu rispettu.
> (Because this rhythm's in my heart,
> And the style's come from my mind,
> But without forgetting my tradition,
> I've coloured it with dialect,
> Because I respect my culture.)

The final extract below introduces what was to become a central motif and metaphor throughout SSS's body of work, *lu sule* (the sun). In equating reggae with the sun, Treble alludes to reggae's inherent connectivity, which manifests itself through its respect for, and emphasis of, diverse roots, cultures, and traditions and its potential to establish a vast and inclusive transnational community.

> Lu reggae cu lu sule,
> La vita mia llucisce e moi te dicu percene,
> ... Ca parla te radici, cultura e tradizione,

120 S. SCARPARO AND M. S. STEVENSON

> Le tenimu diverse ma tutte l'imu rispettare,
> E parla puru de problemi de guerra e amore,
> De quiddhru ca tieni intra e ca a bbessire fore,
> Perciò, in Jamaica ni piace lu reggae,
> In America ni piace lu reggae,
> A Londra in Francia ni piace lu reggae,
> Puru in Italia ni piace lu reggae.
> (Along with the sun, reggae illuminates my life,
> And I'll tell you why,
> ... Because it speaks about roots, culture and tradition,
> Although they're different we must respect them all,
> And it also speaks about problems of love and war,
> About what you feel inside and must express,
> And that's why, in Jamaica they love reggae,
> In America they love reggae
> In London and France they love reggae,
> Even in Italy we love reggae.)

The song's use of dialect as a medium for intercultural dialogue directly contrasted with the Lega Nord's contemporary politicization of dialect as a symbol of cultural isolation and separatism, a point which is discussed in more detail in the following chapter. Thus, the song's interweaving of dialectal lyrics into a spacious, electronic reworking of a Jamaican roots *riddim* provides another example of SSS's deliberate creation of an inclusive Salentine cultural identity.

On the B-side of "Reggae Internazionale," SSS further developed their self-conscious approach to the use of dialect with GgD's ragga-hip hop number, "Punnu Ieu" (I'm Rapping/Toasting). *Punnu* (infinitive *punnare*) derives from a modern rendition of the Salentine verb, *spundare* (*sfondare*: to break down/break through). The verb was adopted by SSS from local football slang as a synonym for "rap," "toast," and "sing" and conveys their understanding of the inherent power of the (dialectal) word. Fittingly, SSS declare that "Punnu Ieu" was their first song to explicitly articulate their understanding of dialect as their most effective means of self-expression and self-realization and of preventing cultural annihilation (in Pacoda 1993, p. 96). Thus, the self-reflexive resistance vernacular of "Punnu Ieu" challenges the national hegemony and its fiction of a homogeneous Italian cultural identity.

Using first-person and direct address, GgD's opening verse proposes a regeneration of dialect through rhythmic (hence, cultural) hybridity as an act of resistance to standardizing views of language:

> Parlu comu ma fattu mama,
> ... Ci sinti? a ddhru sinti? te sienti dire:
> "Parla l'italianu ca lu dialettu nu bbete mutu correttu,"
> Ieu te ticu ca lu ritmu sa mmescatu,
> E le parole nu anu cangiate,
> Ncarra cchiu forte ncarra cu nu sparisci.
> (I speak as my mother made me,
> ... Who are you? Where are you? You hear yourself say:
> "Speak Italian because dialect isn't very proper,"
> I'm telling you that the rhythm is mixed,
> And the words haven't changed,
> Strive harder, strive so you don't disappear.)

The southern register of the track is further embellished by DJ War's sampling of southern folk instruments, specifically *la tamorra* (a type of large tambourine) and *lo scacciapensieri* (a type of Jew's harp).

Subsequently, as in other songs, GgD compares Salento to Jamaica, thus drawing attention to the process of transcultural synthesis at hand and the capacity for both these territories to inspire cultural consciousness. Furthermore, as with previous examples discussed, this comparison ties these two "global Souths" together as being shaped by the oppressive and racist structures of colonialism, along with its diasporic consequences. Hence, the imperatives in the segment below call for awareness of, and attachment to, cultural roots, seeking to reverse the destructive territorial abandonment of economic emigration and inspire new forms of social, cultural, and political action. Also significant is the reappropriation of the pejorative label *terrone* as a marker of a resistant southern identity:

> Nu te scerrare ci sinti,
> Nu te scerrare te ddhru sinti,
> ... Terrone nu lassa' la posizione,
> Dane dane forza a na noa azione,
> De lu meridione scansamu la distruzione.
> (Don't forget who you are,
> Don't forget where you come from,

... *Terrone* don't leave your place,
Give force to a new action,
Let's avoid the destruction of the South.)

This destruction of the South and the hegemonic repression of dialect are explicitly tied to the structures, institutions, and overarching political corruption which define the nation: "Basta cu sta mberda te organizzazione / Ca se spaccia pe na nazione / Quiddhra ca ni cumanda / Ieu dicu ete propiu na brutta banda" (Enough with this shit organization / That passes itself off as a nation / I'm telling you those in charge of us / Are really a nasty mob). Significantly, the reference to the political class (*quiddhra ca ni cumanda*: those in charge of us) as *propriu na brutta banda* (really a nasty mob) is a reinforcement of an earlier political statement made in 1991 by the Venetian dialectal reggae group, Pitura Freska, in their song, "'Na bruta banda": "Cuei che ne comanda li se senpre na bruta banda" (Those in charge of us are still a nasty mob). Through this intertextual reference, GgD establishes an interregional and interlinguistic counter-hegemonic alliance with northern dialectal reggae, inherently undermining the Lega Nord's promotion of dialect as a means of cultural purity and isolationism.

Although Militant P officially left the formation in 1992, between late 1992 and 1994, SSS continued to expand their musical activity and broaden their field of influence. In late November 1992, they supported the most internationally recognized raggamuffin artist of the time, Shabba Ranks from Jamaica, and, in 1993, they toured France with Massilia Sound System and supported the British dub poet, Linton Kwesi Johnson, during his Italian tour. Also in 1993, SSS established their own cultural association and record label, Ritmo Vitale, in Salento, which enabled them to promote musical events and self-produce their work. This development led to the production of *Salento Showcase 1994*, which was recorded in Salento and completely self-produced and self-distributed.

The album was significant not just because it shifted the site of their official cultural production from the North to the South for the first time, but also due to the fact that it gathered together practically the entire Salentine reggae scene (apart from Militant P), including new and present-day SSS members, Nandu Popu and Terron Fabio. Highlighting the breadth and diversity of the collaborative project was the participation of Gopher, Soul Boy, and numerous female vocalists: Lady Ninja, Marilena, Fabiana, and Mad Sabrina.

Salento Showcase 1994 was exceptionally popular in Salento and distributed internationally, being played on French, German, and British radio programmes (Sud Sound System, Liner notes 1996). Although DJ War left the posse during this period, the album's success gave the group additional impetus and led to their organization of cultural and musical events seeking to enrich and reinvigorate Salento. The most significant of these were two festivals in 1994 and 1995, organized under the banner *S.U.D.* (*Suoni Uniti Differenti*) (United Different Sounds). As the title suggests, these festivals sought to establish new and suitably broad connections and exchanges through music, not only bringing together international reggae artists, such as Thriller Jenna and Chubby Rankin, but also the Apulian folk and world music formations of Alla Bua and i Tamburellisti di Torrepaduli and Al Darawish. Moreover, *S.U.D.* gathered some of the leading protagonists in Italy's national posse movement, such as One Love Hi Powa and Villa Ada Posse from Rome, South Posse from Calabria, Piombo a Tempo (ex-Lion Horse Posse) from Milan, and ex-Different Stylee/Struggle's Nico Caldarulo's Suoni Mudù from Bari.

Despite being the most original, recognized, and influential reggae formation of the late 1980s and early 1990s, Sud Sound System formed just one part of a translocal, politicized, and grassroots musical movement that spread throughout the peninsula during this period and which has come to be known as the period of the posses. In the following chapter, we discuss the phenomenon of the posses in light of their continuity with Italy's earlier reggae contexts and their integration of raggamuffin and rap, which resulted in the creation of a new social and political youth movement.

WORKS CITED

Anderson, Benedict. 1983. *Imagined Communities: Reflections on the Origins and Spread of Nationalism*. London and New York: Verso. Print.

Anselmi, William. 2002. From Cantautori to Posse: Sociopolitical Discourse, Engagement and Antagonism in the Italian Music Scene from the Sixties to the Nineties. In *Music, Popular Culture, Identities*, ed. Richard Young, 17–45. Amsterdam: Editions Rodopi. Print.

Bettini, Stefano, and Pier Tosi. 2009. *Paperback reggae: Origini, protagonisti, storia e storie della musica in levare*. Firenze: Editoriale Olimpia. Print.

Campo, Alberto. 1995. *Nuovo? Rock?! Italiano!* Firenze: Giunti. Print.

Capone, Federico. 2003. *Lecce che suona: Appunti di musica salentina*. Lecce: Capone Editore. Print.

———. 2004. *Hip hop, reggae, dance, elettronica*. Roma: Stampa Alternativa. Print.

124   S. SCARPARO AND M. S. STEVENSON

——. 2009. *I canti del Salento*. Lecce: Kurumuny. Print.

Colazzo, Salvatore. 1994. Rap e tarantelle. In *Intervista sul tarantismo*, ed. George Lapassade, 163–173. Maglie: Madona Oriente. Print.

de Kock, Leon. 1992. Interview with Gayatri Chakravorty Spivak: New Nation Writers Conference in South Africa. *A Review of International English Literature* 23 (3): 29–47. Print.

De Martino, Ernesto. 1961. *La terra del rimorso: Contributo a una storia religiosa del Sud*. Milano: Il Saggiatore. Print.

DeNora, Tia. 2000. *Music in Everyday Life*. Cambridge: Cambridge University Press. Print.

Deleuze, Gilles, and Félix Guattari. 1987. *A Thousand Plateaus*. London: Continuum. Print.

Dickie, John. 2012. *Mafia Brotherhoods: Camorra, Mafia, 'ndrangheta: The rise of the Honoured Societies*. London: Sceptre. Print.

Donadio, Francesco, and Marcello Giannotti. 1996. *Teddy-boys, rockettari e cyberpunk: Tipi mode e manie del teenager italiano dagli anni Cinquanta a oggi*. Roma: Riuniti. Print.

Epifani, Mattia, dir. 2011. *Rockman*. Goodfellas. DVD.

Ginsborg, Paul. 2001. *Italy and Its Discontents: Family, Civil Society, State 1980–2001*. London: Penguin. Print.

Gramsci, Antonio. 1997. *Selections from the Prison Notebooks of Antonio Gramsci*. Ed. and Trans. Quentin Hoare and Geoffrey Nowell Smith. New York: International Publishers. Print.

——. 2000. *The Gramsci Reader: Selected Writings, 1916–1935*. Ed. and Trans. David Forgacs. New York: New York University Press. Print.

Harindranath, Ramaswami. 2006. *Perspectives on Global Cultures*. Maidenhead: Open University Press. Print.

Ives, Peter. 2004. *Language and Hegemony in Gramsci*. London: Pluto Press. Print.

Jones, Simon. 1988. *Black Culture White Youth: The Reggae Tradition from JA to UK*. London: Macmillan. Print.

Klein, Gabriella. 1986. *La politica linguistica del Fascismo*. Bologna: Il Mulino. Print.

La musica che arriva dal cuore nel messaggio di Treble. 2011. *LeccePrima*, February 1. http://www.lecceprima.it/eventi/cultura/la-musica-che-arriva-dal-cuore-nel-messaggio-di-treble.html. Accessed 4 May 2013.

Langbauer, Laurie. 1992. Cultural Studies and the Politics of the Everyday. *Diacritics* 22 (1): 47–65. Print.

Lapassade, George, and Pietro Fumarola, eds. 1992. Rap Copy. *Studi e ricerche* 13: 69–98. Print.

Lapassade, Georges, and Philippe Rousselot. 2009. *Rap: Il furor del dire*. Trans. Tobia D'Onofrio. Lecce: Bepress. Print.

Manfredi, Tommaso. 2008. *Dai Caraibi al Salento: Nascita, evoluzione e identità del reggae in Puglia*. Lecce: AGM. Print.

Marshall, Wayne. 2005. Hearing Hip-Hop's Jamaican Accent. *Institute for Studies in American Music* 34 (2): 8–9. http://www.brooklyn.cuny.edu/web/aca_centers_hitchcock/NewsS05.pdf. Accessed 4 June 2013.

Militant, A. 1997. *Storie di Assalti Frontali: Conflitti che producono banditi*. Roma: Castelvecchi. Print.

Mitchell, Tony. 1996. *Popular Music and Local Identity: Rock, Pop and Rap in Europe and Oceania*. London and New York: Leicester University Press. Print.

———. 2000. Doin' Damage in My Native Language: The Use of 'Resistance Vernaculars' in Hip Hop in France, Italy, and Aotearoa/New Zealand. *Popular Music and Society* 24 (3): 41–54. Print.

Pacoda, Pierfrancesco. 1993. L'antagonismo in musica: Posse in azione. In *Posse italiane: Centri sociali, underground musicale e cultura giovanile degli anni '90 in Italia*, ed. Carlo Branzaglia, Pierfrancesco Pacoda, and Alba Solaro, 71–110. Firenze: Editoriale Tosca. Print.

———. 2000. *Hip Hop Italiano: Suoni, parole e scenari del Posse Power*. Torino: Einaudi. Print.

———. 2011. *Salento, amore mio: Viaggio nella musica, nei luoghi e tra i protagonisti del rinascimento salentino*. Milano: Kowalski. Print.

Petrachi, Antonio. 2012. Personal Interview. August 7.

Pizzutilo, Mimmo. 2012. Personal Interview. August 13.

Pizzutilo, Mimmo, and Gianni Galli, eds. 1986. *Ritmo Vitale* 1: n.pag. https://www.dropbox.com/s/l0eucpnpw7ft132/IL_MEGLIO_DI_REBELSOUL. pdf. Accessed 10 Sep 2012.

Potter, Russell A. 1995. *Spectacular Vernaculars: Hip Hop and the Politics of Postmodernism*. Albany: State University of New York Press. Print.

Pugliese, Joseph. 2008. Whiteness and the Blackening of Italy: La Guerra Cafona, Extracommunitari and Provisional Street Justice. *Portal: Journal of Multidisciplinary International Studies* 5 (2): 1–35. http://epress.lib.uts.edu. au/journals/index.php/portal/article/view/702. Accessed 10 July 2013.

Q&A: Massilia Sound System Interview. 2006. *CNN*, December 22: n.pag. http://edition.cnn.com/2006/TRAVEL/12/22/marseille.qa/. Accessed 10 July 2013.

Richardson, Brian. 2001. Questions of Language. In *The Cambridge Companion to Modern Italian Culture*, ed. Zygmunt G. Baranski and Rebecca J. West, 63–80. Cambridge: Cambridge University Press. Print.

Saunders, George R. 1993. Critical Ethnocentrism' and the Ethnology of Ernesto De Martino. *American Anthropologist* 95 (4): 875–893. Print.

Schneider, Jane. 1998. Introduction: The Dynamics of Neo-Orientalism in Italy (1848–1995). In *Italy's Southern Question: Orientalism in One Country*, ed. Jane Schneider, 1–23. Oxford: Berg. Print.

Simonini, Augusto. 1978. *Il linguaggio di Mussolini*. Milan: Bompiani. Print.

Solaro, Alba. 1991. L'hip hop ridà fiato alla musica independente. *l'Unità*, November 13. Print.

Stille, Alexander. 1995. *Excellent Cadavers: The Mafia and the Death of the First Italian Republic*. New York: Pantheon Books. Print.

Sud Sound System. 1996. Liner notes. Sud Sound System. *Tradizioni*. Ritmo Vitale. CD.

treblestudio. 2010. tarantamuffin. Treble and Calura. Live studio recording. *YouTube*, June 17. https://youtu.be/kTU8Gy5xImc. Accessed 3 Mar 2013.

Verdicchio, Pasquale. 1997. *Bound by Distance: Rethinking Nationalism Through the Italian Diaspora*. Madison, NJ: Fairleigh Dickinson University Press. Print.

———. 2005. Introduction. *The Southern Question*. By Antonio Gramsci. Trans. Pasquale Verdicchio. Toronto: Guernica Editions, 1–13. Print.

DISCOGRAPHY

Asher D and Daddy Freddy. 1988. *Ragamuffin Hip-Hop*. Music of Life. LP.

Boogie Down Productions. 1987. *Criminal Minded*. B-Boy Records. LP.

———. 1988. Illegal Business. *By All Means Necessary*. Jive. LP.

———. 1990. *Edutainment*. Jive. LP.

Canzoniere Grecanico Salentino. 1977. Quanno Camini Tie. *Canti di Terra d'Otranto e della Grecia Salentina*. Fonit Cetra. LP.

Clarke, Johnny. 1978. If You Should Lose Me. Clocktower Records. 7-inch.

Fabio, Terron. 1994. La Romanella. Various. *Salento Showcase 1994*. Ritmo Vitale. CD.

Fat Boys. 1985. Hard Core Reggae. Sutra Records. 12-inch.

Pitura Freska. 1991. '*Na Bruta Banda*. Psycho. LP.

Run-D.M.C. 1985. Roots, Rap, Reggae. *King of Rock*. Profile Records. LP.

Struggle. 1987a. Nuclear City. *Struggle to Live*. Self-production. Demo tape.

———. 1987b. *Struggle to Live*. Self-production. Demo tape.

———. 1987c. Struggle to Live. *Struggle to Live*. Self-production. Demo tape.

Sud Sound System. 1991a. Fuecu. Century Vox Records. 12-inch.

———. 1991b. T'à Sciuta Bona. Century Vox Records. 12-inch.

———. 1992a. Punnu Ieu. Century Vox Records. 12-inch.

———. 1992b. Reggae Internazionale. Century Vox Records. 12-inch.

CHAPTER 5

The Rise of the Posses and the Power of the Word

As discussed in the preceding chapter, the term "posse" was appropriated from Jamaica and New York as a means of self-identification by various independent musical collectives, which emerged throughout Italy between the end of the 1980s and the beginning of the 1990s. In turn, the media promptly adopted this term as a generic label for an often-disparate range of artists and musical styles that tended to blur the boundaries between the aesthetically and culturally related forms of reggae and rap. Focusing on their involvement with the early 1990s student movement, *la Pantera* (the Panther), in this chapter we trace the development of the posses and analyse the transregional and anti-racist cultural politics of groups such as the Roman Onda Rossa Posse, the Florentine il Generale and Ludus Pinsky, the Turinese Torino Posse (TO.SSE), and the Neapolitan 99 Posse and Almamegretta.

At that time, the anti-institutional and counter-informational use of music was rooted in the autonomous spaces of the *centri sociali* and *radio libere*, which, as discussed in previous chapters, were inherited from the youth counter-cultures of the late 1970 and 1980s. Tony Mitchell writes that "the Italian posses emerged as the prevailing soundtrack to the disruptions and dislocations of the 1990s" (1996, p. 149) and that they could even be seen as "one of the main cultural catalysts of a political renaissance of oppositional Italian youth movements" (2001, p. 200).

© The Author(s) 2018
S. Scarparo, M. S. Stevenson, *Reggae and Hip Hop in Southern Italy*, Pop Music, Culture and Identity,
https://doi.org/10.1007/978-3-319-96505-5_5

According to Mitchell, in fact, the posses "represented a diversified 'national popular' musical movement as widespread and important as the protest-inflected *cantautori nuovi* (new singer-songwriters) of the late 1970s" (1996, p. 149).

This interpretation of the posses as a widespread movement of cultural and political significance on par with the *cantautori nuovi* was echoed in contemporary Italian commentary, both in the press and in specialized literature (Pacoda 1996, p. 7; Bettini and Tosi 2009, p. 233; Castaldo 1993a, p. 37). For example, Ernesto Assante from the daily newspaper, *la Repubblica*, referred to the posses as *nuovi cantastorie* (new troubadours), arguing that by reclaiming dialects, local cultures, and social commitment, they formed a movement that represented the freshest and sharpest contemporary musical reality (1992, p. 41). Also in la Repubblica, Gino Castaldo labelled the music of the posses as the new folk music and the most authentic music of the time, further stating that the posses were a true and proper movement of violent and radical cultural opposition (1993a, p. 37, 1993b, p. 31, 1993c, p. 31). Similarly, Gabriele Ferraris argued in *la Stampa* that the posses reprised and renewed the commitment of the political song of the 1960s and 1970s (1992b, p. 35). Moreover, in the *Corriere della Sera*, Gloria Pozzi stressed that the posses did not simply make music but carried out political criticism, reportage, and social denunciation (1992, p. 31).

Yet, although the use of music to popularize social and political messages displayed obvious continuities with the *canzone d'autore* and political folk of the 1960s and 1970s, as demonstrated by the music of Sud Sound System and others, the posses' link to the reggae and punk revolutions of the 1980s signalled a decisive break with the political music of earlier decades. The translocal posse scenes also responded to the need for widespread musical renewal due to the disengagement and commercialization of the mainstream cultural contexts of the 1980s. Similar to the "free music" movement of the late 1970s, the posses stood in opposition to the commercial music industry and its promotion of celebrity, representing "the triumph of solidarity" and a rejection of star worship in favour of a return to collective movements (Pacoda 1993, p. 72). Highlighting the (g)local significance of their musical approach, the posses typically identified themselves either in relation to their geographical provenance, for example Salento Posse and Torino Posse, or in relation to their originating autonomous context, such as the *centri sociali* and *radio libere*, for example, Isola Posse All Stars (*Isola nel Kantiere*) and, Onda Rossa Posse (*Radio Onda Rossa*, ROR).

Although Bettini and Tosi explain that the posse phenomenon marked a sudden acceleration of Italian reggae (2009, p. 233), scholarly and journalistic work dedicated to the phenomenon has typically failed to recognize the vital role played by reggae both within and as a precursor to the posse movement. In fact, throughout the early to mid-1980s, Italy's translocal reggae scenes had already been referring to themselves as "posses" (e.g., the Bari Posse and the Savona Posse). Like the interconnected punk scenes of the time, these early reggae scenes established independent and self-managed networks of distribution, concert organization, and musical production. The underground reggae and punk contexts of the 1980s thus laid the foundation for the national explosion of the posse movement, which formed an almost symbiotic relationship with Italy's network of *centri sociali* and *radio libere*, and adopted an explicitly political approach to musical expression and practice.

Pasquale Verdicchio argues that reggae and rap music have been adopted by "youth internationally as a critique of a transnational dominant culture," and this "horizontality of resistance, or extra-national movement, is representative of an instance of the practical aspects of Gramsci's concept of 'national popular'" (1997, p. 167). Adopting this transnational perspective, he proposes further that Gramsci's "national popular" be extended to an "(inter)national popular" in order to "properly represent the terms of horizontality ... across national boundaries" expressed by reggae and rap (Verdicchio 1997, p. 168). Indeed, as Verdicchio points out, (southern) Italian reggae and hip hop undermine "the fiction of 'Italian culture' through the elaboration of ... a sphere of discourse that values the local alongside the global" (2006, n.pag.). Through this relationship between the global and the local, reggae and rap reassert "subaltern cultures in dialogue with other peripheral cultures" (2006, n.pag.).

This broad notion of the national popular rejects racist and fascist connotations by offering "resistance to nationalized notions of culture that ... deny diversity" through non-official networks and alliances that instead oppose nationalist interests and acknowledge differences (Verdicchio 1997, pp. 168, 144). Hence, a national popular culture emerges organically and collaboratively from below in opposition to institutional culture imposed from above. Consequently, it stands in direct opposition to examples of coercive nationalism and imperialism, which seek to enforce a national culture (Verdicchio 1997, p. 173). Joseph Pugliese further articulates the transcultural potential of these musical alliances by declaring that

130   S. SCARPARO AND M. S. STEVENSON

southern Italian reggae and rap articulate "transoceanic connections between the black Atlantic and the black Mediterranean," confirming "a transatlantic connection" as well as "a transmediterranean reconnection with African and Arab culture" (2008, p. 19).

These transatlantic and transmediterranean connections, in turn, fostered cultural flows within and across Italy. The posse movement was defined by a vertical dynamic unifying South and North in opposition to Italy's hegemonic discourses, narratives, and cultural identities. Emblematic examples from the South (Naples and Salento), the Centre (Florence and Rome), and the North (Genoa, Turin, and Venice) show how the continued transculturation of reggae, particularly raggamuffin reggae, further resisted and influenced hegemonic cultural and informational flows. The increasing translocal collaborations between North and South, and the South's growing agency and authority within the movement, further challenged the North's traditional cultural dominance over the South. Thus, by establishing translocal (interregional) and glocal (international) connective marginalities, the posse movement proposed a new model of national unity and local culture that welcomed cultural and social diversity, providing models of social and racial integration (Castaldo 1993a, p. 37).

LA PANTERA, RADIO ONDA ROSSA, AND THE AUTONOMIST ROOTS OF THE ROMAN POSSES

As had happened in various locations, such as Bari (see Chap. 3) and Bologna (see Chap. 4), the autonomous 1980s punk scene paved the way for the politicization of "black" music in Rome during the late 1980s and early 1990s. However, more than in any other Italian location, in Rome, reggae and rap were given an explicitly political impetus through their symbiotic relationship with the brief but highly significant national student movement of 1989/1990, popularly known as *la Pantera*. The movement adopted the slogan, "*la Pantera siamo noi*" (we are the Panther), after a panther, which had escaped from the zoo, had been glimpsed prowling the streets of Rome. The moniker and image of the panther were also appropriated in order to evoke the militancy of the Black Panthers, a point discussed in more detail below. Moreover, the students had been inspired by the recent images of young Berliners knocking down the Wall and the student massacres in Tiananmen Square (Denaro 2006, p. 6).

The first student occupation of the university in Palermo was inspired by the parlous material condition of the university and the Socialist minister Antonio Ruberti's attempt to increase the privatization and corporatization of tertiary education. It was feared that the less commercially productive universities would rapidly lose ground, leading to greater inequality, particularly for students in the South (Denaro 2006, p. 44). Massimiliano Denaro explains that this opposition to privatization was part of a more general fear of the *berlusconizzazione* of culture, seen to be the most corrosive example of neoliberal or free-market capitalism (2006, p. 7). The movement also sought access to free and independent information, which had been undermined by Berlusconi's concentrated media ownership. This opposition to Berlusconi's neoliberalism *all'italiana* had been a defining characteristic of Italy's autonomous cultural and political contexts of the 1980s, and was to influence heavily the outlook and practices of the posses.

The Palermitan mobilization rapidly stirred interest within Italy's other universities, beginning with the occupation of Rome's la Sapienza on January 15, 1990. For a period of 100 days, every Italian university had at least one faculty occupied, something which had never even occurred during the grand ferment of the 1970s (Denaro 2006, p. 5). By the end of January, there were already 150 faculties occupied throughout the country and the movement had a national assembly. Denaro explains that although the universities of the Centre-South responded better to the call for occupation than those in the North (2006, p. 38), *la Pantera* signalled the birth of a national student movement (2006, pp. 38–39). This national explosion of the movement might be understood in terms of what Katsiaficas refers to as the "eros effect": "a sudden intuitive awakening of massive opposition to the powers-that-be" (1997, p. v).

The students in the South of Italy were the most marginalized and disadvantaged in the country, and supported by the town's first *centro sociale* in Palermo, *Montevergini*, the Sicilian capital remained the movement's "beating heart" (Denaro 2006, p. 33). However, it was in Rome, where reggae/raggamuffin and rap had merged with the autonomous cultural spaces of the *centri sociali* and *radio libere*, that *la Pantera* found its most expressive outlet. Central to this Roman narrative were *Radio Onda Rossa* (Red Wave Radio), which had been established in 1977 by the dominant tendency within the Roman autonomist scene in Via dei Volsci, San Lorenzo,[1] and the legendary *centro sociale, Forte Prenestino*, which was

---

[1] Located near la Sapienza University, San Lorenzo is an area with strong proletarian and leftist roots.

occupied in 1986 by a group of autonomists and punks from the socioeconomically marginalized and drug-ridden Centocelle district. *Radio Onda Rossa* (*ROR*) brought their microphones into the occupied faculties—which they renamed the "Sakoa" (Arts Faculty) and "Aldo il Moro" (Political Sciences)—and invited students onto their transmissions, while also documenting initiatives and demonstrations (*Radio Onda Rossa*).

The story of *ROR* is central to the grassroots and counter-hegemonic dissemination of reggae and rap in Rome and throughout Italy. Defining itself as a "militant" or "revolutionary" radio station rather than a "free" one, *ROR* was a mouthpiece for a variety of marginal groups, from anarchists to feminists, and advocated a range of political issues and causes throughout the 1980s.[2] Moreover, *ROR* employed an "open microphone" policy, whereby any person or group was invited to gain access to the airwaves. This practice was to become a fundamental aspect of the live music performances of the posses. However, it was not until around 1986 that *ROR* merged music and politics through its links with the growing punk scene and the second wave of *centri sociali* occupations.

Contemporaneous to this new wave of social centre occupations was *ROR*'s newfound involvement in Rome's growing underground music scene. A group of young *autoriduttori* from the San Lorenzo area, which included Paolo "Sego" Occidentale and Attilio Caminiti, introduced two formative reggae programmes, "Rebel Soul" and "Daje Pure Te" (You Do It Too), at the station during the late 1980s and early 1990s. Wanting to solidify further the link between music and political practice, they also introduced to *ROR* a varied nightly musical programming of reggae, afro, ska, punk, rap, and funk titled "Rumori Molesti" (Disturbing Noises). This cultural shift at the radio was significant and demonstrated a rejection of the rigid approach of the previous generation of militants, who were mistrustful of imported and commercially produced musical styles.

As part of the new musical programming at *ROR*, Militant A and his friends, Castro X and NCOT, conducted the programme "Funk Theology," which promoted the politics and culture of hip hop through a process of cultural translation. This process merged the black militancy of

---

[2] Some of the political matters which the radio advocated throughout the 1980s were the support of FIAT workers in the face of post-industrial restructuring in 1980, the support of the Lebanese resistance against Israel in 1982, the support of a popular anti-nuclear referendum after the Chernobyl disaster in 1986, and the wave of occupations *of centri sociali* throughout Italy in the second half of the 1980s (see *Radio Onda Rossa*).

THE RISE OF THE POSSES AND THE POWER OF THE WORD 133

groups like Public Enemy with the marginal local traditions of the extra-parliamentary Left. As Militant A recounts: "on the radio we pushed hip hop, translated texts, extracts of books by the ... Black Panther Party" (Militant A 1997, p. 27). Their decision to begin rapping in Italian during their programme was positively received by their audience, and they subsequently named themselves, Onda Rossa Posse (ORP), in 1988, and began performing in the expanding *centri sociali* network. Symbolizing their transatlantic and interracial connective marginalities, they adopted as their insignia a five-pointed star encasing a panther, which was almost identical to that of the Black Panther Party.

During the student occupation of la Sapienza, there were numerous reggae dancehall sessions (Nano 1997, p. 6), and ORP often performed at these parties and distributed their lyrics on flyers (Militant A 1997, p. 34). As a result of these performances, one of their most antagonistic tracks, "Batti il Tuo Tempo" (Beat Your Own Time), became the anthem of *la Pantera*. A textual and contextual analysis of "Batti il Tuo Tempo" highlights the continuities and contrasts between the protest music of previous generations and that of the late 1980s and early 1990s. The opening bars convey the intertextual interplay of the posses' music by sampling the ethereal pan-pipe notes from Ennio Morricone's theme for Sergio Leone's cinematic classic, *Once Upon a Time in America* (1984). This transmedia sample not only symbolically underscores the Italo-American connection of "Batti il Tuo Tempo," but since the film chronicles the lives of Jewish youths from the ghettos of New York who rise to prominence as gangsters, it can also be seen to evoke a subtext of marginality.

An abrupt male voice, which shouts the self-identifying exclamation "ONDA ROSSA POSSE!," soon shatters the meditative atmosphere created by the pan-pipes as the heavy hip hop beat kicks in. The juxtaposition of the peaceful and light melody of the pan-pipes with the heavy bassline-driven, up-tempo beat, sampled from New York rapper Kool Moe Dee's "I Go to Work" (Jive, 1989), augments the semantic impact of the urgently rapped chorus and verses. Despite the profound formal and aesthetic contrasts between the political folk music of the 1960s and 1970s and "Batti il Tuo Tempo," in terms of its sociopolitical function and anti-institutional and anti-capitalistic sentiment, ORP's *la Pantera* anthem recalls Paolo Pietrangeli's Marxist folk song, "Contessa," which became the anthem of the 1968 student-worker protest movement and was officially recorded in 1970.

134 S. SCARPARO AND M. S. STEVENSON

These parallels are particularly striking in terms of the two songs' galvanizing choruses. ORP's pressing, succinct, and aggressive spoken-word command—"Batti il tuo tempo per fottere il potere" (Beat your own time, to fuck up Power)—might be understood as an updated version of Pietrangeli's more melodic, more verbose, less colloquial, yet no less subversive chorus:

> Compagni, dai campi e dalle officine,
> Prendete la falce e portate il martello,
> Scendete giù in piazza e picchiate con quello,
> Scendete giù in piazza e affossate il sistema.
> (Comrades from the fields and workshops,
> Take the sickle and bring the hammer,
> Go down into the *piazza* and beat with them,
> Go down into the *piazza* and bring down the system.)

However, whereas "Contessa" uses second person plural imperatives, the use of the second person singular in "Batti il Tuo Tempo" underscores the 1980s shift in emphasis onto the individual and the private realms. Furthermore, the use of the imperative, *batti* (beat), in ORP's chorus, self-reflexively draws attention to the political significance of the hip hop beat, thus demonstrating a clear break with the staid acoustic guitar accompaniment of "Contessa."[3]

The belligerent rapid-fire vocal delivery and hard-hitting lyrics of the ensuing verses of "Batti il Tuo Tempo" complement the militant beat and represent a call to action against corrupt institutional power. The incendiary and emotive language is permeated by an angry and indignant tone, providing critical commentary of the current sociopolitical context. Those in power are variously referred to as *assassini* (murderers), *maiali* (swines), *odiosi uomini fottuti* (odious fucked up men), *bastardi senza dignità* (bastards without dignity), and a number of historical events are cited as examples of corruption and repression.

In the first verse, there is a reference to the disproportionately aggressive and unlawful clearing out of Milan's historic *centro sociale*, *Leoncavallo*, on August 16, 1989, which is interpreted as an example of corrupt collusion between capitalist and political interests. At the request

---

[3] Speaking about the intrinsically political quality of the hip hop beat, Jazz drummer Max Roach has said: "The rhythm was very militant to me because it was like marching, the sound of an army on the move. We lost Malcolm, we lost King and they thought they had blotted out everybody. But all of a sudden, this new art form arises and the militancy is there in the music" (Lipsitz 1994, p. 38).

of the development company, Scotti, Milan's magistrate, Pierluigi Stolfi, had signed an order for the forced evacuation of the site.[4] Although its occupants had been in discussions with the local council to seek a peaceful solution for months, on the day of the evacuation, around 150 military police descended upon the site with tanks, helicopters, and fire engines, launching teargas and making 26 arrests (Solaro 1993, p. 37). Scotti immediately sent in bulldozers and caterpillars without council authorization, destroying all the internal structures of the centre, such as the kindergarten and the personal effects of its occupants (Solaro 1993, p. 38). The conspicuously absent Socialist mayor of Milan, Paolo Pillitteri, flew to Tunisia to stay with his brother-in-law and former Socialist prime minister, Bettino Craxi. Pillitteri proceeded to depict *Leoncavallo*'s occupants as terrorists and heroin addicts while saying nothing about the legality of the evacuation (Solaro 1993, p. 39). Both Craxi and Pillitteri were later convicted during the *mani pulite* (clean hands) investigation into systematic political corruption during the early 1990s.

The implication of corruption and collusion in relation to the *Leoncavallo* affair is made more explicit in the second verse of "Batti il Tuo Tempo," which associates economic and institutional power with the criminal and anti-democratic tendencies of the 1980s, and cynically refers to those in power as *maestri dei disastri* (masters of disasters). In particular, the lyrics allude to the various conspiracies and cover-ups during the 1980s involving occult forces, right-wing elements of the Italian State, neo-fascist terrorists, and, allegedly, NATO. The two specific examples given, the *triangolo di Ustica*, or *strage di Ustica* (Ustica massacre), and the *strage di Bologna* (Bologna massacre), both took place in 1980 and, according to "Batti il Tuo Tempo," initiated *dieci anni di menzogne* (ten years of lies).

The first of these incidents involved the mysterious crashing of an Italian commercial flight into the Tyrrhenian Sea between Ponza and Ustica, which killed all of its 81 passengers. In 1989, a team of scientists concluded that it had been struck by a missile (Cowell 1992, n.pag.), and, in 1999, an exhaustive investigation by Judge Rosario Priore concluded that the plane had probably been caught in a dogfight between NATO jet fighters and Libyan MiG-23s. He also claimed that, at the behest of NATO, his and previous investigations into the disaster had been deliberately obstructed by the Italian military and members of the

---

[4] One of the very first *centri sociali*, *Leoncavallo*, was occupied in 1975 in an abandoned pharmaceutical factory. Stolfi later admitted to having signed the order without even knowing what *Leoncavallo* was.

136   S. SCARPARO AND M. S. STEVENSON

secret services.[5] Over the years, several Air Force officials were investigated for concealing evidence, and four generals were tried for high treason and for obstructing investigations (Cowell 1992, n.pag.). The difficulties faced by the investigators and the victims' relatives in receiving complete, reliable information from the Italian state led to the expression, *muro di gomma* (rubber wall). In 2010, Italy's president, Giorgio Napolitano, stated that the incident involved subversive plots and also international schemes, together with dishonest conduct on behalf of the organs of the state (in Smargiassi 2010, p. 10). The massacre remains a crime without convictions.

The events surrounding the *strage di Bologna* are equally murky. The bombing of Bologna station was the final major act in the many neo-fascist terrorist bombing massacres of innocent civilians, known as *stragismo* (from the term *strage*: massacre), dating back to the 1969 bombing of Piazza Fontana, in Milan, and together forming part of the so-called strategy of tension. This strategy was directed at containing Communism in Italy by creating "an atmosphere of subversion and fear in the country so as to promote a turn to an authoritarian type of government" (Bull 2007, p. 19). Exploding on the morning of August 2, 1980, the bomb killed 85 people and wounded more than 200. Although the attack has been materially attributed to the neo-fascist terrorist organization, *Nuclei Armati Rivoluzionari* (Armed Revolutionary Nuclei), the type of explosives used and the political climate of the strategy of tension hinted at involvement by the Italian secret services. The secret service chief, Pietro Musumeci, and the financier, Licio Gelli, were later condemned for attempting to mislead the police inquiry into the bombing.

Gelli was the head of the anti-democratic and anti-communist Masonic lodge, Propaganda Due (P2), which was publicly uncovered in the following year and shed new light onto the strategy of tension. A fervent fascist during his youth, Gelli had fought alongside the Nazis during the last phase of the Second World War and with the fascists in Spain as a volunteer. Gelli set up the P2 Lodge in order to reverse the leftward trend that was taking place during the 1970s, when strikes were widespread, the student protest movement was in full swing, and the Communist Party's

---

[5] In September 2011, the Palermo civil tribunal ordered the Italian government to pay 100 million euro in civil damages to the relatives of the victims for failure to protect the flight and for concealing the truth and destroying evidence, and, in January 2013, Italy's top criminal court confirmed that the flight was brought down by a stray missile (Smargiassi 2010, p. 10).

votes had almost surpassed those of the Christian Democrats (Stille 2006, p. 67). Using the P2 Lodge, Gelli assembled many of the most powerful and unscrupulous members of Italy's governing class, including more than a dozen generals in the Army and Air Force, the heads of military intelligence and foreign espionage, three ministers of the government, the commander of the Treasury Police, leading figures in the *Carabinieri* (military police), the presidents of several prominent Italian banks, and leading figures in industry and the world of information, including Berlusconi and the owner of the *Corriere della Sera*, Angelo Rizzoli (Stille 2006, p. 68).

Through the Banco Ambrosiano, Gelli brokered massive under-the-table payments to Craxi's Socialist Party and instigated the purchase of a large share of the Rizzoli-*Corriere della Sera* group, so that he could exercise influence on the paper's direction as a kind of "de facto owner" (Stille 2006, p. 69). All such examples of collusion and corruption demonstrated that below the surface of Italian democracy there "lay a secret history, made up of hidden associations, contacts and even conspiracies" (Ginsborg 2001, p. 144).

Thus, "Batti il Tuo Tempo" must be understood as a reaction against an actual social and political context in which hegemonic forces continuously and deliberately undermined democracy and justice. The two rhetorical questions at the end of the song's final verse—"Dove sono gli illegali? / Chi protegge noi da voi, da questi criminali?!" (Where are the illegals? / Who protects us from you, from these criminals?!)—intend to act as a thought-provoking denunciation of what was perceived to be a criminal state. They also simultaneously draw attention to the irony of this same state's criminalization of the *centri sociali*, which in fact provided the cultural and social services that the state itself had repeatedly failed to deliver.

THE RESPONSE TO THE *LEGA NORD* AND RACISM

In what is arguably the first-ever Italian raggamuffin LP, *Stupefacente* (Wide 1991),[6] the Florentine il Generale and Ludus Pinsky confronted the issue of growing repression and racism in Florence with the song, "Foglio di

---

[6] *Stupefacente* plays on the word's double meaning between "amazing" and "drug." Also released in 1991 was the Bolognese raggamuffin artist Lele Gaudi's debut album, *Basta Poco* (It Doesn't Take Much), on the multinational Polygram/Mercury label. Gaudi was the most commercially successful and one of the most vocally gifted of Italy's raggamuffin pioneers. However, due to its predominantly sentimental themes and pop aspirations, his work will not be the subject of discussion. Lele Gaudi was also a founding member of Tubi Forti Productions, which produced Sud Sound System's debut recordings.

Via" (Expulsion Order).[7] Bettini explains that the song was also inspired by an episode involving Sandro Favilli, who was the bassist for their previous historic punk band, I Refuse It, and founder of Wide Records, who had been expelled from Florence by the police with a *foglio di via*, precisely because he was a punk. Bettini highlights that the frequent harassment and expulsion of African immigrants and punks from Florence led to interracial solidarity between the two groups (Personal interview), and so new connective marginalities were born in the Tuscan capital as a result of increasing institutional intolerance and repression. Featuring the instrumental backing of the Ludus Dub Band, "Foglio di Via" fittingly establishes a narrative about two youths, one white and one black, who are racially harassed by a shopkeeper and then given a *foglio di via* by the police.

Il Generale also declared that the song was inspired by the broader issue of growing racism throughout Italy, which he directly linked to the rise of the Northern Leagues (in Signorini 1992, p. 33). Franco Rocchetta founded the *Liga Veneta* in 1979, and in 1984 Umberto Bossi founded the *Lega Lombarda*. However, these were just two of numerous neolocalist leagues that had begun to flourish during the 1980s due to popular resentment towards corruption and inefficiencies within the centralized Italian state. In the 1987 national elections, the *Lega Lombarda* gained representation in the Italian parliament for the first time, with Bossi elected to the Senate and Giuseppe Leoni to the Chamber of Deputies.

Leaders of the various leagues sought to politicize language, and their demands for regional autonomy were "articulated through an affirmation of local dialects and culture" (Zaslove 2011, p. 55). They maintained that dialects "should be considered authentic languages and that the colonization of the central state and its bureaucracy was destroying this essential link to local and traditional culture" (Zaslove 2011, p. 85). Thus, whereas the use of dialect by Sud Sound System and other groups was inspired by subaltern cultural "Others" and formed part of an inclusionary and intercultural dialogue, the Northern Leagues emphasized their local languages and identities as markers of cultural and racial superiority and exclusivity.

To compete in the European elections, Bossi formed the *Alleanza Nord* (Northern Alliance) in 1989 by merging his *Lega Lombarda* with the regional leagues from Veneto, Piedmont, Liguria, Emilia-Romagna,

---

[7] A *foglio di via* is a legal measure which can be applied to exile both Italian and non-Italian citizens from a specific district for an extended period of time, even for minor offences.

and Tuscany. Under the collective title *Lega Nord*, the movement tripled its electoral support in the 1990 regional elections (Zaslove 2011, p. 55). The *Lega Nord* promoted a "regionally specific 'ethnic' neo-liberalism" (Levy 1996, p. 20) based on "positivist constructions of Northern racial superiority and Southern inferiority" (Verdicchio 2005, p. 16). The movement viewed unification as a mistake and contrasted what it perceived were the northern values of "entrepreneurship, efficiency, the capacity to work hard and to save" with those of what they claimed was a "lazy and parasitic South" (Ginsborg 2001, p. 175). Consequently, the so-called *terroni* from the South and the *extracomunitari* (non-Europeans) from abroad, who had arrived in the North as economic refugees, were all unwelcome. Disturbingly, Bossi himself declared that assimilation "could not apply to black immigrants" with whom "it would be impossible to build an ethnic link without generating grave racial tensions within society" (in Ginsborg 2001, p. 176).

Bossi understood that using local dialects along with everyday street language and slang could serve as a powerful tool to break the codes of the dominant political discourse (Zaslove 2011, p. 85). The posses' musically mediated politics, which framed vernacular language, dialectal expressions, and popular references within a "black" musical aesthetic, directly contrasted Bossi's adoption of the language of the street, bars, and football stadiums within a popularist and discriminatory discourse. As discussed in the previous chapter, Sud Sound System's "Fuecu" is one such example of the use of dialect to create a self-reflexively local perspective, which adapted colloquial expressions such as *punnu* from Salentine football slang, along with lines from a popular football chant, as part of a discourse underlining the continuum between one's own cultural roots and those of cultural and racial "Others."

Another crucial example of the use of music as a vehicle to promote diversity and cultural exchange was "Ragga Soldati" (Ragga Soldiers 1992). Produced in collaboration with Africa Unite's Madaski, at his Spliff a Dada Studio in Pinerolo, "Ragga Soldati" provides an innovative example of the alliances that were taking place in opposition to nationalist and regionalist racisms. Connecting the South (Sicily), Centre (Florence), and North (Pinerolo), "Ragga Soldati" features il Generale's Florentine vernacular alongside the Sicilian dialect of DJ Kote Giacalone (currently performing as Jaka, and from now on referred to in this chapter as Giacalone). The blending of these dominant and subaltern languages through a process of transregional collaboration symbolically constructs a new model of national unity based on an

140 S. SCARPARO AND M. S. STEVENSON

acentric and multiple understanding of Italian identity and culture. Furthermore, as indicated by the lyrics transcribed below, the song self-consciously frames raggamuffin reggae as an independent, rebellious, message-oriented, transnational, and anti-racist cultural weapon within the wider posse movement. As such, the lyrics can be understood to articulate the (inter)national popular horizontality of reggae music outlined by Verdicchio (2006).

> Ragga soldati da nessuno comandati,
> ... Rime coscienziose, liriche culturali,
> ... Della parola, ti dico, solo siamo armati,
> ... Tutte le posse muovono, reggae-ribelle,
> ... Guarda, c'è un naziskin, ci vuole un pezzo appropriato
> ... Zucca vuota, cranio rasato,
> Il nuovo razzismo dev'essere fermato.
> ... Reggae, raggamuffin in dialetto locale,
> Per un messaggio internazionale,
> Senza distinzioni di colore, di linguaggio o di nazione.
> (Ragga soldiers commanded by no-one,
> ... Conscious rhymes, cultural lyrics,
> ... I tell you, we're armed with lyrics only
> ... All the posses move, rebel-reggae,
> ... Look, there's a nazi skin, an appropriate song is required,
> ... Empty noggin, shaved head,
> The new racism must be stopped,
> ... Reggae, raggamuffin in local dialect,
> For an international message,
> Without divisions of colour, language or nation.)

The final three lines are particularly noteworthy since, in direct contrast to the insular and segregating use of local dialect by Bossi and the *Lega Nord*, they explicitly posit local, dialectal raggamuffin as a vehicle for a wide-reaching and non-discriminatory message.

In 1992, the collaborative and transregional anti-racism of the posses reached its apex through the Torino Posse (TO.SSE) and their 12-inch release on the independent Milan-based label, Vox Pop. The record contained two vocal tracks—"Legala" (Tie It Up), A-side, and "Da Bun" (Truly), B-side—together with their dub versions. The two recordings, both produced by Madaski, were the product of a broad alliance bringing together Briggy Bronson (Savona), Militant P (Sud Sound System,

Bari/Salento), Papa Ricky (Salento), il Generale (Florence), Giacalone (Sicily/Florence), Lele Gaudi (Bologna), Aloisha (Casino Royale, Milan), Bobo Boggio (Fratelli di Soledad, Turin), Luca Morino (Mau Mau, Turin), Geki (Niù Tennici, Verona), and a little-known female rapper named Lori.

One of the guiding forces behind the formation of the TO.SSE was Paolo "Paolone Aka" Ferrari, who was a DJ on *Radio Torino Popolare* and a music journalist, and his friend Lucampione, who asked the founding members of Africa Unite, Bunna and Madaski, to form a raggamuffin posse. As already mentioned in Chap. 3, Africa Unite was founded in 1981 as Africa United in Turin's provincial town of Pinerolo during Italian reggae's first wave. Between the 1950s and 1970s, mass migration from the South to Turin had transformed it into the "third largest Southern city" (Però 2006, p. 213), and the parentage of Bunna (Piedmontese father and Calabrian mother) and Madaski (Piedmontese mother and Sicilian father) both reflected and embodied the very mixing between the South and North opposed by Bossi's movement.

Inspired by Bob Marley and examples of British reggae, such as Steel Pulse and Linton Kwesi Johnson, Africa Unite remains Italy's most longevous and arguably most recognized reggae band. Their first demo was released in 1984, while their first self-produced EPs, *Mjekrari* and *'Llaka*, were released in 1987 and 1988 respectively. Their first LP, *People Pie*, was released in 1991. Reflecting the previously discussed tendencies of early Italian reggae, throughout this initial period they performed almost entirely in English.[8] During the late 1980s, Africa Unite supported and had been associated with the *centri sociali* network. In 1989, they had performed a street concert after the evacuation and destruction of *Leoncavallo*, and they commemorated this event in 1991 with their English language song "Lionhorse Possee" (New Tone Records). Despite this tangible link with alternative cultural contexts of the 1980s, it was the advent of *la Pantera* and the posses that inspired the band's understanding of the communicative and political potential of reggae music. In the words of Bunna: "After the era of the 1970s *cantautori*, the desire to reclaim the 'serious' song which delivers messages had returned" (in Bunna et al. 2011, pp. 76–77).

---

[8] Their only Italian language song had been "Nella Mia Città" (In My City), which appeared on *Mjekrari* and fittingly articulated a local narrative about the everyday marginalization of life in Pinerolo.

After accepting the invitation to form the raggamuffin-style Torino Posse, Bunna and Madaski initiated a project which sought to unite the various (trans)local scenes. This collaborative project was organized as part of a counter-informational campaign leading up to the April elections of 1992 (Bunna et al. 2011, p. 77). The A-side track, "Legala," embodies the transcultural and transregional aspirations at the heart of the project. The song's melodic and tongue-twisting chorus—"Lega la Lega, lega la Lega, legala la Lega"—translates as "tie up" or "bind" the League and unequivocally calls for direct action. While the refrain's phonetic structure facilitates the expression of a Jamaican-style rhythmic and lingual dexterity, it is also idiosyncratically Italian, making an ironic play on the homonyms *Lega* (League) and *lega* (the imperative second person form of the verb *legare*: to tie up/bind). Although the electronic raggamuffin *riddim* of the song is self-consciously modern and based on a foreign model, the use of a female chorus, which intermittently repeats *lega la Lega*, can be understood to evoke the folk singing of the *mondine*, the exploited female rice pickers of the Northern Po Valley. The folk quality of the song is further reinforced by its locally inspired vocal melodies and sparing use of concertina. This linguistic and rhythmic juxtaposition of the local and the foreign, and of the modern and the traditional, evokes a sense of openness and dialogue which directly challenges the self-preserving and closed localism of the League. Further articulating the posse movement's rhizomatic redistribution of cultural flows and its subversion of the historic imbalance between North and South, the glocal syncretism of the *riddim* appears to have been inspired by the (previously discussed) early recordings of Sud Sound System, such as "T'à Sciuta Bona" and "Fuecu."

The various vocalists alternate throughout the song to express their disrespect for the *Lega* and their forceful rejection of its dangerous and divisive racism. The didactic nature of the production is manifest in the series of imperative and declarative sentences contained in the following extract:

> Lega la Lega, sì, non lasciarla scappare,
> Perché il razzismo è difficile da fermare,
> ... Divisione, razzismo è divisione
> ... Quando l'unica strada è rispetto e integrazione,
> Non si può, e non si può,
> Vivere in un paese se è razzista.
> (Tie up the League, yes, don't let it escape,
> Because racism is difficult to stop,
> ... Division, racism is division,

THE RISE OF THE POSSES AND THE POWER OF THE WORD   143

… When the only way is respect and integration,
One cannot, and one cannot,
Live in a country if it's racist.)

Importantly, the phenomenon of *la Lega* is subsequently framed as a national problem, and one which reflects a broader, corrupt, and anti-democratic political and economic hegemony comprising fascists, *mafiosi*, Socialists, and Christian Democrats.

As stated above, the northern autonomist leagues politicized language by maintaining that dialects were an essential link to a separate local cultural identity, and Bossi combined dialect with colloquial and idiomatic expressions both to establish popular appeal and to distinguish himself from the mainstream parties. A particularly crude and chauvinistic example of this was Bossi's catchphrase, *La Lega ce l'ha duro* (The League's got a stiff one). Throughout "Legala," and the B-side collaboration, "Da Bun," there is a self-conscious use of slang and dialect which seeks to counter Bossi and his League's use of local and vernacular language as a means of stirring up opposition to diversity. For example, "Legala" uses Bossi's own language as a weapon against his racist ideology: "La Lega attacca ma non è vero che 'ce l'ha duro' / Il razzismo non ha, non ha, non ha futuro" (The League attacks but it's untrue that 'it's got a stiff one' / Racism has no, has no, has no future). Furthermore, the League's movement is colloquially referred to as a *sporca fregatura* (sleazy swindle), and towards the end of the song all of the vocalists unite to sing a juvenile football stadium-like chant ridiculing potential *leghisti*: "Chi vota la Liga, porta tanta sfiga" (Whoever votes for the League, is a massive loser).

In "Da Bun," the use of popular language is even more intricate. The chorus contains a vulgar use of the Piedmontese dialect to playfully deride *leghisti* as *cujun* (dickheads, lit. testicles). The dimwitted nature of the League's rhetoric is further ridiculed through the use of anti-intellectual language:

> Di quello che dice la Lega,
> A me non me ne frega,
> Sono tutte idiozie,
> Non me ne importa una sega.
> (I don't give a damn,
> About what the League says,
> It's totally idiotic,
> I don't give a toss [lit. wank] about it.)

144 S. SCARPARO AND M. S. STEVENSON

Importantly, the verses of "Da Bun" also integrate Piedmontese side by side with the Salentine and Sicilian dialects of Papa Ricky and Giacalone, which has symbolic resonance due to the fact that Piedmont was the colonizing force behind the unification of Italy and the ensuing suppression of the South's cultures and economies. Fittingly, Giacalone's verse raises the issue of Sicilian emigration, arguably one of the main consequences of the North's economic exploitation and dominance of the South. Thus, the song's core anti-racism and promotion of a harmoniously diverse national cultural identity are embodied both in linguistic form *and* content.

The record was distributed throughout Italy's various regions by the artists themselves, and Bunna declares that it made a considerable impact (in Bunna et al. 2011, p. 77). According to Giacalone, the project represented an unsurpassed example of the collaborative spirit and wide-reaching impact of the period (in Bunna et al. 2011, p. 78). The project also signalled a turning point for Africa Unite; not only did it motivate them to begin to sing in Italian, but it even inspired Bunna and Madaski to run an election campaign as candidates for *Rifondazione Comunista* (PRC, Communist Refoundation Party), during which they sung accompanied by a sound system (Madaski in Bunna et al. 2011, p. 79).[9]

THE MOVEMENT'S BROADENING INFLUENCE AND VISIBILITY

A series of live events and mass gatherings, taking place in the lead up to and soon after the 1992 elections of April 5 and 6, further demonstrated that the posse movement reached its most collaborative phase during a particularly volatile period in institutional Italian politics. On March 26, the satirical Milanese left-wing weekly, *Cuore*, sponsored an anti-League and anti-racist concert in Milan during which the TO.SSE and friends performed in front of 1000 people. The following evening in Turin, an event representing the culmination of the entire posse era took place at the *centro sociale*, *Murazzi del Po* (Bettini and Tosi 2009, p. 234). This self-managed event was organized with the Al Ard Association in support of the Palestinian Intifada and gathered together Sud Sound System (Salento), il Generale (Florence), Papa Ricky (Salento), Briggy Bronson (Savona), the TO.SSE (Turin), Lele Gaudi (Bologna), and more than 4000 spectators (with at least another 1000 outside). The event lasted

---

[9] *Rifondazione Comunista* was the smaller of the two parties emerging from the dissolution of the Italian Communist Party in 1991.

almost until dawn with "Legala" being the most enthusiastically received song (Campo 1992, p. 25).

The following evening, another mass gathering, *La Notte dei Marziani Italiani* (The Night of the Italian Martians), was held at Turin's Palasport in front of 6000 spectators. The concert united artists from all over Italy, some less deeply rooted in the posse scene than others: Pitura Freska (Venice), Isola Posse All Stars (Bologna), Sa Razza (Sardinia), Carrie D and Devastatin' Posse (Turin), the Aeroplanitaliani (Turin/Bologna), Lele Gaudi (Bologna), Mau Mau (Turin), Casino Royale (Milan), Nuovi Briganti (Sicily), and Frankie hi-NRG MC (Perugia).

The considerable popularity and widespread media coverage granted to these two events brought to light a number of issues that were beginning to arise from the growing mainstream exposure and recognition of the nation's musical underground. The self-managed raggamuffin event at *Murazzi del Po* was a faithful representation of the autonomous and organic roots of the early phase of the posse movement. As Gabrielle Ferraris explains, in the cavernous spaces of the *centro sociale*, "one inhaled smoke and sweat and the free and wild air of the *centri sociali* where the posses were born" (1992a, p. 17). In contrast, *La Notte dei Marziani Italiani* was held in an "official" and highly policed space, indicating a "definitive passage from 'underground' semi-illegality to the foreground of the pop music scene" (1992a, p. 17).

A momentous gathering in Salento, during the summer months (June–July) of 1992, further attested to the counter-cultural and counter-hegemonic vitality of the movement. The youth from Sud Sound System and the Salento Posse took charge of an enormous green space and manor farm on the Adriatic coast, between Otranto and San Foca. For two months, they transformed it into "the largest and most effective creative laboratory" in the history of Italian reggae and rap (Pacoda 1996, pp. 38–39). Via word of mouth in Italy's *centri sociali* and clubs, the occupation became a site of cultural pilgrimage and exchange for youth from all over Italy and for key components of the national posse movement from South to North: the Salento and Bari Posses, Militant A and One Love Hi Powa from Rome, the entire posse tied to *Isola Nel Kantiere*, the Lion Horse Posse from Milan, and members of Turin's scene (Pacoda 1996, p. 39). The improvised evening dancehalls, which attracted thousands of youth and showcased reggae and rap, unfolded without any official authorization and were powered by an electric generator. Innumerable vocalists were accompanied either by selectors or live bands until dawn, converting the peripheral rural setting in the deep South into a nationally significant hub of cultural production.

As a means of conveying the autonomous and culturally significant nature of the occupation, the gathering was referred to with the dialectal term, *Mantagnata*, meaning a site which is conveniently sheltered from the wind. What took place at the *Mantagnata* was something very similar to the free music festivals in Italy during the 1970s (Pacoda 2011, p. 8). However, whereas these festivals, such as those organized by *Re Nudo*, predominantly took place in the North and drew young Italians from all over the peninsula, including the South, on this occasion, the cultural flow was reversed, and the South was transformed into the centripetal counter-cultural centre. Pacoda argues further that this rural festival not only founded Salento's reputation as "the new Jamaica," thus confirming its cultural prestige and authority within Italy's reggae-hip hop scene, but it was also the catalyst for the subsequent boom in local tourism (2011, p. 88). The fact that an event organized illegally in such a peripheral southern location, showcasing a marginal musical culture, was able to have such a broad and lasting influence attests to the "national popular" impetus of this period.

During this same period, the internal conflict arising from the growing resonance of the posse movement outside autonomous and anti-institutional contexts began coming to the fore. Within the movement, there was an inherent tension between the desire to effect broad counter-cultural change and the need to increase visibility and, in turn, collaboration with the cultural and commercial mainstream. On July 24, 1992, the music magazine, *Velvet*, and the Department of Culture, together with elements of the business sector, staged another mass concert at Rome's Stadio Olimpico, which drew at least 5000 spectators and brought together many of the peninsula's raggamuffin and rap acts. The fact that the show was part of a bill dominated by the commercial industry and sponsored by the Socialist Party caused apprehension amongst those invited. As a consequence of its institutional and commercial ties, Sud Sound System, Isola Posse All Stars, Nuovi Briganti, 99 Posse, and Assalti Frontali (ex-Onda Rossa Posse) all dissociated themselves from the initiative.

Due to this general unease, the organizers decided to grant free entry and dedicate the event to the recently murdered anti-Mafia magistrate, Paolo Borsellino (a questionable act given the Socialists' alleged courting of the Mafia and the emerging details of endemic corruption within the

THE RISE OF THE POSSES AND THE POWER OF THE WORD   147

party). During the Torino Posse's performance, however, Assalti Frontali hijacked the stage and exhibited a large banner with the words: "No hypocrisy." During their 15-minute occupation of the stage, they denounced the festival's organizers as music *mafiosi* and encouraged the audience to come instead to the *centri sociali* (Militant A 1997, p. 83).

Between 1991 and 1993, as the cultural push from below became more powerful, the long-standing underground-mainstream dichotomy was further problematized and subverted. The success of self-productions, such as "Batti il Tuo Tempo," and the independent releases on Bologna's Century Vox Records label, like "Fuecu," reverberated within the Italian record industry and dominant cultural channels. Between 1991 and 1992, Isola Posse All Stars, Papa Ricky, Nuovi Briganti, Pitura Freska, 99 Posse, and Sud Sound System all appeared on Rai 3's widely followed satirical television programme, *Avanzi*, for which Century Vox Records also produced the theme music.[10] Arguably the most significant of these musical appearances took place in 1992, when Sud Sound System performed on the show for the second time in two years. On this occasion, the Salentine posse delivered one of Militant P's lyrical compositions—"Video politica" (Video politics)—over the "T'à Sciuta Bona" *riddim*.[11] By self-reflexively critiquing the televisual medium, this live and nationally broadcasted performance captured the historical influence and visibility of the posses and the complex dialectic they had established between the margins and the mainstream.

Also in 1992, Century Vox Records released the groundbreaking compilation, *Fondamentale Vol. 1*, which collated all of the label's numerous raggamuffin and rap productions to date. In the same year, the following compilations were also released: *Italian Posse: Rappamuffin d'Azione*, which focused on the hybrid and politicized nature of the movement and was released on Naples' independent dance label, Flying Records, and the more club-oriented *Italian Rap Attack*, on Bologna's independent dance label, Irma Records.

At this time, the commercial recording industry awoke to the fact that the posses represented the renewal of the youth music market, and the

---

[10] Broadcast between February 3, 1991, and March 1993, every episode of *Avanzi* showcased a live performance from an unknown or emerging musical group or artist. In 1992, *Avanzi* won a *Telegatto* as the TV revelation of the year.

[11] The video of this performance can be found on the YouTube channel, irie2012 (see Works Cited list).

large record companies began "bombarding" the offices of Century Vox with financial offers (Pacoda in Lapassade and Fumarola 1992, p. 94). This inversion of cultural authority marked an important shift, since for the first time the commercial, or mainstream, industry was forced to defer to the cultural underground. Somewhat ironically, a primary case in point was Berlusconi's label, RTI Music, which released two compilations in 1992: *Sotterranei Italiani* (Underground Italians), featuring il Generale, and *Ragga Radio Station (11 Atti Originali Di Raggamuffin Italiano)*, featuring the cult classic "Rubbai" (I Stole), by Milan's Krama Possee, and Briggy Bronson's only recorded Italian language singles. Furthermore, in 1993, RTI Music licensed il Generale's second album, *Guarda la Luna e Non il Dito*, and Lele Gaudi released his second pop-raggamuffin album, *Gaudium Magnum*, with the multinational Polygram/Mercury label.

Considering the autonomous roots of the posse movement within the *centri sociali* and *radio libere*, together with the politicized history of Italian youth music dating back to the 1960s and 1970s, this blurring of the boundaries between the underground and the mainstream was bound to create tensions and heated debate. As previously discussed, ideological opposition to the commercialization of culture was inbuilt into the *centri sociali*'s governing ethical codes of *autoproduzione* (self-production) and *autogestione* (self-management). Within the posse movement, the *centri sociali* "were indicators of authenticity, political militancy, and street credibility" (Mitchell 2001, p. 197), and artists who did not have their roots in these contexts were often criticized for their perceived inauthenticity. The newfound cultural hegemony of these politicized contexts even motivated Jovanotti, who had come to represent the most politically disengaged trends in the 1980s youth culture and the most commercial strand of reggae and rap, to begin releasing socially committed songs from 1992.

In 1993, tensions rose to the surface between those who were totally opposed to industry encroachments into the posse scene, such as Rome's Assalti Frontali and One Love Hi Powa, and those willing to collaborate with the industry to varying degrees, such as Bologna's Century Vox Records (the pioneering label had decided to sign a distribution deal with the multinational, Sony). On January 27, the national left-wing newspaper, *l'Unità*, published an article signed by Assalti Frontali, One Love Hi Powa, 00199, and AK47 entitled, "Le posse romane contro i colossi musicali" (The Roman Posses Against the Musical Giants). In the article, these groups "excommunicated" from the movement those who had signed with majors and called for a reinforcement of the practices of self-management (*autogestione*). The result of this reaffirmation of *autogestione* and *autoproduzione* by the Roman posses was the setting up of the production/distribution *Cordata per l'autorganizzazione* (Network for self-management), at *Forte Prenestino*. Another example of opposition to the industry's advances was *Leoncavallo*'s launching of a series of self-produced and self-managed CDs through the organization of a live concert (featuring One Love Hi Powa and 99 Posse) outside Milan's San Vittore Prison. Confirming the politics of this section of the movement, the concert advocated the release of political prisoners and AIDS-afflicted inmates while also protesting against the legislations that granted leniency to corrupt politicians.

THE POSSE MOVEMENT HITS THE SILVER SCREEN

Also in 1993, the posse movement received its highest level of "official" recognition. Academy Award-winning director, Gabriele Salvatores, included a number of artists in the soundtrack to his film, *Sud* (*South*, 1993), and the soundtrack went on to win a prestigious *Nastro d'Argento* (Silver Ribbon) film award. Set in a peripheral small town deep in Italy's South, *Sud* was Salvatores' most socially engaged film to date and was largely inspired by the autonomous cultural and political renewal initiated by the *centri sociali* and the posses. Salvatores claimed that the posses were "the voice of the new cultural political commitment" (in Bellizi 1993, p. 48) and that their music had "influenced" and "nourished" his film (in Fusco 1993, p. 29). Salvatores officially presented the film's soundtrack at *Leoncavallo*, much to the chagrin of Milan's *Lega Nord* mayor, Marco Formentini, who had based his election campaign on vehement opposition to the historic social centre. This was a watershed moment, since it invested an unprecedented level of cultural legitimacy to the *centri sociali* and further demonstrated the posse movement's considerable influence on the cultural hegemony of the time.

The film takes the perspective of three unemployed southerners and an unemployed Eritrean, who inadvertently uncover collusion between the local political baron and the Camorra during an armed school occupation in protest against government neglect. In line with Salvatores' aim to represent the South as a symbolic Gramscian space where the forgotten people of the world live (in Fusco 1993, p. 29), almost all the raggamuffin and rap artists chosen for the soundtrack were from the South: Papa Ricky and Nandu Popu from Salento and 99 Posse, Bisca, and Possessione from

150 S. SCARPARO AND M. S. STEVENSON

Naples. Also asked to participate in the film were Assalti Frontali, who, despite their reservations about Berlusconi and Mario Cecchi Gori's financing of the film, produced the title track, "Sud," which plays during the opening title sequence. However, in line with their anti-industry stance, Assalti Frontali prohibited the song's release on the official, Sony-distributed, soundtrack, instead releasing it in 1994 through the previously mentioned *Cordata per l'autorganizzazione*.

The two other most prominent songs in the film are 99 Posse's "Curre Curre Guaglió" (Run Run Man, 1993) and Papa Ricky's Salentine version of the classic "'O Sole Mio," "Lu Sole Mio" (My Sun), which had been originally released in 1992 by Century Vox Records.[12] Although "Lu Sole Mio" bears little of Papa Ricky's trademark lyrical militancy, its Salentine reinvention of a Neapolitan classic synthesizes "Jamaican cadences and Mediterranean melody" (Pacoda 1996, p. 121). Consequently, it represents an important example of the transculturation and glocalization of southern Italian reggae during this period. Indeed, echoing the work of Sud Sound System, Papa Ricky explained that in the song the sun represented "the last true unifying element in a society whose disintegration is in full view" (in Perboni 1993, p. 48). The song's spoken-word introduction explicitly states the non-discriminatory symbolism of the sun: "'Lu Sole Mio' non è mica una canzone per solo meridionali, ca lu sole scalda tutta la terra, e quindi sfruttiamolo tutti quanti assieme questo calore" ("Lu Sole Mio" isn't just a song for southerners at all, because the sun warms the whole land, and so let's all make use of this warmth together).

"Lu Sole Mio" is integrated into one of *Sud*'s most poignant scenes where, in celebration of their victory, the occupiers begin to sing the traditional Neapolitan version in acapella before Papa Ricky's version is seamlessly layered over the top. Significantly, in a clearly symbolic scene, the Eritrean character, Munir, who embodies the racist history of Italian colonialism, venerates the sun to the accompaniment of Papa Ricky's melodic chorus.

The raggamuffin song, "Curre Curre Guaglió," was written by 99 Posse[13] after Salvatores had asked them to compose a piece which spoke about Naples and the experience of its *centro sociale*: *Officina 99*. In a

---

[12] "Lu Sole Mio" also features the guest vocals of Treble, from Sud Sound System.

[13] The founding members of 99 Posse were Luca "'O Zulù" Persico (vocals), Massimo "JRM" Jovine (bass guitar), Marco "Kaya" Messina (DJ), Sacha Ricci (keyboards), and Claudio "Klark Kent" Marino (drums).

THE RISE OF THE POSSES AND THE POWER OF THE WORD   151

mixture of Italian and Neapolitan, 99 Posse narrate the story and motivation behind the occupation of the *centro sociale* that had given them their name. As well as accompanying the film's closing credits and featuring in its official trailer, the track was used as the centrepiece for one of the film's most significant narrative moments.[14] After the inhabitants of the town publicly demonstrate their support for the occupation, the chorus and third verse provide indignant and emotive accompaniment to the protagonists' actions, while they reinforce their barricades, instituting a link between the fictional occupation portrayed in the film and the real occupations of the *centri sociali* (99 Posse in Campo 1995, p. 89).

NEW NEAPOLITAN SOUNDSCAPES

Officina 99 was an abandoned garage in the working-class Neapolitan suburb of Gianturco and was occupied on May 1, 1991, by around 500 students and unemployed citizens. Although it was soon evacuated, it was reoccupied later that year and gained further support from the homeless and factory worker movements. In the early 1990s, the lack of social services and high levels of unemployment, marginalization, and exploitation, which inspired such occupations, were particularly pronounced in the South. In 1990, the number of unemployed youths aged between 14 and 29 in the South stood at 44.1 per cent, compared with 14.6 per cent in the Centre-North (Ginsborg 2001, p. 22), and, in 1991, overall unemployment stood at over 15 per cent throughout most of the South, while throughout most of the North it was below 5 per cent (Levy 1996, p. 3).

99 Posse's first self-produced 12-inch was released in 1992 on the independent hip hop label, Crime Squad. The title of the record alone, *Dì Original Trappavasciamuffin Stailì*, linguistically foregrounds the process of transculturation at play. The Jamaican Patois expression *di original stylee* (the original style) is phonetically Italianized to become *dì original stailì*. Furthermore, there is the use of a compound dialectal neologism: *trappavasciamuffin*; *trappa* derives from the Neapolitan expression *trappano*, which refers to a yokel, while *vascia* or *vascio* can either denote low in stature or refer to the tenement housing of the Neapolitan lumpenproletariat. Consequently, *trappavasciamuffin* might be understood to stand for a very direct, unrefined, and egalitarian

---

[14] In 2013, a censored version of the lyrics to "Curre Curre Guagliò" was also included in an anthology of Italian literature for secondary schools.

Neapolitan raggamuffin vernacular, which, through its synthesis of local and foreign non-official cultural-linguistic idioms, creates connective marginalities that challenge dominant and homogenizing tendencies. In this regard, it can be understood as a parallel to the syncretic resistance vernacular created by Sud Sound System, which we discussed in the previous chapter.

The themes and style of the two vocals tracks on the EP, "Rafaniello" (Radish) and "Salario Garantito" (Guaranteed Salary), are openly critical of Italian politics. Using the Neapolitan word for radish as a symbol of those who are "red outside but white inside," "Rafaniello" critiques the local federation of the *Rifondazione Comunista* (Communist Refoundation Party). The metaphor, which is based on the colour distinction between Communists (red) and Christian Democrats (white), implies that while the party claimed to be Communist, it was really part of the hegemonic political structure governed by the Christian Democrats, which is condemningly referred to as *o partit' ca mettete e bombe a Piazza Fontana* (the party that planted the bombs in Piazza Fontana). Hence, similarly to the examples in "Batti il Tuo Tempo," this reference explicitly links Italy's political hegemony to the atrocities of the strategy of tension.

"Salario Garantito" provides an example of the melodically Mediterranean and dialectal *trappavasciamuffin staili* of 99 Posse's early work. The lyrics use an indignant first person voice to link the economic precariousness of underemployed and unemployed Neapolitan (and southern) youth, and their exploitation by the economic system, to the posse's defining non-conformism and political antagonism:

> Nun me piace stà società me fà schif' é faticà,
> No nun voglio faticà sul' pe me fà sfruttà,
> E nun voglio sturià (studiare) sulament' pé sfunnà,
> ... A me me piac' é sturià pe capì é cose comm' stann',
> Sent' ò bisogn'é luttà contr'à stù stat' che è tirann',
> ... Vogl'ò salario garantit'.
> (I don't like this society, work makes me nauseous,
> I don't want to work because it's exploitation,
> And I don't want to study just to make it big,
> ... I like studying so I understand how things work,
> I need to fight against this tyrannical state,
> ... I want a guaranteed salary.)

THE RISE OF THE POSSES AND THE POWER OF THE WORD   153

99 Posse's first album, *Curre Curre Guagliò* (Esodo Autoproduzioni, 1993), was self-produced with the collaboration of Sergio "RadioGladio" Messina. Riding the wave of the posse's cinematic exposure, the album sold more than 50,000 copies in a few months, and, in 1994, it further marked the arrival of the musical underground in the "official sphere" by winning a *Targa Tenco* award for best dialectal work (Campo 1995, pp. 90, 91).[15] The album employs an intercultural "aesthetic of fusion" (Dawson and Palumbo 2005, p. 168). Such an aesthetic blends the black transatlantic styles of raggamuffin, rap, funk, soul, and jazz with the sounds of the Neapolitan and Arabic Mediterranean to articulate an understanding of cultural and racial identity that inherently embraces diversity. To this end, after the title track, there is a reprisal of "Salario Garantito," titled "Salario Qawali." A Qawali (or Qawwali) is a form of Islamic musical poetry, and the recitation of the first four lines and chorus of "Salario Garantito" with Arabesque intonation, and to Middle Eastern-style musical accompaniment, poetically conveys the link between the economic exploitation of the South and its racialization as an Oriental "Other," which we discuss in previous chapters.

However, the album's most powerful transcultural alliance is created through the composition, "Napolì" (Naples). The fundamental hybridity of "Napolì" renders it unclassifiable using standard generic definitions. The eclectic mix of instrumentation combines congas, saxophone, electric bass, birbinet (a type of reed instrument used in European folk music), the *ocarina emiliana* (a small flute native to the Emilia-Romagna region), and the *cennamella calabra* (a Calabrian bagpipe). The latter three of these instruments are played by Daniele Sepe, who had been a key figure in Naples' political folk/world music scene since playing on the historical record, *Tammurriata dell'Alfasud* (I Dischi del Sole, 1976), with Gruppo Operaio E Zèzi in the 1970s. The performance of this multicultural ensemble moulds an Arabesque soundscape, which, when combined with the dialectal, Mediterranean style of its raggamuffin toasting and jazzy Afrobeat-style saxophone, conveys a militant and syncretic aesthetic of Middle Eastern-African-Southern "Otherness."

This rhythmic sense of otherness, which establishes a musical dialogue with the racialized discourses informing the ongoing economic exploitation and marginalization of the South, finds its semantic articulation in the

---

[15] On March 25, 2014, a remake of the album featuring various guest artists, *Curre Curre Guagliò 2.0: Non un Passo Indietro* (Musica Posse), was released.

154   S. SCARPARO AND M. S. STEVENSON

lyrics to "Napolì." Instead of a formal chorus, there is a rhythmical chant-like repetition of the city's name, which, together with a bleak description of the daily struggles of its marginalized youth, creates a perilous sense of tension that reflects their daily struggle for survival: "Napolì, criature vuttate 'mmiez' 'a na vi' / Napolì, crisciute cu 'e pippate 'e cucaì' / Napolì, guagliune ca se fanno l'eroì'" (Naples, children devoured in the streets / Naples, grown up snorting cocaine / Naples, youth that shoot up heroin).

Another vital component of Naples' burgeoning underground music scene was the reggae/dub/world outfit, Almamegretta,[16] which also had ties with *Officina 99* and 99 Posse. The name of the group, which was taken from an archaic Latin dialect and means "migrant soul," expressed their multilayered musical aesthetic based on stylistic and cultural synthe-ses. Such fusions of diverse styles brought together Neapolitan language and musical roots with hip hop, raggamuffin, and dub reggae, soul, funk, and various North African, Middle Eastern, and Mediterranean styles, thus endorsing the growing multicultural reality of Italy.

Almamegretta's practice of combining diverse musical styles and genres is articulated by the group's drummer, Gennaro Tesone: "Almamegretta is a musical project that wishes to put together things which are seemingly different, like the Jamaican rhythm alongside melodies from the Mediterranean, North Africa or from the East" (in Marchesano 1994, n.pag.). According to Marco Santoro and Marco Solaroli, this combina-tion of styles emphasized the historical otherness of southern Italy, and, in so doing, Almamegretta aimed to build "a collective cultural memory as a base for a socially constructed, historically situated and, above all, politi-cally connoted identity whose condition could be linguistically defined and crucially expressed through … music" (2007, p. 477).

In 1991 the group gave a successful performance at the Arezzo Wave festival promoting young musical talent, and in September 1992 they recorded an EP comprising four tracks, which was released by the inde-pendent label, Anagrumba, under the title, *Figli di Annibale* (Hannibal's Children). The record gave the group a certain visibility, and its syncretic sonorities were strongly marked by dub reggae and raggamuffin. Almamegretta's musical discourse, which subverted geocultural barriers of

---

[16] In the period discussed, Almamegretta comprised the following members: Gennaro Della Volpe (aka Raiss, vocals), Gennaro Tesone (drums), Tonino Borrelli (bass), Giovanni Mantice (guitar), Paolo Polcari (keyboards).

THE RISE OF THE POSSES AND THE POWER OF THE WORD   155

distance (and difference), not only drew upon global black forms, such as reggae, but also foregrounded "the African roots of local musical traditions" (Dawson and Palumbo 2005, p. 170). Similarly, to Sud Sound System (and Different Stylee before them), Almamegretta believed that there was a certain affinity between reggae and local musical traditions: "Reggae is melancholic, languid music played in minor chords, like Neapolitan music, and therefore it is closer to our sensibility than other styles" (in Campo 1995, p. 93).

While there were raggamuffin and hip hop influences in their early work, the group were especially attracted to the unconventional expressive qualities of dub, establishing what has been referred to as *dub mediterraneo* (Campo 1995, p. 91). Almamegretta's reframing of local language and musical traditions through fusion with other global influences from the Mediterranean region, and beyond, had its roots in the politically inspired 1970s Neapolitan folk revival of the Nuova Compagnia di Canto Popolare and Gruppo Operaio E Zèzi, as well as in the dialectal jazz, funk, and blues fusion of Napoli Centrale and Pino Daniele.[17] Almamegretta's lead vocalist, Raiss, stresses that they sought to recover traditions that had been annihilated by the economic system and unite them with the new cultures brought by immigrants escaping their own economic hardships (in Milioni 1994, n.pag.). Thus, whereas for the *Lega Nord* African immigration signified a degenerative and polluting threat to local cultural identity and traditions, for groups like Almamegretta it represented a *regenerative* and enriching outcome with the potential to reinvigorate local culture and identity.

As an anthem celebrating cultural and racial diversity, the title track of their debut EP, "Figli di Annibale," merits detailed discussion as the group's musical manifesto. The song was inspired by Malcolm X's 1964 speech about African-American history. In this speech, the black nationalist leader drew parallels between poor Italo-Americans and poor African-Americans by claiming that the dark complexion of the former was the result of Hannibal's occupation of large tracts of the Italian peninsula

---

[17] Raiss declares his respect for Pino Daniele's pioneering fusions during the 1970s and 1980s and in particular his album appropriately named "Nero a metà" (Half Black, 1980), dedicated to Mario Musella, the Neapolitan "black" music pioneer from the Showmen, who was the product of an amorous war-time encounter between a Native American father and a Neapolitan mother (in Milioni 1994, n.pag.). Interestingly, another crucial member of the Showmen was James Senese, who was the child of an African-American soldier and a Neapolitan father and went on to found Napoli Centrale.

156 S. SCARPARO AND M. S. STEVENSON

during the Second Punic War. Raiss explains that when he read this speech he decided to rearrange it over a dub reggae rhythm (in Milioni 1994, n.pag.).

"Figli di Annibale" explicitly refers to the fact that Hannibal invaded the Italian peninsula from the North by crossing the Alps and must therefore be understood as a directly antagonistic response to the *Lega Nord*, which, in rejecting southern Italians and African immigrants alike, based its provincial ethno-nationalism on a notion of cultural and racial purity. The subversive black aesthetic of the song is reinforced by the menacing rhythmic chanting of "Africa! Africa! Africa! Africa! Africa! Africa! Africa! Africa!" before the first verse begins. The choice to use standard Italian rather than Neapolitan, something which was rare for Almamegretta, is indicative of the national framework of its rhetorical discourse:

> Annibale grande generale nero,
> Con una schiera di elefanti attraversasti le alpi,
> ... Restò in italia da padrone per quindici o vent'anni,
> Ecco perché molti italiani hanno la pelle scura,
> Ecco perché molti italiani hanno i capelli scuri,
> Un po' del sangue di annibale è rimasto a tutti quanti nelle vene.
> (Hannibal great black general,
> Crossed the Alps with an army of elephants,
> ... He ruled in Italy for fifteen or twenty years,
> This is why many Italians have dark skin,
> This is why many Italians have dark hair,
> A bit of Hannibal's blood has remained in all our veins.)

Echoing Malcolm X's statement—"This is why you find many Italians dark—some of that Hannibal blood"—Raiss takes the argument one step further by stating that some of Hannibal's blood remains in the veins of *all* Italians, regardless of complexion, hair colour, and, of course, latitudinal position.

In the following section, the use of direct address personalizes the discourse for the listener, calling on him/her to form a new understanding of their cultural heritage: "Se conosci la tua storia sai da dove viene il colore / Del sangue che ti scorre nelle vene" (If you know your history you know where the colour / Of the blood that runs through your veins comes from). The lyrics also adapt Malcolm X's references to the handful of black American troops who spread their genes throughout Europe in just a few years during and after the Second World War, commenting that, likewise,

THE RISE OF THE POSSES AND THE POWER OF THE WORD   157

widespread genetic mixing must have occurred also during the 15–20 years of Carthaginian occupation of the Italian peninsula:

> Durante la guerra pochi afroamericani,
> Riempirono l'europa di bambini neri,
> Cosa credete potessero mai fare in venti anni di dominio militare,
> Un'armata di africani in italia meridionale?
> (During the war a handful of African-Americans,
> Filled Europe with black babies,
> What do you think an army of Africans in southern Italy,
> Could do in twenty years of military rule?)

The use of a rhetorical question in the final two lines encourages the listener to reflect on this contentious argument, which was supported by the fact that two of Naples' most influential musicians of the 1960s and 1970s, Mario Musella and James Senese, were the children of Native American and African-American fathers, respectively.

Through the collective classification of southerners as the children of Hannibal with both Mediterranean and African blood—"Ecco perchè noi siamo figli di annibale / Meridionali figli di annibale / Sangue mediterraneo figli di annibale / Sangue di Africa" (That's why we are the children of Hannibal / southerners the children of Hannibal / Mediterranean blood children of Hannibal / The blood of Africa)—Hannibal becomes an emblematic figure of African cultural roots in the South. Thus, as Pugliese argues, the contentious question of southern racial difference is connected "back to another history that only figures, in hegemonic Italian histories, in terms of a military figure that was ultimately vanquished by the power of Rome" (Pugliese 2007, n.pag.). Hence, Almamegretta's view of southern history suggests an alternative reading of official history that "transforms Umberto Bossi's contemptuous declaration of the South as Africa into a point of pride" (Verdicchio 1997, p. 166). In so doing, the group also seeks to configure a new Neapolitan identity which transcends simplistic stereotypes of the city and its inhabitants.

In terms of both its lyrical content *and* musical form, therefore, "Figli di Annibale" provides a musically mediated counter-history and alternative model of Italian culture and identity based on intercultural/interracial solidarity and exchange. As Almamegretta explain, this cultural hybridity is not only inescapable but also a key to survival (in Amenta 1994, n.pag.). However, rather than seeking to create a meta-narrative of its own, the

158 S. SCARPARO AND M. S. STEVENSON

track provides "an ironic attack on notions of racial purity" (Mitchell 2001, p. 205), a fact which was reinforced by its rerelease on their first album with a question mark after the title.

To conclude, the posses discussed in this chapter represent important examples of creative transcultural and (g)local opposition to Italy's underlying power imbalances and racisms. Their activities reinforced the national popular quality of the movement and its capacity to articulate progressive intercultural alliances and exchanges. Although in the most militant contexts there was vehement resistance to attempts by the cultural mainstream to appropriate and exploit the movement's innovative vitality, such attempts were in fact a testament to the posses' counter-hegemonic potential and their growing cultural significance and recognition. Indeed, their ability to transcend alternative and autonomous spaces allowed them to influence mainstream music spheres and cultural institutions. While the period between 1991 and 1994 was the most widely influential period of the posses, as we discuss in the following chapters, their legacy endures through groups and artists still active today.

Works Cited

99 Posse. 1993. CD Cover. *Curre Curre Guagliò*. Esodo Autoproduzioni. CD.

Amenta, Daniela. 1994. Almamegretta: Animamigrante. *Mucchio Selvaggio*, March: n.pag. in Rassegna stampa, *Official Website Almamegretta*. Almamegretta. March 24, 2009. http://www.almamegretta.net/index.php/rassegna-stampa/42-animamigrante/67-almamegretta-animamigrante. Accessed 3 June 2013.

Assante, Ernesto. 1992. Rapper italiani all'attacco. *la Repubblica*, March 26. http://ricerca.repubblica.it/repubblica/archivio/repubblica/1992/03/26/rapper-italiani-all-attacco.html?refresh_ce. Accessed 25 Sep 2013.

Bellizi, Marco. 1993. Leoncavallo a Roma. *Corriere della sera*, October 15. Print.

Bettini, Stefano. 2012. Personal Interview. September 6.

Bettini, Stefano, and Pier Tosi. 2009. *Paperback reggae: Origini, protagonisti, storia e storie della musica in levare*. Firenze: Editoriale Olimpia. Print.

Bull, Anna Cento. 2007. *Italian Neofascism: The Strategy of Tension and the Politics of Nonreconciliation*. New York: Berghahn Books. Print.

Bunna, et al. 2011. *Trent'anni in levare: Storia della storia di Africa Unite*. Genova: Chinaski. Print.

Campo, Alberto. 1992. Pace, amore e libertà ecco il popolo ragamuffin. *la Repubblica*, April 1. http://ricerca.repubblica.it/repubblica/archivio/repubblica/1992/04/01/pace-amore-liberta-ecco-il-popolo.html. Accessed 25 Sep 2013.

THE RISE OF THE POSSES AND THE POWER OF THE WORD   159

————. 1995. *Nuovo? Rock?! Italiano!* Firenze: Giunti. Print.

Castaldo, Gino. 1993a. Democratiche posse tra rabbia e commozione. *la Repubblica*, October 16. http://ricerca.repubblica.it/repubblica/archivio/repubblica/1993/10/16/democratiche-posse-tra-rabbia-commozione.html?ref=search. Accessed 25 Sep 2013.

————. 1993b. Grida dalla Century Vox. *la Repubblica*, February 4. http://ricerca.repubblica.it/repubblica/archivio/repubblica/1993/02/04/grida-dalla-century-vox.html. Accessed 25 Sep 2013.

————. 1993c. L'Italia contro, unita nelle posse. *la Repubblica*, February 4. http://ricerca.repubblica.it/repubblica/archivio/repubblica/1993/02/04/italia-contro-unita-nelle-posse.html?ref=search Accessed 25 Sep 2013.

Cowell, Alan. 1992. Italian Obsession: Was Airliner Shot Down? *New York Times*, February 10. http://www.nytimes.com/1992/02/10/world/italian-obsession-was-airliner-shot-down.html. Accessed 7 Nov 2013.

Dawson, Ashley, and Patrizia Palumbo. 2005. Hannibal's Children: Immigration and Antiracist Youth Subcultures in Contemporary Italy. *Cultural Critique* 59 (1): 165–186. Print.

Denaro, Massimiliano. 2006. 1990. Il Movimento studentesco della 'Pantera.' Diss., Università di Pisa. http://www.quellidiinformatica.org/upload/39/0/tesifinita.pdf. Accessed 9 Aug 2013.

Ferraris, Gabriele. 1992a. Basta col rock classico, trionfa il rap. *La Stampa*, March 30. http://www.archiviolastampa.it/component/option,com_lastampa/task,search/mod,libera/action,viewer/Itemid,3/page,17/articleid,0825_01_1992_0087_0017_11551146/. Accessed 27 Nov 2013.

————. 1992b. Le canzoni con rabbie di sempre. *La Stampa*, September 12. http://www.archiviolastampa.it/component/option,com_lastampa/task,search/mod,libera/action,viewer/Itemid,3/page,35/articleid,0842_01_1992_0250_0035_25198013/. Accessed 28 Nov 2013.

Fusco, Maria P. 1993. Sud, la voglia di essere 'contro.' *la Repubblica*, October 9. http://ricerca.repubblica.it/repubblica/archivio/repubblica/1993/10/09/sud-la-voglia-di-essere-contro.html?ref=search. Accessed 25 Sep 2013.

Ginsborg, Paul. 2001. *Italy and Its Discontents: Family, Civil Society, State 1980–2001*. London: Penguin. Print.

irie2012. 1992. Sud Sound System live: 'Video politica' (T'à sciuta bona riddim: 1992). Rai Tre. Live television performance. https://youtu.be/BIsh69edw-A. Accessed 18 Dec 2012.

Katsiaficas, Georgy. 1997. *The Subversion of Politics: European Autonomous Social Movements and the Decolonization of Everyday Life*. Oakland: AK Press. Print.

Leone, Sergio, dir. 1984. *Once Upon a Time in America*. Warner Bros. DVD.

Levy, Carl. 1996. Introduction: Italian Regionalism in Context. In *Italian Regionalism: History, Identity and Politics*, ed. Carl Levy, 1–33. Oxford: Berg. Print.

160 S. SCARPARO AND M. S. STEVENSON

Lipsitz, George. 1994. *Dangerous Crossroads: Popular Music, Postmodernism, and the Poetics of Place*. London: Verso. Print.

Marchesano, Nino. 1994. Tamurriata psichedelica. *Tutto*, March: n.pag. in Rassegna stampa, *Official Website Almamegretta*. Almamegretta. March 24, 2009. http://www.almamegretta.net/index.php/rassegna-stampa/42-animamigrante/62-tammurriata-psichedelica. Accessed 3 June 2013.

Milioni, Stefano. 1994. Noi, figli di Annibale. *Frigidaire* February 2: n.pag. in Rassegna stampa, *Official Website Almamegretta*. Almamegretta. March 24, 2009. http://www.almamegretta.net/index.php/rassegna-stampa/42-animamigrante/66-noi-figli-di-annibale. Accessed 3 June 2013.

Militant A. 1997. *Storie di Assalti Frontali: Conflitti che producono banditi*. Roma: Castelvecchi. Print.

Mitchell, Tony. 1996. *Popular Music and Local Identity: Rock, Pop and Rap in Europe and Oceania*. London and New York: Leicester University Press. Print.

———. 2001. Fightin da Faida: The Italian Posses and Hip Hop in Italy. In *Global Noise: Rap and Hip Hop Outside the USA*, ed. Tony Mitchell, 194–222. Middletown: Wesleyan University Press. Print.

Nano, Rankis. 1997. *Come again: vibrazioni dal basso*. Roma: Edizioni XOA autoproduzioni. Print.

Pacoda, Pierfrancesco. 1993. L'antagonismo in musica: Posse in azione. In *Posse italiane: Centri sociali, underground musicale e cultura giovanile degli anni '90 in Italia*, ed. Carlo Branzaglia, Pierfrancesco Pacoda, and Alba Solaro, 71–110. Firenze: Editoriale Tosca. Print.

———. 1996. *Potere alla parola: Antologia del rap*. Milan: Feltrinelli. Print.

———. 2011. *Salento, amore mio: Viaggio nella musica, nei luoghi e tra i protagonisti del rinascimento salentino*. Milano: Kowalski. Print.

Perboni, Elia. 1993. 'O sole mio', reggae leccese. *Corriere della Sera*, March 5. Print.

Però, Davide. 2006. The Left and the Construction of Immigrants in 1970s Italy. In *Speaking Out and Silencing: Culture Society and Politics in Italy in the 1970s*, ed. Anna Cento Bull and Giorgio Adalgisa, 212–226. London: Legenda. Print.

Pozzi, Gloria. 1992. Niente panico: La protesta urla a suon di rap. *Corriere della Sera*, March 31. Print.

Pugliese, Joseph. 2007. White Historicide and the Returns of the Souths of the South. *Australian Humanities Review* 42: n.pag. http://www.australianhumanitiesreview.org/archive/Issue-August-September%202007/Pugliese.html. Accessed 20 June 2013.

———. 2008. Whiteness and the Blackening of Italy: *La Guerra Cafona, Extracommunitari* and Provisional Street Justice. *Portal: Journal of Multidisciplinary International Studies* 5 (2): 1–35. http://epress.lib.uts.edu.au/journals/index.php/portal/article/view/702. Accessed 20 June 2013.

Salvatores, Gabriele, dir. 1993. *Sud*. Penta Film. DVD.

THE RISE OF THE POSSES AND THE POWER OF THE WORD   161

Santoro, Marco, and Marco Solaroli. 2007. Authors and Rappers: Italian Hip Hop and the Shifting Boundaries of Canzone d'Autore. *Popular Music* 26 (3): 463–488. Print.

Signorini, Ricki. 1992. "Il Generale." *Flash.* February: 32–33. Print.

Smargiassi, Michele. 2010. Napolitano: strage di Ustica senza colpevoli. *La Repubblica,* June 27. http://ricerca.repubblica.it/repubblica/archivio/repubblica/2010/06/27/napolitano-strage-di-ustica-senza-colpevoli. html?ref=search. Accessed 27 Nov 2013.

Solaro, Alba. 1993. Il cerchio e la saetta: Centri sociali occupati in Italia. In *Posse italiane: Centri sociali, underground musicale e cultura giovanile degli anni '90 in Italia,* ed. Carlo Branzaglia, Pierfrancesco Pacoda, and Alba Solaro, 11–70. Firenze: Editoriale Tosca. Print.

Stille, Alexander. 2006. *The Sack of Rome: Media + Money + Celebrity = Power = Silvio Berlusconi.* London: Penguin. Print.

Verdicchio, Pasquale. 1997. *Bound by Distance: Rethinking Nationalism through the Italian Diaspora.* Madison, NJ: Fairleigh Dickinson University Press. Print.

———. 2005. Introduction. *The Southern Question.* By Antonio Gramsci. Trans. Pasquale Verdicchio. Toronto: Guernica Editions, 1–13. Print.

———. 2006. Horizontal Languages and Insurgent Cultural Alignments: National Popular Culture and Nationalism. *This Nothing's Place.* March 1. http://light-zoo.blogspot.com.au/2006/03/horizontal-languages-and-insurgent.html. Accessed 4 Mar 2011.

Zaslove, Andrej. 2011. *The Re-Invention of the European Radical Right: Populism, Regionalism, and the Italian Lega Nord.* Montréal: McGill-Queen's University Press. Print.

DISCOGRAPHY

99 Posse. 1992a. *Dì Original Trappavasciamuffin Stailì.* Crime Squad. 12-inch.

———. 1992b. Rafaniello. Dì Original Trappavasciamuffin Stailì. Crime Squad. 12-inch.

———. 1992c. Salario Garantito. *Dì Original Trappavasciamuffin Stailì.* Crime Squad. 12-inch.

———. 1993a. *Curre Curre Guagliò.* Esodo Autoproduzioni. CD.

———. 1993b. Curre Curre Guagliò. *Curre Curre Guagliò.* Esodo Autoproduzioni. CD.

———. 1993c. Napolì. *Curre Curre Guagliò.* Esodo Autoproduzioni. CD.

———. 1993d. Salario Qawali. *Curre Curre Guagliò.* Esodo Autoproduzioni. CD.

———. 2014. Curre Curre Guagliò Still Running. Feat. Alborosie, and Mama Marjas. *Curre Curre Guagliò 2.0: Non Un Passo Indietro.* Musica Posse. CD.

Africa United. 1987a. *Mjekrari.* Spliff A Dada Records. EP.

———. 1987b. Nella Mia Città. *Mjekrari.* Spliff A Dada Records. EP.

——. 1988. *'Llaka*. Spliff A Dada Records. EP.

——. 1991a. Lionhorse Possee. *People Pie*. New Tone Records. LP.

——. 1991b. *People Pie*. New Tone Records. LP.

Almamegretta. 1993a. *Figli di Annibale*. Anagrumba. EP.

——. 1993b. Figli di Annibale. *Figli di Annibale*. Anagrumba. EP.

Assalti Frontali. 1994. Sud. Cordata per l'autorganizzazione. 7-inch.

Assalti Frontali et al. 1993. Le posse romane contro i colossi musicali. *l'Unità*, January 27. Print.

Daniele, Pino. 1980. *Nero a Metà*. EMI. LP.

Dee, Kool Moe. 1989. I Go to Work. *Knowledge Is King*. Jive. LP.

Fondamentale Vol. 1. 1992. Century Vox Records. LP.

Gaudi, Lele. 1991. *Basta Poco*. Mercury. LP.

——. 1993. *Audium Magnum*. Mercury. CD.

Generale, il, and Ludus Dub Band. 1993. *Guarda la Luna e Non il Dito*. Wide Records/RTI Music. LP.

Generale, il, and D.J. Kote Giacalone. 1992. Ragga Soldati. Wide Records. 12-inch.

Generale, il, and Ludus Pinsky. 1991a. Foglio di Via. *Stupefacente*. Wide Records. LP.

——. 1991b. *Stupefacente*. Wide Records. LP.

Gruppo Operaio E Zèzi. 1976. *Tammurriata dell'Alfasud*. I Dischi del Sole. LP.

Krama Possee. 1992. Rubbai. *Ragga Radio Station (11 Atti Originali Di Raggamuffin Italiano)*. RTI Music. LP.

Messina, Sergio. 1990. RadioGladio. Self-produced. Cassette.

Onda Rossa Posse. 1990. Batti il Tuo Tempo. *Batti il Tuo Tempo*. Self-produced. 12-inch.

Pietrangeli, Paolo. 1970. Contessa. *Mio Caro Padrone Domani Ti Sparo*. I Dischi del Sole. LP.

Ricky, Papa. 1992. Lu Sole Mio. Century Vox Records. 12-inch.

Sud Sound System. 1991a. Fuecu. Century Vox Records. 12-inch.

——. 1991b. T'à Sciuta Bona. Century Vox Records. 12-inch.

Torino Posse. 1992a. Da Bun. Vox Pop. 12-inch.

——. 1992b. Legala. Vox Pop. 12-inch.

Various. 1992a. *Italian Posse: Rappamuffin d'Azione*. Flying Records. LP.

——. 1992b. *Italian Rap Attack*. Irma Records. LP.

——. 1992c. *Sotterranei Italiani*. RTI Music. LP.

CHAPTER 6

Southern Echoes of the Posses in Sardinia: Sa Razza

In preceding chapters, we argued that reggae had provided marginalized Italian youth with a music that helped them articulate their political values and create local and global communities which in turn empowered them, and their listeners, with agency. The convergence between reggae, ragga-muffin, and rap, exemplified by the Salentine group Sud Sound System, gave rise to the posse movement of the late 1980s and early 1990s. In turn, the period from 1992 to the late 1990s has been recognized as a transitional period, where independent Italian hip hop and reggae scenes evolved beyond the period of the posses (Lutzu 2012, p. 349).

It is within this context that in the marginal Italian island of Sardinia, hip hop, reggae/raggamuffin, and fusions between these genres emerged as a means of critiquing power structures and foregrounding marginal voices and languages. Arguably, the most influential Sardinian group to bridge these two periods were Sa Razza. In this chapter, we examine the ways in which Sa Razza used rap music as a form of cultural expression designed to reclaim agency for disenfranchised Sardinian youth. To this end, we undertake a visual and thematic analysis of selected tracks and video clips with a focus on linguistic choices, reference to local and global contexts, and the musical and stylistic processes of transculturation and cultural fusion they carry out. Hence, in our discussion, we explore how cultural, social, and political discourses, particularly those surrounding Sardinia, are framed and narrated through the synthesis of images and music.

© The Author(s) 2018
S. Scarparo, M. S. Stevenson, *Reggae and Hip Hop in Southern Italy*, Pop Music, Culture and Identity,
https://doi.org/10.1007/978-3-319-96505-5_6

163

Sa Razza released their first vinyl in 1991 for the independent label Century Vox, a 12-inch mix that established the crew as one of the best-known rap groups in Sardinia. They became known nationally when the track "In Sa Ia" (In the Street) was included in the 1992 various artists compilation *Fondamentale Vol. 1* (Fundamental Vol. 1, Century Vox Records) which also featured Sud Sound System's "Fuecu" (Fire). Between 1991 and 1998, Sa Razza participated in numerous concerts and jam sessions throughout Italy and Sardinia. Notably, in 1993 they were the opening act for the Beastie Boys in Reggio Emilia and in 1998 for Guru in Turin. Until they disbanded in 2003, Sa Razza produced a total of six official releases under several formations, among which are the most famous albums, the 1996 *Wessisla* for Undafunk (Turin) and, in 2001, *E.Y.A.A.* for Cinevox/Cinenova (Rome).

Sa Razza disbanded after the release of the EP *Grandu Festa* (Big Party, Nootempo Records), and the group's founding member Alessandro Sanna, aka Quilo, together with rapper and producer Micio P founded the Malos Cantores. In 2004, Malos Cantores released *Un Gran Raap Sardo* (A Great Sardinian Raap, Nootempo Records) and in 2006 *Musica Sarda* (Sardinian Music, Nootempo Records). Malos Cantores have collaborated and worked with a number of well-known groups and artists, such as Sud Sound System, Caparezza (guests of his second album), J-Ax, Cor Veleno, Kurtis Blow, and many more. In 2017, Sa Razza's Ruido and Quilo reunited to perform at several concerts in order to celebrate the 20th anniversary of the release of their album *Wessisla*, which at the time of its release sold over 15,000 copies.

Quilo is still active today, after more than 25 years, with his solo projects and as MC/selector with artist Randagiu Sardu. In 2008, he founded the production company Nootempo (see http://www.nootempo.net/), which he defines as a *non etichetta* (a no-brand/record label). Indeed, the mission statement on Nootempo's website states that "Nootempo Sardinia factory" is not "a standard production label" but, rather, "an independent media factory" where artists collaborate to develop and produce art projects, events, and video productions. As stated on its website, Nootempo functions as a collective of artists with no masters ("non ci sono Padroni"), in which everyone involved stands for a new vision of music production. Nootempo's artists are not interested in becoming famous. As they state, "ours is a silent assembly line" that does not manufacture "stars of the show," and the artists involved in the collective are not obsessed with fame (see http://www.nootempo.net/).

The Nootempo website also affirms that they believe in free art and creative commons, as they believe that the unencumbered sharing of cultural production helps to diminish both geographic and emotional and intellectual distances between people across the world. Nootempo, they assert:

> builds bridges and not walls. From the local to the global we try to maintain our identity, exchange knowledge, participate in, and build, cultural interactions. We are free Cultural Workers and every sound or visual work is designed to spread our Identity, to promote independent Music, Events and Artistic Expression. (see http://www.nootempo.net/)

The Nootempo collective works with a graphic design studio (undas.net) and a production team (FishEye Sardinia Media Productions) and to date has produced and released eight original albums and two independent docu-films on DVD. It has fostered the growth of diverse Sardinian artists such as Randagiu Sardu, electro-folk Bentesoi duo, singer-songwriter Claudia Aru, and eclectic DJ/producer Gangalistics.

Sardinia has a number of peculiarities that are directly relevant to the conditions that have favoured the spread of reggae, raggamuffin, hip hop, and rap music in other parts of southern Italy. Like Apulia, as previously discussed, Sardinia has a highly developed and distinctive musical tradition, as well as a long history of colonial oppression. It is also afflicted by especially low youth employment rate (averaging just over 44.7 per cent according to 2009 Eurostat data), with data provided by the Sardinian Regional Ministry of Employment indicating that in 2017 unemployment of people under 24 years of age reached the staggering levels of 56 per cent (http://www.olbia.it/disoccupazione-giovanile-sardegna-istruzione-master-13-04-2017). Moreover, according to 2011 Eurostat data, Sardinia has the lowest levels of tertiary educational attainment across the whole EU, about 16.15 per cent (http://ec.europa.eu/eurostat/web/regions/overview).

Sardinia is the second-largest island in the Mediterranean, with enough ecological diversity and with a land mass of 270 kilometres on the north-south axis and 145 kilometres east to west to "sustain a substantial population and foster the development of complex societies" (Dyson and Rowland 2007, p. 1). Many Sardinians are proud to define their island as located at the centre of the Mediterranean region. This conviction, which is presumably about a geographic location, invokes a cultural centrality that positions the island within a historically significant region beyond its otherwise marginal cultural, geographic, and political location in relation to the Italian peninsula.

Indeed, Stone Age archaeological remains, as well as the presence of dolmen, menhir, and funeral monuments, indicate that Sardinia shared elements of a broader Western European culture. Large stone buildings called *nuraghi*, unique to Sardinia and dotted across the island, along with holy well temples and bronze statuettes found mainly inside or around *nuraghi*, attest to the existence of a distinctive Sardinian civilization that evolved during the Bronze Age. Archaeological evidence suggests that this civilization was part of a Mediterranean trading community (Dyson and Rowland 2007, p. 96). During the eighth century BC, the Phoenicians, who controlled an extensive trading network in the Mediterranean, founded a number of cities and settlements in the south and west of Sardinia. For instance, the island's capital city, Cagliari, was founded by them. At that time, Sardinia was significant because it was located in the Western Mediterranean between Carthage, Spain, the river Rhône, and the areas belonging to the Etruscan civilization (Brigaglia et al. 2006, p. 27).

From 238 BC to the Middle Ages, Sardinia was part of the Roman Empire. Following the disintegration of the Western Roman Empire, however, parts of the island were occupied by the Vandals, became part of the Byzantine Empire, and were subjected to periodic raids by the North African Saracens. For a relatively brief period, from the ninth to the fifteenth centuries, Sardinia was ruled by autonomous administrative organizations called the Sardinian *giudicati*. They were sovereign states governed by rulers called Judges (in Sardinian they were called *Judics*) and did not follow the feudal system prevalent in other European kingdoms. Hence, historians claim that in the context of the Middle Ages, the Sardinian *giudicati* were uncharacteristically democratic and enjoyed respect in medieval Europe (Cojana et al. 1994, p. 101). The *giudicati* were defeated by the Spanish Crown of Aragon, and it is believed that the so-called Battle of Sanluri, on June 30, 1409, marked their end and, for many, also the end of Sardinian self-rule and the loss of independence (Casula 1994, p. 372). Accordingly, Sardinia became known as the Kingdom of Sardinia under the Crown of Aragon and the Spanish Empire until 1720 when it was assigned to the Piedmont's House of Savoy, only to become part of the newly unified Kingdom of Italy in 1861.

Following the unification of Italy, Sardinia, like other regions of the South, was "reduced to the status of a semi-colonial market, a source of savings and taxes" and was kept "disciplined" by "pitiless repression of every mass movement, with periodical massacres of peasants" (Gramsci 1997, p. 94). In his "Notes on Italian History," Gramsci, who was born and grew up in Sardinia, reported that in the Sardinian Congress of 1911 it was claimed that "many hundreds of millions had been extorted" from the island "in the first fifty years of the unitary state, to the advantage of the mainland" (1997, pp. 71–72). In light of this history, Sardinia has had, and continues to have, independentism and autonomist movements. As early as 1903, editorials in the Socialist newspaper *Il giornale di Oristano* suggested that Sardinia should leave the Kingdom of Italy in order to become an independent socialist state (Bomboi 2014, p. 112). The first organized autonomist movement, the *Partito Sardo d'Azione* (the Sardinian Action Party), was formed in 1920 in the aftermath of the First World War and was made up primarily of war veterans who felt strongly that Sardinia had little to gain from being part of the Kingdom of Italy (Bomboi 2014, pp. 112–13).

Indeed, as Gramsci claimed, the North was an "octopus" which enriched itself "in direct proportion to the impoverishment of the economy of the South" (1997, p. 71). Yet, according to Gramsci, not being able to understand how even after being "liberated" the South remained poor, the "ordinary person from the North came to believe that it must have to do with biological inferiority" (1997, p. 71). Hence, Gramsci famously stated that "in the North there persisted the belief that the Mezzogiorno was a 'ball and chain' for Italy, the conviction that the modern industrial civilization of Northern Italy would have made greater progress without this 'ball and chain'" (1997, p. 71). These assumptions were to determine the complex relationship of pride, on the one hand, but also shame, on the other hand, that characterize the ways in which Sardinians relate to the mainland. In particular, this has affected their attitudes towards their native Sardinian language.

As a result of the Roman domination, Latin prevailed as the main language spoken on the island, eventually developing into the present-day Sardinian language, called *Sardu* (Casula 1994, pp. 110–14). Sardinian (*Sardu*) is not a dialect but is considered to be a distinct Romance language, related to Italian but not easily understood by mainland Italians. There is also an enclave of Catalan that is still spoken in the town of Alghero. According to Adriano Bomboi, *Sardu*, in its local variations, is spoken by about 70 per cent of the adult population and by about 13 per cent of youth (2014, p. 16). The two main varieties of *Sardu*, called

Logudorese and *Campidanese*, from the names of the regions in which they are spoken, account for the majority of speakers. Despite its recognition by the Italian state as a minority language, *Sardu* does not enjoy the status of co-official language that other minority languages have in other parts of Italy, such as French in the Aosta Valley and German in the Trentino-Alto Adige/Südtirol region (Bomboi 2014, p. 16).

As with other Italian regional contexts discussed in previous chapters, in Sardinia many rap, reggae, and raggamuffin artists rap and sing in *Sardu*, using its local varieties, or they alternate and move between Sardinian, Italian, and often English and Jamaican Patois. Their lyrics focus primarily, albeit not exclusively, on local issues, such as unemployment, Sardinian history of colonial exploitation, and political autonomy. Moreover, instead of performing mainly at *centri sociali* (social centres), which never took hold in Sardinia, it is common to hear many artists and groups perform at local festivities in honour of the village's patron saint. Every village of Sardinia has a patron saint with its own festival and its own organizing committee. Traditional Sardinian music and improvised poetry have always been part of these festivals, and since the 1970s most festivals have also included events dedicated to youth. Whereas in the 1970s and 1980s these usually involved ballroom dancing and in the 1990s rock and pop bands, in recent years, rap music, and to a lesser extent reggae and raggamuffin, have become popular at these festivals, and it is not rare to hear these artists perform alongside traditional Sardinian musicians (Lutzu 2012, pp. 353–54).

The Pride of Rapping in Sardinian: "In Sa Ia"

The issue of linguistic choice in the social and political context of Sardinia is complex and is inevitably bound up with the processes through which standard Italian was, and still is, institutionalized in civil society. It is generally believed that it was Dante, the author of the *Divina Commedia* who, in the treatise *De vulgari eloquentia* (written in 1306 but only published in 1529), claimed to have discovered, rather than to have invented, the language of a nation that only came into existence politically more than five centuries later (Joseph 2004, p. 99). Significantly, then, for the development of standard Italian, the Florentine dialect that was adopted was a literary language "not rooted in common usage" (Ruzza 2000, p. 172); its prominence, as mentioned in our discussion of Sud Sound System's use of Salentine language in Chap. 4, being a direct result of the literary prestige of Florentine authors of the Renaissance (Ruzza 2000, p. 172). Scholars estimate that at the time of Italian unification (1861), only 2.5 per cent of the total population spoke a language that could be called Italian (Ruzza 2000, p. 172).

Linguistic historians have shown "that national languages are not actually a given, but are themselves constructed as part of the ideological work of nationalism-building" (Joseph 2004, p. 94). Hence, it comes as no surprise that successive Italian post-unification governments have attempted to suppress all local dialects and languages, depriving them of official status and using bureaucratic and educational institutions as vehicles through which they constructed the linguistic ideology of standard Italian as a shared national aspiration. This practice became official during the Fascist regime, when the use of dialects and minority languages was banned from public life, although it continued to be used in everyday life by most Italians. The 1948 constitution introduced a new official tolerance towards minority languages, with Article 6 stating that the Republic protected linguistic minorities through appropriate legislations (Kinder 2000, p. 453).

In effect, whereas the responsibility to support local dialects and languages has since been devolved to regional governments, the Italian state has "adopted a non-interventionist, passive stance in relation to the question of dialect usage and maintenance of minority languages" (Kinder 2000, p. 453). Indeed, as mentioned, with the exception of the regions of the Aosta Valley and Trentino-Alto Adige/Südtirol, standard Italian remains the official language of the national bureaucracy, the national education system, the mass media, and the Catholic liturgy. Social and political factors such as mandatory schooling, the ubiquity of mass and social media, and the spread of bureaucracy have increased substantially the number of habitual speakers of standard Italian. Italy, however, has retained a "form of widespread diglossia" as the "switch from dialect to standard language depends upon situational factors that include knowledge of the linguistic background of the other speakers, the perceived social status of the other speakers, the degree of intimacy with the speakers, and the selection of topic of conversation" (Ruzza 2000, p. 176).

When compared to other European countries, moreover, it appears that diglossia is not common among the educated classes in Italy, indicating that standard Italian is the language of upward social mobility. As the linguist Carlo Ruzza argues, "in a country where mass education is relatively recent, speakers are often keen to symbolize a decisive break with what could be perceived as a membership of a peasant subculture" (2000,

p. 176). Similarly, Quilo points out that linguistic policies and the institutionalization of standard Italian have contributed to promulgating the message that Sardinian is boorish. Consequently, this perception is reflected through Sardinian language whereby the word *su civili* (the civilized) refers to standard Italian, hence implying that Sardinian is the opposite, that it is the language of the savage. This use of the word *su civili* was particularly popular during the Fascist regime when Sardinian was banned from public life (Quilo, Personal interview).

For Quilo, the power of being a rapper comes from what he calls "the power of the word" (Personal interview), which he defines as the power to communicate and express emotions, ideas but also frustrations and anger. Quilo recounts how in the late 1980s he started by writing rap lyrics in English, emulating North American models (Personal interview). Yet, in the early 1990s, during the period of the posses, and at a time in which Italian rappers started to sing in Italian and to adapt rap music to the "Italian socio-political context" (Lutzu 2012, p. 349), Quilo and his fellow members of Sa Razza were smitten by the example of Sud Sound System's singing in their Salentine language. Hence, Sa Razza began to write and rap in their native Sardinian language. Following Sa Razza's example, others started to rap in Sardinian, and, like Sa Razza, they often alternate Sardinian with Italian or English, Spanish, or, in one case, even German. They all use Sardinian slang, distorted by Italianisms and neologisms.[1]

In his study of Sardinian hip hop, Marco Lutzu comments that the social context of Sardinia in which "the bilingualism of certain areas inexorably leaves space to diglossia, rapping in Sardinia is a desired and conscious choice, a choice that is always highlighted" (2012, p. 359). For Quilo, the choice to rap in Sardinian foregrounds a desire to regain and to claim pride for Sardinian culture and language. According to Quilo, Sardinians have developed a strong "sense of inferiority" in relation to mainland Italians and have turned their low self-esteem into a litany of woes: "we are poor, we are insular, we are marginal and far away" (Personal interview). By contrast, given that language is essential to our daily life but

---

[1] Groups and artists who use Sardinian language or a combination of various languages include Dr Drer & CRC Posse (mainly from Cagliari, the capital city of the island), the rap group Menhir (originally from Nuoro, the main town of inland Sardinia), the rappers Balentia (named after the Sardinian word that means courage and valour, and which was often used to describe the traits of Sardinian bandits). For a discussion of language use by these and other Sardinian artists, see Lutzu 2012.

is also crucial for fostering inclusion and self-belief (Carmichael 2000, p. 285), Quilo points out that he views Sardinian language as a *richezza* (wealth), refusing to adopt the commonly held view that speaking Sardinian marks one as necessarily marginal.

Building on the success of their debut self-produced cassette, Sa Razza's first 12-inch mix explores the aforementioned local themes of language and culture through an interpretation of Afro-American and Afro-Jamaican styles. Similar to Sud Sound System's first 12-inch production ("Fuecu"/"T'à sciuta bona"), also issued on the pioneering Bolognese label (see Chap. 4) in the same year, and which fused hip hop, reggae/raggamuffin, and Salentine language for the first time on vinyl, Sa Razza's seminal record marked the foundation of a Sardinian musical discourse that was to be developed and refined for years to come.

Produced by the Sardinian-born DJ Gruff (Sandro Orrù), who was a pioneer and a key player in the mainland hip hop contexts of Turin and Bologna, "In Sa Ia" (In the Street, A-side) and "Castia in Fundu" (Look Down in Depth, B-side) feature live instrumentation from Milan's Casino Royale. Both tracks reference and integrate hip hop's essential funk and soul elements, incorporating both live ("Castia in Fundu") and sampled ("In Sa Ia") breakbeats together with live rhythm and bass guitar. Adding to the textual layers of the two recordings, DJ Gruff employs scratching and sampling over both tracks, while the funk-inflected "Castia in Fundu" contains a raggamuffin interlude to evoke a stylistic fusion which was typical both of the posse era and of the influential productions of Sud Sound System (see Chap. 4). Although neither track openly cites or samples Sardinian musical traditions, as Sa Razza's later productions would do, the use of Sardinian language and cultural references nevertheless imbues the release with a distinct local dimension.

"In Sa Ia" (In the Street) encapsulates the group's preoccupation with the alienating loss of pride in the local culture and language, as experienced by disenfranchised Sardinian youth. The title, in fact, refers to "the street" as the literal, as well as symbolic, space of marginalization, violence, and wasted potential. Rapped in Sardinian language, with verses delivered in combination by Quilo (identified as Speaker KG) and Su Rais, the track showcases DJ Gruff's virtuosic eclecticism. Commencing with a classic funk breakbeat that is overlaid with dark, almost extra-terrestrial, synthesizer notes which hint at the "otherness" of the vocalists and underscore the gravity of the ensuing message. A syncopated scratch cuts in a jarring soulful scream that ushers in a driving funk bassline and rhythm guitar, framing the urgent opening lines "ascurtami" (listen to me), "ascurta sa boxi mia su chi seu nendi da s'arruga" (hear my voice, what I am saying is coming from the hood) "da sa ia" (from the street) "sa cantada e basta no d'apu inventara, fradi miu ascuta no seu nendi una catzara" (this song is not made up, my brother hear me I am not talking shit).

While the intensity of Quilo and Su Rais' vocal phrasing and delivery enhance the urgency of the message, the rappers' use of the imperative, combined with the direct and informal second-person address (listen to me), establishes their desire to stand as uncompromising harbingers of truth. Significantly, they claim such authority because their knowledge comes from the reality of the street (*da sa ia*), and as such it conveys the collective and, presumably authentic, wisdom and experiences shared by those who come from that space. To this end, the appellative (*fradi miu*, my brother) aims to reinforce the connection between the rappers and all those who, like them, come from the street. Similarly, the subsequent verses, which use the first-person pronoun to narrate a number of ills afflicting those who come from the street, emphasize the rappers' wish to frame the experience of alienation and disenfranchisement as a shared reality:

> non tengu traballu
> non tengu dinai
> sceti su tantu bastu cantu bastat po campai
> s'alternativa è custa
> emmigrai assusu
> sa fabrica è serrada
> sa miniera non c'è prusu
> ma sa terra mia no da bollu abandonai
> mi depu acuntentai de mi fai sfrutai?

> (I've got no work
> I've got no money
> only enough to survive
> these are the choices
> migrate to the North
> the factory's closed
> the mine's gone
> but I don't want to abandon my land
> do I have to get used to being exploited?)

In the subsequent verses, Quilo and Su Rais switch from first-person back to the second-person address, commenting on the importance and self-conscious choice of expressing their message in Sardinian: "e in sardu ti du nau 'tzerriendi" (and I'm telling you this in Sardinian). This explicit reference to Sardinian language introduces the exhortation to be strong and proud, in order to survive: "furriari" (fight back) the rappers order, "non abarrisi firmu, moviri!" (don't stand still, move!). This call to action is justified by the first-person observation that "nci seu nàsciu nci seu bìviu e sa segunda dommu mia / ma deu no bollu morri" (I was born and raised here, this is like my second home but I don't want to die), "morri in sa ia" (die in the street). The repetition of "morri" (to die) underscores the urgency and the need to react by conjuring up strength and pride. Once again, the return to the first person invokes the shared plight and connection between the rappers and their listeners, which has remained a trademark of hip hop discourse as it has moved around the globe (Morgan 2016, p. 135), and has been adopted and adapted by rappers in diverse locations such as the Netherlands (Pennycook 2006), the Ukraine (Helbig 2014), Australia (Ministrelli 2017), and Japan (Sterling 2010).

Notably, the musical backing to the chanted chorus—"andu, andai, andu a nc'aturai in sa ia, bastascendi in sa ia" (where to go if we don't stay in the street, loitering in the street)—exhibits a marked variation in mood, as a sparser breakbeat, rolling bass riffs, and repeated scratches are accompanied by uplifting piano notes and pan-pipe synths to create a lighter tone which reinforces the key themes of defiance, cultural pride, and the potential for Sardinian agency. By contrast, however, later lines remind the listener that "eh, no bastat mari bellu" (the beautiful sea is not enough) / "po ponni a postu totu" (to make everything ok) since, "s'istadi est acabara" (when the summer finishes) / "su sardu esti giai mortu" (the Sardinian is already dead) / "giai mortu" (already dead) / "mortu e scarèsciu, custu cazz'e situazioni giai m'ari arrèsciu ma sa ia è sempri bista" (dead and forgotten, I'm sick of this fucking situation, but the street is always the same). The repetition of "mortu" (dead) in relation to the Sardinian language, giving rise to the frustration with life on the margins, is soon contrasted by the affirmation that "su rap slai in sardu nc'arrikedi de prusu" (rapping in Sardinian makes us richer), thus highlighting the rappers' faith in the existentially and culturally revitalizing powers of the Sardinian language. Hence, the ensuing verses urge the listener to defend Sardinian ("su sardu du depis difendi") and clearly state that "custa è sa casa poita seus rappendi" (this is the reason why we're rapping) and, crucially, position the Sardinian language as "s'unica speràntzia po sa genti mia" (the only hope for my people) / "sopravvivi innoi" (to survive here) / "sopravvivi in sa ia" (to survive in the street).

Survival, however, depends on coming together, "sardu cun su sardu" (Sardinian with Sardinian); hence the second-person address turns into a plural "us" in "feus unu carràxiu e si feus intendi" (let's make a ruckus and be heard) but returns to the second-person address in the ensuing lines addressed to the "fradi" (brother) in order to urge him to keep going ("no ti depis firmai"), to be courageous ("agat su coràgiu"), and to demonstrate willpower ("sa fortz'e volontai"). Ultimately, the aim, as urgently rapped by both Quilo and Su Rais, is to demand "rispetto" (respect). It is significant that "rispetto" is in Italian. It precedes a series of lines in which the rappers, adopting the aggressive and uncompromising stance of the streetwise ghetto youth, change addressee and, instead of addressing their "fradi," talk directly to those whom they feel are benefitting from their marginalization: "ci du depis donai, du scisi deu su sardu e ti nci fatzu cravai" (You have to give it to us, you know that I'm Sardinian and I can crush you) / "e ti càstiu beni in faci" (I look straight into your eyes) / "no ti seu timendi, si sighis seghendi ti seu giai arroghendi" (I'm not afraid of you, I'm after you and gonna break you).

A variation on the lighter music of the chorus continues in the concluding verses, in which the rappers reach the conclusion that "s'unicu orizonti (the only horizon) / "ei s'unica via" (the only way) / "a contu fatu, abarrara sa ia" (when all things are considered, is still the street). The repetition of "sa ia" (the street) leads into the final chorus—"andu, andai, andu a nc'aturai in sa ia, bastascendi in sa ia" (where to go if we don't stay in the street, loitering in the street)—which is repeated four times with the previously noted shift in musical mood. The positive message of the track, therefore, is to be found in the potential role that a newly discovered pride in Sardinian culture, as expressed through the Sardinian language, can play in reclaiming "the street" as a shared space and experience beyond marginalization and alienation.

Fighting from Below: "Stiamo Giù"

As a result of the 1946 referendum, Italy became a republic, and in 1948 Sardinia obtained the status of autonomous region. This status, however, while providing Sardinians with the opportunity to enact a high level of self-governance, was never fully realized, as in practice, successive regional governments have failed to take advantage of many of the provisions provided to them by the status of autonomous region (Bomboi 2014, p. 101). Consequently, to this date, most Sardinians consider the autonomy granted to them since 1948 as inadequate to their needs (Bomboi 2014, p. 101). In the absence of a coordinated and nuanced political strategy capable of addressing the local needs of the island in accordance with the specificities of its history, geography, and economy, all major initiatives concerning the economic development of Sardinia following the Second World War have been initiated by the Italian central government. Ignoring the diverse histories and cultures that characterize the southern regions of Italy, the South (*il mezzogiorno*) was viewed as an internally homogeneous block and, significantly, as a problem requiring a solution. Hence, Sardinia, along with the regions located below Rome, has remained a part of the so-called southern question, which, as discussed in previous chapters, has framed the political, social, and cultural discourses about the South of Italy since the nineteenth century (see Schneider 1998; Gramsci 1995).

With financial assistance provided by the International Bank for Reconstruction and Development, the Italian government initiated a massive programme of industrialization, known as the *piano di sviluppo del mezzogiorno* (development plan for the South), that aimed to address the perceived "backwardness" of the South in relation to the North, together with the imbalances in terms of standard of living that existed between the two areas (Ferrandino et al. 2014, pp. 21–22). A number of large industrial complexes, consisting mainly of oil refineries and petrochemical productions, were built across the island with a view to create employment and wealth. Nonetheless, the transport costs required to cross the seas to reach the mainland, as well as the international oil crisis of the early 1970s, determined the failure of the industrial project. Given that a large number of farmers and shepherds left their lands to become factory workers, agriculture also failed to develop as a modern industry, as had happened in the central and northern regions of Italy. Consequently, as referenced in Sa Razza's track "In Sa Ia," many unemployed factory workers and their families migrated to the industrial cities of the North of Italy or to Germany, France, and Belgium. Meanwhile, in the aftermath of the Italian economic miracle in the late 1950s and early 1960s, and more recently since the spread of low-cost air travel, the tourism industry has provided much-needed employment, albeit seasonal, and for the most centred around coastal areas.

Moreover, the mining industry had been a primary contributor to the economies of the south-western regions of Sardinia, including in large part the region of Sulcis, also known as Sulcis-Iglesiente from the name of its main town, Iglesias. This mining area was already important for the extraction of the minerals lead, zinc, and silver at the time of the Phoenicians and continued to be significant until the closing of the mines in the early 1990s. The dominance of the mining industry, particularly after Sardinia became part of the House of Savoy in the late 1770s, led to the construction of roads, railways, and dams in the mining regions (see http://whc. unesco.org/en/tentativelists/5003/) and attracted workers from other parts of the island as well as the mainland. The mines were owned by foreign companies, and most of the minerals extracted in Sardinia were exported to the mainland and abroad where they were treated, processed, and sold at high prices to, among others, Sardinia itself.

The mines, in fact, merely supplied raw materials, as the mining companies could extract minerals at low cost in Sardinia but placed them on the market at competitive prices (see http://www.sardegnaminiere.it/). The low costs for the extraction of minerals were due to the exploitation of the miners, including large numbers of women and children, who often worked under inhumane conditions and received very low wages. Reacting against their exploitation, since the late 1880s, Sardinian miners joined the workers' movement and organized strikes. Famously, three miners were killed in the strike that took place in the Buggerru mine in September 1904, and seven were killed by the military police and the royal guards in Iglesias in 1920 (see http://www.sardegnaminiere.it/gli_scioperi.htm). More recently, in 1949 a strike at Montevecchio lasted a total of 47 days, and in 1961 the miners occupied the shafts in order to secure better working conditions. Finally, in 1991, seeking to force the Italian government to provide assistance in view of the inevitable closure of the mines, miners organized prolonged strikes and occupations of shafts.

Following the closure of the mines, the Sardinian regional government established a geo-mining, historical and environmental park which received support from UNESCO. The park was officially recognized by the Sardinian regional Minister for the Environment and Land Protection, and the Minister for Industry, Education and Research, on October 16, 2001. The objectives of the park are "the protection and the valorization of the technical-scientific, historical, cultural and environmental heritage of the whole set of assets present within the park" (UNESCO n.d.). Under the auspices of the park, many of the disused mines and the, now abandoned, mining villages where the miners used to live have been turned into museums, becoming specimens of industrial archaeology. Despite the lofty objectives of the geo-mineral park, however, many of the abandoned villages and disused mines look like ghost towns, with crumbling buildings, scarred and visibly polluted excavated land sites, and decaying equipment, acting as reminders of a conflicted past and of a difficult present. Indeed, since the mining industry has not been replaced by alternative sources of employment, the former mining regions are struggling to survive.

Accordingly, widespread unemployment and social malaise after the collapse of the mining industry were fertile breeding ground for the emergence of Sa Razza, whose members came from the Sulcis region. As Quilo, states:

> I am from Sulcis, therefore, my home ground since I was a young boy was the Sulcis region. Sulcis has been a land in the grip of a profound crisis since the 1990s; this unfinished and failed industrial dream that the inhabitants of this region have turned into a chimera: that is, the mine as if it were the only solution to all evils, to all problems. And that is where the project of Sa Razza was born. Because where there is discomfort there is need to find self-expression in order to survive and communicate. (Personal interview)

Track four from the album *E.Y.A.A.*, "Stiamo Giù" (We are Staying Down Here, 2002), available on YouTube, deals directly with the history of mining in the Sulcis. "Stiamo Giù" is the most streamed Sa Razza track on Spotify (with approximately 41,000 streams) and its accompanying video clip has approximately 140,000 views on YouTube. The track's enduring popularity attests to the significance of its message but also to the impact of the music, the lyrics—rapped in a mix of Italian and Sardinian—and the evocative video clip, which was shot on location in a disused mine in Iglesias. As if arriving to the viewer through an otherworldly transmission, the clip commences with a medium shot of Quilo, whose image sharpens from blurred focus to see him materialize inside an abandoned mine. For the first eight bars, sparse and foreboding musical backing consists of erratically echoing scratches, dramatic synthesized strings, and metronomic cymbal. The images intercut between Quilo, as he raps the refrain—"ci da gherramos ci da ghettamos" (we fight, we go down)—in a voice as if distorted through a distant megaphone, and eerie long shots of the dilapidated mine. The diagonal and horizontal panning shots of the abandoned mine are accompanied by the disembodied chanting of a male choir that evokes the ghosts of former miners. This visual and aural juxtaposition thus establishes a link between the past miners and the present hip hop crew, while the sombre melody of the chanting choir further reinforces the haunting, almost gothic, quality of the music.

This sequence of shot/reverse shot, alternating the panning shots of the mine with blurring medium shots of the crew with Quilo in the foreground, continues throughout the opening eight bars and as the beat kicks in, serving to reinforce the spectral ambience and the continuity between Sa Razza and the miners who used to work in the mine, including those who lost their lives during the strikes in other mines. As additional layers of dramatic electronic strings enhance the disquieting mood, the quick interchange between reverse low- and high-angle shots which frame the mine and the crew, as well as Quilo on his own, provides visual commentary on the ensuing lines: "sempre sotto sto" (I'm always under) / "come minatore schiavo ayo calamos" (like a mining slave let's go down) / "ci da gherramos aunde su sole no splende de asutte e terra battiegliero" (we fight where the sun doesn't shine, fighting underground). These lines reinforce the track's central motif of the miner as fighter and of mining work as work that requires fighting spirits, which had been introduced by the refrain "ci da gherramos ci da ghettamos" (we fight, we go down) and which continues throughout the track. Hence, Quilo rhymes: "combatto stando" (I am fighting) / "sotto mando no comando espando rime sotto ma" (under here I don't rule but I keep rhyming) / "la cavesa vado alzando sotto ma me sto pesando" (I am raising my head from under but I am thinking).

The use of rapid internal rhymes in the first person, alongside a reflexive reference to rhyming, equates the miner with the rapper and the rapper with the miner, thus linking the combative spirit of the miner with that of the rapper, who battles through his rhymes. The shared plight of the rappers and the miners is established at the beginning of, and is emphasized throughout, the track by the use of the pronoun "ci" (we) repeated twice in the refrain "ci da gherramos ci da ghettamos." The link between Quilo and the miner is further emphasized visually by a high-angle shot of Quilo as he raps "sempre sotto sto" (I am always under). The high-angle shot serves to give the impression that Quilo actually stands underground (i.e., below the camera) as the camera's low angle also makes him look smaller, disempowered, as the miners had been.

Nonetheless, subsequent frontal medium shots of the crew, with Quilo in the foreground moving close and looking straight into the camera, underscore the MC's defiance as he declares: "non mi fido di chi mi vende luce" (I don't trust who sells me light) / "luce in cambio di bucce" (light in return for scraps) / "la mia voce produce brace sotto più sotto aunde la pressione schiaccia predator notturno capocaccia nella giungla sarda vendo cara la pellaccia di sa razza" (my voice produces embers under and below, where the pressure crushes the nocturnal predator head-hunter in the Sardinian jungle, I sell dearly the skin of this people) / "gente vera che non porta maschere" (truthful people who don't wear masks). The reference to "sa razza" as people who don't wear masks, while invoking the crushing pressure of the compressor room, which was a mainstay in the mines that made use of machinery requiring compressed air in order to work, once again establishes a connection between Sa Razza and the miners, attributing qualities of truthfulness to both.

Subsequently, the chorus, rapped by all members of the group, declares: "stiamo giù noi vogliamo stare giù / qui giù saremo sempre di più / il nostro fuoco brucia ancora e tu cala nel loco asutta dove nos gherrammos" (we are down, we want to stay down / here our numbers will grow / our fire still burns and you come down below where we are fighting). With these lines, the chorus refers to the strikes in which the miners occupied the shafts and also to the actual fighting spirit required to work in the mines. Significantly, the camera alternates between high- and low-angle shots of the crew. This suggests that the miners are both powerful in their group solidarity, as the camera positioned on a low-angle configures them as authoritative, and powerless in their struggle against the mining companies. Their powerlessness is conveyed by the high-angle shots that frame them from above, diminishing them, and also by the fact that Sa Razza are rapping inside the ghostly abandoned mine.

Later in the track, Raio takes over from Quilo and with aggressive demeanour, looking straight into the camera, declares that, presumably a northerner, "guarda dall'alto verso il basso l'isolano giù sulcitano meridiano" (looks down from above the islander down under, southerner from Sulcis). In this segment of the track, the "giù" (down under), which had previously referred to the mine, now stands for the South and more specifically for Sardinia and the Sulcis. The trope of the northerner who looks down on the southerner can be traced back to long-standing European attitudes that extend beyond Italy. As Maria Bonaria Urban points out, the North-South dichotomy operated at a number of levels: "at the largest scale between the North and South of Europe, in specific terms between neighbouring nations and within single nations" (2013, p. 26). Dominant ideologies of Romanticism in the nineteenth century, which coincided with the unification of Italy, successfully codified the cultural supremacy of the North based on Nordic mythology and medieval Christendom. According to Urban, in fact, while the "less Romanised" northern regions of Europe "appeared destined for progress and development," "those of the Mediterranean basin, identified with the splendour of ancient civilisation," were seen as "old and bound to the past, slaves to vice and immorality and fated to inexorable decline" (2013, p. 26). Attempting to position itself as belonging to the North, the newly unified Kingdom of Italy adopted this North-South dichotomy "as the pillar of the post-unification popular imagination," thus casting the South as "the centre of the pre-modern, in contrast to the rest of Italy, which was seen as the locus of civilisation" (Urban 2013, pp. 26–27).

Ultimately, this dichotomy underpinned the European mind-set in relation to their colonial possessions, therefore linking the South with Africa and with Latin America, and in recent times with the notion of the global South more generally. Reclaiming and reinterpreting these connections in light of renewed cultural pride, in subsequent verses of "Stiamo Giù," a clear reference to a presumed Sardinian descent from the Spanish establishes a connective marginality with the Latinos of the global South: "voglio restare così striscio coi gomiti nel fango" (I want to stay crawling with my elbows in the mud) / "stimo il mio rango tengo ramengo" (I am proud of my ancestry and I remember) / "de dinastia de sardo-ispano m'espando finchè quaggiù saremo sempre di più" (I come from the Sardinian-Hispanic and I am expanding till down here there will be more of us) / "giù c'è la base ferma le fondamenta" (down here there is a stable base, the roots).

This reference to the Sardinian-Hispanic connection is a recurring theme and stylistic feature of the album *E.Y.Y.A.* and had marked the work of Sa Razza since their first album, *Wessisla* (1996). Since this album, released on Undafunk records (the independent label founded by Quilo and the DJ-producer, Trizta), the Sardinian crew had set themselves apart from the majority of Italian acts of that period by taking their cues from West Coast G-funk or gangsta-funk. Importantly, this context boasted seminal Hispanic rappers, such as Kid Frost, who had released bilingual hit "La Raza" in 1990, and Cypress Hill, who in the same year released

"Latino Lingo" with its references to a funky use of "Spanglish." In turn, Sa Razza undertook their own search for Sardinian-Hispanic slang (Pacoda 2000, p. 48), which in the case of *E.Y.Y.A.* reached its culmination in the form of a playful transcultural synthesis. This synthesis combined Spanish/ Latino slang and cultural and musical references to Mexico with Sardinian and Italian language and musical samples of, and lyrical references to, local folk traditions, simultaneously reinforcing parallel experiences of marginality and Sardinian cultural identity.

CREATING COMMUNITIES: "GRANDU FESTA"

As exemplified by Sa Razza, a peculiarity of the Sardinian scene is that it originated in provincial and rural villages rather than the ghettos of large urban centres. Nonetheless, like youth all over the world who, according to Tony Mitchell, use hip hop as a vehicle for "global youth affiliations" and as a tool for "reworking local identity" (Mitchell 2001, pp. 1–2), Sardinian artists also used hip hop, rap music, and raggamuffin as a means to create communities. As Quilo explains, "I fell in love with a music genre but also with a community made up of DJs, graffiti artists, breakers, and rappers" (Personal interview).

The notion of a shared community had also been central to the political song, which, as Alessandro Portelli has shown, deteriorated partly as a result of the gradual fragmentation of the notion of community that underpinned its production and reception (Portelli 1983). In actual fact, it is commonly acknowledged that any understanding of the relationship between popular culture and community is complicated by a plurality of individual choices and communication flows, in which individuals are no longer part of a single community, and individual identity is increasingly formed by a combination, different from person to person, of factors such as age, gender, political, and religious affiliations, use of leisure time, and relationship with the mass media (Portelli 1983, p. 217). Thus, according to Portelli, since many workers in the age of the internet and social media are more readily involved in multiple musical contexts, and not just those associated with workers, the political song of the workers' movement, since the late 1970s, has lost a cohesive reference community, remaining suspended halfway between progressive folklore and show business (in Fanelli 2015).

182   S. SCARPARO AND M. S. STEVENSON

By contrast, drawing strength from the tension between cultural homogenization and cultural heterogenization that Arjun Appadurai has defined as "the central problem of today's global interactions" (1990, p. 5), Sardinian rappers such as Quilo were able to construct a reference community that, in turn, allowed them to claim agency, connections across multiple musical contexts, and belonging through music. Quilo explains how he was mesmerized by the sounds of what he calls "black music, that is, Jazz, Soul and Funk," because, in his mind, "everything comes from that. And then Jamaican DJs introduced the practice of speaking over the music, and from there we ended up with rap music. It is about the way you express yourself in rhymes. It was very fascinating to me. I felt inside a community" (Personal interview).[2]

This desire to belong to a community is seconded by all of the artists interviewed by Roberto Pili in his documentary, *Ca4Arts. La storia della cultura hip hop di Cagliari e Provincia* (The History of Hip Hop Culture in Cagliari and its Surrounds). Moreover, as Micio P from Sa Razza states, rap has been instrumental for many in that it provided a means through which they could voice, and thus make sense of, their experience of violence, drugs, trauma, and marginalization (in Pili).[3] Micio P, however, makes a clear distinction between Sa Razza's treatment of these themes and the ways in which commercial hip hop, particularly gangsta rap, consolidates stereotypes in relation to gender, class, and racialized identities.[4] Focusing on the controversial involvement of corporate interests that have come to dominate commercial hip hop, Fahamu Pecou, in fact, argues that the repetitive loop of tracks "by the same artists who rap about the same things: money, women, drugs, and crime" dominate commercially produced and distributed rap music. Hence, according to Pecou, "the music, like the images, offers an aesthetic that reifies many

---

[2] As discussed in Chap. 4, during the mid- to late 1980s, a new wave of Jamaican immigration to New York led to increasing hybridization between reggae and rap, as exemplified by the influential Bronx artist KRS-One's fusion of rap and reggae on the album, *Criminal Minded* (B-Boy Records, 1987). The formative influence of *Criminal Minded* and its spread of transnational "black" connective marginalities are attested to by the fact that this album directly inspired the UK's first ragga-hip hop hybrid the very next year: Daddy Freddy and Asher D's *Ragamuffin Hip-Hop* (Music of Life, 1988).

[3] Pili's documentary covers the past 20 years of hip hop activity in Cagliari, featuring all of the main artists and groups involved in what he defines as "the four arts" of hip hop: breakdancing, DJ'ing, rapping/MC'ing, and graffiti writing.

[4] For discussions about controversies surrounding commercially available hip hop, see Rose 2008; Malone and Martinez 2015; Helbig 2014.

traditionally racist, yet consumable stereotypes about black culture" (2015, pp. 105–06).[5]

It is through this interplay between "blackness as symbol and blackness as lived" (Sterling 2010, p. 28) that Sardinians, like others around the globe who have appropriated and adapted hip hop culture and rap music to their specific circumstances, negotiate multiple layers of belonging at both local and global levels. In the most immediate way, local and global belongings are exhibited through the adoption of gestures and fashion styles. On the one hand, Sardinian artists wear items of clothing and adopt gestures that identify them as part of a global hip hop community. On the other hand, they often wear elements of clothing that belong to a recognizable Sardinian tradition, such as *su bonete* (a beret), drape the Sardinian flag over the tables on which their turntables rest, or, in some cases, during their performances, make gestures that recall those of the Sardinian traditional *tenore* singers (Lutzu 2012, pp. 354–55).[6] This investment in the "ideology of authenticity" characterizes hip hop culture around the world (Pennycook 2006, p. 103), and in the case of Sa Razza, fashion styles and gestures are designed to mark their authenticity as hip hop artists but also as Sardinian hip hop artists.

As with their adoption of hip hop fashion and gestures, Sa Razza also, for the most part, follow global hip hop conventions in terms of musical backing and structure of their tracks, while also adding some elements of Sardinian traditional music to evoke a local resonance. Although these elements do not radically change their tracks' musical structure, they play a significant role at a symbolic level (Lutzu 2012, p. 357). They contribute to creating an imagined community distinguished by the discourses of connective marginality that symbolically link Sardinian youth with their counterparts in other disenfranchised parts of the world, such as Latinos in Los Angeles, while also constructing a community generated through the recognition of shared affiliations and experiences. The choice to rap in Sardinian language underscores their desire to claim and celebrate

---

[5] Likewise, in his discussion of dancehall and reggae in Japan, Marvin Sterling argues that blackness in consumerist Japan is "a commodity that is largely devoid from its human referents, to be enjoyed through, for example, the playful consumption of dancehall music" (2010, p. 4).

[6] Sardinian *tenore* singers take their name from the style of their singing called the *cantu a tenore*. Lutzu describes this style of singing as a "polyphony of oral tradition sung by four men and typical of the central areas of the island. Usually the soloist, or one or more components of the accompanying choir, covers his ear with his hand while singing" (2012, p. 355).

184   S. SCARPARO AND M. S. STEVENSON

"Sardinianess" as a source of strength and also as a means to foster unique engagement with their hip hop community. To this end, as shown in our discussion of "In Sa Ia" and "Stiamo Giú," Sa Razza replace the obsession with stories of violence, drugs, and brutal lifestyles typical of North American rap music (Pennycook 2006, p. 103) with a focus on specifically Sardinian issues, such as emigration, loss of linguistic and cultural patrimony, the collapse of the mining industry, and the North and South racial and economic divide within Italy.[7]

Sa Razza's final release, the EP *Grandu Festa* (Big Party), exemplifies these preoccupations. With its reflexive reference to hip hop's roots, transcultural impact, links to local and global power dynamics, and its ironic, playful but also critical take on Sardinian themes, culture, and music, the video clip of "Grandu Festa," the EP's title track (2003, available on YouTube), has multiple layers of meaning. The video starts with DJ Nike driving a car inside a NATO military base. This is a clear reference to a controversial issue of great interest in Sardinia. The island, in fact, has a disproportionate number of NATO military bases, created in large part for missile and weapon testing. They account for 60 per cent of all Italian, NATO and non-NATO military installations and occupy more than one-third of the island's land and sea territory (Beeley 2016, n.pag.).[8] Controversially, the media and public opinion are increasingly of the view that the immediate surroundings of many of the military bases are afflicted by above-normal levels of illnesses such as cancers of the lymphatic systems and natal genetic malformations (Zucchetti 2006, p. 83). Accordingly, local protest against the bases has grown increasingly strong.

Evoking this controversy surrounding the military bases, the video clip of "Grandu Festa" casts DJ Nike as a sort of undercover agent involved in a classified mission to a "secret NATO military zone." Accompanied by a burly security guard, DJ Nike, dressed in a dark suit and cap, imperiously passes security checkpoints with two briefcases. As his security keeps watch, and in a climate of suspense reminiscent of the cinematic genres of thriller and espionage, DJ Nike opens his briefcases to reveal a turntable

---

[7] The focus on local themes and the use of a local language is not unique to Sa Razza. As hip hop scholars have demonstrated, the turn to local languages and themes is characteristic of the modes of indigenization and syncretism that exemplify the global spread of hip hop (see Bennett 2000; Pennycook 2006; Helbig 2014).

[8] According to Vanessa Beeley, fishing and navigation around Sardinia are suspended during military drills and naval exercises; thus NATO's control of Sardinia extends to around 7200 square miles beyond the land boundaries (2016, n.pag.).

and a mixer. He sets these iconic hip hop tools on an empty table and tweaks a dial on the mixer to initiate the sending of a transmission through the digital satellite control system, which is, in fact, a computer monitor. Through the computer screen, we see that the transmission is sent through "vinilic sound control software" by the "selector," in a reference to hip hop's Jamaican roots. As the DJ/selector begins to scratch the vinyl, the monitor displays that this transmission forms part of the mission "Grandu Festa" and is being beamed from Sardinia, Italy, to "the Rest of the World." As the camera zooms into a satellite image of the map of Sardinia on the computer screen, thus identifying the island and in particular the south-western part of the island as the source of the signal, the soundtrack introduces a traditional Sardinian rhythm.

Subsequently, the camera cuts to a frontal close-up shot of an accordion, an iconographic instrument widely used in traditional Sardinian music and also inserted in the musical backing. This is followed by a quick sequence of long and medium shots of the rappers performing activities associated with farming and dressed in a mix of hip hop and Sardinian clothes, alternating with shots of farm animals such as roosters, hens, and goats. The overall effect of these establishing shots, along with the inclusion of well-known Sardinian rhythms, is both playful and ironic but also somewhat nostalgic. After the first eight bars, a hip hop beat and funky bass drop in perfect synchronism with the traditional tempo to create an original and high-energy synthesis between old and new, local and foreign. Upon this transition, the camera focuses on Quilo, wearing *su bonete* (the Sardinian beret) but using the hand gestures and body postures of global hip hop culture, as he moves around the farmyard, declaring in Italian: "scendiamo dall'ovile" (we come back from the sheepfold) / "sardacci come pochi" (hardcore Sardinians like few others) / "faccio saltare i culi in aria da Cagliari a Milwaukee" (I kick arse from Cagliari to Milwaukee).

The allusion to the shepherds as harbingers of genuine Sardinianess is tied to representations of Sardinia that invariably identify the pastoral world of sheep farming and of shepherds as icons of traditional Sardinian identity (Urban 2013, p. 9). The shepherds, moreover, have often been associated with brutal customs such as the code of honour and the *vendetta* (Urban 2013, p. 22). Such customs, in turn, have often codified them as outlaws and as bandits.[9] Significantly, then, the transition from

---

[9] Vittorio De Seta's 1961 Neorealist film, *Banditi a Orgosolo* (*Bandits in Orgosolo*), provides a well-known example of this cultural imagining of Sardinian shepherds.

the pronoun "we," when referring to the shepherds in "scendiamo dall'ovile" (we come back from the sheepfold), to the first person of "faccio saltare i culi" (I kick arse) establishes a dialogic relationship of authenticity, belonging, and affinity between the Sardinian shepherds, identified as hardcore Sardinians, and the rapper, who is characterized by his aggressive and threatening stance. Accordingly, the pejorative suffix ("sardacci") chosen to define the shepherds as true Sardinians has undertones of violence, thus resonating with established representations of Sardinian shepherds but also with the global hip hop gangsta persona of the rapper. Hence, the reference to his ability (or threat) to "kick arse" from Cagliari, which marks him as Sardinian, to Milwaukee, which links him to international, US hip hop and rap music in general.

In subsequent verses, Quilo moves between the kitchen, the outdoor barbeque area, and back to the kitchen, which is adorned with Sardinian rural household items such as the wooden table and the cutting board used to serve the Sardinian dish of piglet. In this setting, Quilo changes to the imperative form, asking for "sa cardiga e su schironi" (the grill and the spit), emblematic of the cooking style of Sardinian food. These scenes feature scantily clad female dancers, wearing parts of Sardinian traditional clothes, making a tongue-in-cheek reference to the sexist tropes of rap video clips. Similarly, the repeated "grandu festa" (big party) and the Sardinian "tra la la," chanted by all in the chorus, reinforce the link between the foundational hip hop trope of the street/block party and the Sardinian festival. The refrain of the chorus, "grandu festa," continues on as the camera cuts to medium and long shots of Quilo and Micio P MC'ing at a hip hop party and promptly cuts back to an image of DJ Nike, who at that time was Italian DMC champion, performing turntable tricks in the transmission room of the NATO base. The computer monitor indicates that the signal is being received by Jamaica, as a superimposed image shows three young Jamaicans hearing the signal, and then the three rappers climb into a smoke-filled Cadillac reminiscent of a Cheech and Chong film.

Immediately after the first chorus, the camera moves to Raio, whose session is being beamed from the popular Chia-Masua beach in southern Sardinia. The subsequent images of beach life and long shots of idyllic sunsets over the sea are often used by Sardinians to boast about their island to themselves but also to others; and they are also the tourist industry's most commonly used images of Sardinia. Here we see Raio, holding a surfboard on the beach, surfing and returning to the shore in a wetsuit in order to admire a beautiful young woman who walks by. Taking on the controversial, albeit widespread, sexist attitude typical of rappers around the globe, Raio comments on the "tipa che sfoggia le zinne" (chick showing off her tits).

The second chorus takes the viewers back to the setting of the hip hop party, as the three Jamaicans arrive to begin dancing and Micio P is beamed in from a skatepark. In this sequence, we see skateboarders and breakdancers, one of which wears a Sardinian flag singlet, graffiti murals, and a posse of young men drinking in the street. As Micio P struts through the skateparks, he celebrates his rapping in Sardinian language by stating: "non as cumprendiu ca / in dognia modu festeggiu" (don't you get it that whichever way I party), "tu ses su mellus / deu seu cantadori deis gaggius" (you are better than me, I am the storyteller of the boorish) / "grandu festa rappendi" (rapping at the big party) / "immoi is B-boys" (now is B-boys).

Micio P's reference to himself as the "cantadori deis gaggius" is significant on a number of levels. In the first instance, the use of the word "cantadori" alludes to the Sardinian *cantadoris*. These are improvising freestyle poets, belonging to a variety of traditions present on the island and still active to this day. Sardinian rappers often claim direct descent from the *cantadores*, arguing that, despite originating in the 1970s with the Afro-American minorities of the New York ghettos, rap had already been a part of the Sardinian poetic tradition (Lutzu 2012, p. 362). In particular, Lutzu speculates that this identification between rap and the tradition of improvised poetry stems from "the similarity between the term 'rap' and 'repentina,' an improvised poetical tradition typical of southern Sardinia" (2012, p. 362). The raggamuffin/rap artist Randagiu Sardu, discussed in the subsequent chapter, also claims a connection between the two, arguing that "we must remember that the *repentina*, that is rhyming, has always been a part of the Sardinian cultural tradition" (Personal interview).[10]

The use of the term *gaggius*, in the second instance, functions in similar ways to Pizzutilo's Different Stylee and Sud Sound System's reappropriation of the pejorative label *terrone* (dirty peasant) as a marker of southern identity, as discussed in Chaps. 3 and 4, respectively. The term *gaggius*,

---

[10] Lutzu comments that the propensity to claim a link between local traditions and rap is not new to the Sardinian case, as it is common to places which have a strong tradition of oral poetry. According to Lutzu, journalists and scholars also "in an excessively simplistic way" connect rap with traditions such as the *Griot* of western Africa and the *Majdoub* of the Maghreb (Lutzu 2012, p. 363).

188   S. SCARPARO AND M. S. STEVENSON

however, is a Sardinian rather than Italian, or northern Italian, label and refers to the ways in which Sardinians think of themselves. Specifically, the term is commonly used to describe those who are perceived to be of lower class and lacking sophistication. These are traits often associated with those who speak Sardinian in their everyday interactions, come from rural villages, and look Sardinian; that is, they are short in stature and have a darker completion. In other words, to be *gaggius* is to be *excessively* Sardinian.

The term, therefore, parallels the process of othering initiated during the unification of Italy, which, as we discussed in previous chapters, is shared by southern Italians in relation to their northern compatriots. In Chap. 3, we argued that such a process has generated an enduring experience of self-estrangement that marks southern Italians. Yet, as Sa Razza's reappropriation of the label *gaggius* suggests, further layers of othering are at work in relation to Sardinians. They are generally configured as belonging to the South, hence sharing with southern Italians the presumed "Africanness" that many northern Italians have assigned to the South since unification (see Chap. 3). However, due to their remote location relative to the mainland, their distinct cultural traditions and their language, which is not readily intelligible to fellow Italians, Sardinians are codified as doubly other in relation to the rest of Italy. More significantly, Sardinians also see themselves as such: that is, *in* the South but not *of* the South, *in* Italy but not *of* Italy. Accordingly, Micio P's self-declared status of "cantadori deis gaggius," and also of rapper, in that he is "grandu festa rappendi" (rapping at the big party), makes explicit the correlation between rap music and the Sardinian cultural tradition. This correlation, in turn, underscores the process through which hip hop and rap music, similarly to the process we discussed in relation to reggae in previous chapters, allows for the creation of connective marginalities. Through this connective marginality paradigm, disenfranchised and self-marginalized Sardinians interpret hip hop culture and rap music as global signifiers of social exclusion and, as such, adopt rap as a conscious declaration of *difference* from the cultural mainstream and also from mainland Italy.

Paradoxically, then, Sa Razza self-consciously embrace a music scene underpinned by global cultural flows and global chains of signification, while at the same time using it to reclaim localized cultural identity and local authenticity. Indeed, the spread of hip hop, and especially the acritical adoption of North American hip hop motifs, can be understood as inherent to the process of cultural colonization by the US. The video clip and the lyrics of "Grandu Festa," however, provide a self-reflexive response to this dynamic. On the one hand, the military base that opens and closes the video clip of "Grandu Festa" represents the process of US military and also cultural colonization of Sardinia. DJ Nike's infiltration and appropriation of the base to disseminate a new and distinctive Sardinian hip hop aesthetic, on the other hand, symbolically resists and reverses dominant global flows. The irony and playfulness of the video indicates, therefore, a self-conscious understanding of the dialogic process of glocalization inherent in their use of hip hop, while simultaneously celebrating hip hop's capacity to create new transcultural communities, languages, and identities.

The EP *Grandu Festa* marked the end of Sa Razza's production as a group. Their legacy, nonetheless, endures to this day, and as we discuss in the next chapter, their music, language choice, and mentoring influence have continued to inspire the next generation of Sardinian artists.

Works Cited

Appadurai, Arjun. 1990. Disjuncture and Difference in the Global Cultural Economy. *Public Culture* 2 (2): 1–24. Print.

Beeley, Vanessa. 2016. NATO's Military Enslavement and Toxic Invasion of Sardinia. https://thewallwillfall.org/2016/07/14/natos-military-enslavement-and-toxic-invasion-of-sardinia/. Accessed 27 Aug 2017.

Bennett, Andy. 2000. *Popular Music and Youth Culture: Music, Identity and Place*. London: Macmillan Press. Print.

Bomboi, Adriano. 2014. *L'indipendentismo sardo: le ragioni, la storia, i protagonisti*. Cagliari: Condaghes. Print.

Brigaglia, Manlio, Attilio Mastino, and Gian Giacomo Ortu. 2006. *Storia della Sardegna. Dalle origini al Settecento*. Rome: Laterza Editore. Print.

Carmichael, Cathie. 2000. Conclusions: Language and National Identity in Europe. In *Language and Nationalism in Europe*, ed. Stephen Barbour and Cathie Carmichael, 280–289. Oxford and New York: Oxford University Press. Print.

Casula, Francesco Cesare. 1994. *La Storia di Sardegna*. Sassari: Carlo Delfino Editore. Print.

Cojana, Maria Luisa, et al. 1994. *Almanacco scolastico della Sardegna*. Cagliari: Edisar Editrice. Print.

De Seta, Vittorio. 1961. *Banditi a Orgosolo*. Titanus. Film.

Dyson, Stephen L., and Robert J. Rowland Jr. 2007. *Archaeology and History in Sardinia from the Stone Age to the Middle Ages: Shepherds, Sailors, and Conquerors*. Philadelphia: University of Pennsylvania Press. Print.

Fanelli, Antonio. 2015. http://www.treccani.it/enciclopedia/il-canto-sociale-dai-dischi-del-sole-alle-posse/. Accessed 29 Aug 2018.

190 S. SCARPARO AND M. S. STEVENSON

Ferrandino, Vittoria, Maria Rosaria Napolitano, and Daniela Manetti. 2014. *Storia d'impresa e imprese storiche:una visione diacronica.* Milan: Franco Angeli.

Gramsci, Antonio. 1995. *The Southern Question.* Trans. Pasquale Verdicchio. West Lafayette, IN: Bordighera Incorporated. Print.

———. 1997. *Selections from the Prison Notebooks of Antonio Gramsci.* Ed. and Trans. Quentin Hoare and Geoffrey Nowell Smith. New York: International Publishers. Print.

Helbig, Adriana N. 2014. *Hip Hop Ukraine: Music, Race, and African Migration.* Bloomington: Indiana University Press. Print.

Joseph, John E. 2004. *Language and Identity: National, Ethnic, Religious.* Hampshire and New York: Palgrave Macmillan. Print.

Kinder, John. 2000. Language Policy. In *Encyclopedia of Contemporary Italian Culture,* ed. Gino Moliterno, 452–454. London and New York: Routledge. Print.

Lutzu, Marco. 2012. *Su RAAP:* Sardinian Hip Hop Between Mass Culture and Local Specificities. *Journal of Mediterranean Studies* 91 (2): 349–366. Print.

Malone, Christopher, and George Martinez, eds. 2015. *The Organic Organizer: Hip Hop, Political Development, and Movement Culture.* New York and London: Bloomsbury. Print.

Ministrelli, Chiara. 2017. *Australian Indigenous Hip Hop: The Politics of Culture, Identity, and Spirituality.* New York and London: Routledge. Print.

Mitchell, Tony. 2001. Introduction: Another Root-Hip-Hop Outside the USA. In *Global Noise: Rap and Hip Hop Outside the USA,* ed. Tony Mitchell, 1–38. Middletown: Wesleyan University Press. Print.

Morgan, Marcyliena. 2016. 'The World is Yours': The Globalization of Hip Hop Language. *Social Identities: Journal for the Study of Race, Nation and Culture* 22 (2): 133–149. Print.

Pacoda, Pierfrancesco. 2000. *Hip Hop Italiano: Suoni, parole e scenari del Posse Power.* Torino: Einaudi. Print.

Pecou, Fahamu. 2015. Whirl Trade: The Peculiar Image of Hip Hop in the Global Economies. In *The Organic Organizer: Hip Hop, Political Development, and Movement Culture,* ed. Christopher Malone and George Martinez, 99–110. New York and London: Bloomsbury. Print.

Pennycook, Alastair. 2006. Language, Localization, and the Real: Hip-Hop and the Global Spread of Authenticity. *Journal of Language, Identity and Education* 6 (2): 101–115. Print.

Pili, Roberto. n.d. *Ca4Arts. La storia della cultura hip hop di Cagliari e Provincia.* Nootempo and Fisheye Sardinia Media. Film.

Portelli, Alessandro. 1983. Tipologia della canzone operaria. *Movimento operaio e socialista* 2: 207–224. Print.

Quilo. 2016. Personal Interview. December 6.

Rose, Tricia. 2008. *The Hip-Hop Wars: What We Talk About When We Talk About Hip-Hop—and Why It Matters.* New York: Basic Civitas Books. Print.

Ruzza, Carlo. 2000. Language and Nationalism in Italy: Language as a Weak Marker of Identity. In *Language and Nationalism in Europe*, ed. Stephen Barbour and Cathie Carmichael, 168–182. Oxford and New York: Oxford University Press. Print.

Sa Razza. 2002. Sa Razza–Stiamo Giù UFFICIALE! Sardegna! *YouTube*, February 23, 2009. https://www.youtube.com/watch?v=qWgi_O4JOyA. Accessed 9 Mar 2018.

Schneider, Jane. 1998. Introduction: The Dynamics of Neo-Orientalism in Italy (1848–1995). In *Italy's Southern Question: Orientalism in One Country*, ed. Jane Scheider, 1–23. Oxford: Berg. Print.

Sterling, Marvin. 2010. *Babylon East: Performing Dancehall, Roots, Reggae, and Rastafari in Japan*. Durham, NC: Duke University Press. Print.

UNESCO. n.d. Sulcis Iglesiente. http://whc.unesco.org/en/tentativelists/5003/. Accessed 9 Mar 2018.

Urban, Maria Bonaria. 2013. *Sardinia on Screen: The Construction of the Sardinian Character in Italian Cinema*. Amsterdam: Rodopi. Print.

Zucchetti, Massimo. 2006. Environmental Pollution and Health Effects in the Quirra Area, Sardinia Island (Italy) and the Depleted Uranium Case. *Journal of Environmental Protection and Ecology* 7 (1): 82–92. Print.

DISCOGRAPHY

Asher D and Daddy Freddy. 1988. *Ragamuffin Hip-Hop*. Music of Life. LP.

Boogie Down Productions. 1987. *Criminal Minded*. B-Boy Records. LP.

Cypress Hill. 1991. Latin Lingo. Ruffhouse Records. LP.

Fondamentale Vol. 1. 1992. Century Vox Bologna. LP.

Kid Frost. 1990. La Raza. *Hispanic Causing Panic*. Virgin Records. LP.

Malos Cantores (Quilo and Micho P). 2004. *Un gran Raap Sardo*. Nootempo Records. CD.

———. 2006. *Musica Sarda*. Nootempo Records. CD.

Sa Razza. 1992a. Castia in Fundu. Century Vox Records. 12-inch.

———. 1992b. In Sa Ia. Century Vox Records. 12-inch.

———. 1992c. In Sa Ia. *Fondamentale Vol. 1*. Century Vox Records. LP.

———. 1996. *Wessisla*. Undafunk Torino. CD.

———. 2002a. *E.Y.A.A.* Cinevox/Cinenova. CD.

———. 2002b. Stiamo Giù. *E.Y.A.A.* Cinevox/Cinenova. CD.

———. 2003. *Grandu Festa*. Nootempo Records. EP.

Sud Sound System. 1991. *Fuecu*. Century Vox Records, 12-inch.

———. 1992. Fuecu. *Fondamentale Vol. 1*. Century Vox Records. LP.

CHAPTER 7

The Legacy of the Posses Beyond Genres and Across Generations: Randagiu Sardu, Mama Marjas, Claudia Aru

It has become a truism to argue that present reggae and hip hop scenes in Italy have lost the political impetus of the 1980s and 1990s, becoming more commercialized, less authentic, and lacking in social commitment. The period in discussion has coincided with and been shaped by the rise of new technologies and media platforms that have facilitated the production as well as the consumption of music. Indeed, the advent of the internet and social media has diversified the ways in which music is produced and consumed as well as how individuals "listen to music, are affected by music, use music, create meanings of music, and develop lifestyles around music" (Nowak 2016, p. 5). Websites like YouTube and Facebook and streaming services like Spotify and Mixcloud exemplify the way in which the internet and social media have irrevocably changed the processes through which music brings people together while also allowing a larger number of consumers and producers of music to connect across time and space as a public and as a creative community. In fact, for those who have access to the internet, music posted online offers entrance to a wide range of musical genres and scenes irrespective of geography and mobility. Online access to music also provides audiences with the tools to leave comments, engage in debate, and deliberate with each other. Additionally, the internet has provided independent musicians with greater freedom from commercial distributors. Moreover, the retrospective online archiving of

© The Author(s) 2018
S. Scarparo, M. S. Stevenson, *Reggae and Hip Hop in Southern Italy*, Pop Music, Culture and Identity,
https://doi.org/10.1007/978-3-319-96505-5_7

songs and tracks from previous generations has facilitated the creation of a collective musical memory that has enabled intergenerational dialogue.

All of these factors have played a central role in the development of new and musically diverse artists in Italy. Many of these new voices combine musical, linguistic, social, and political elements, typical of groups such as Different Stylee, Sa Razza, Sud Sound System, and the other collectives of the posse era discussed in previous chapters, with local and transnational rhythms and styles. In this chapter, we focus in particular on the examples of three such artists from Sardinia and Apulia and argue that their distinctive blend of various global as well as local musical and oral traditions distinguishes them as some of the most interesting interpreters of the legacy of reggae and hip hop music in southern Italy today.

Each of the three artists we focus on in this chapter, however, can be interpreted as inheriting but also redefining the legacy of the posses in different ways. Strongly influenced by Sa Razza and still collaborating with Quilo, Randagiu Sardu represents a contemporary Sardinian version of the fusion between reggae and hip hop that was central to the groups we discussed in previous chapters. Mama Marjas reinterprets Italian reggae and the posses by constructing a self-conscious discourse linking Jamaican popular music, African, and African diasporic music, with southern Italy. Less obviously linked to reggae and reggae-influenced hip hop, Claudia Aru's music would not be possible without Sa Razza's pioneering example of self-production, along with their deliberate, self-reflexive, and ironic use of Sardinian language, themes, and customs.

Thus, through our analysis of the linguistic, thematic, and visual styles, as well as the independent contexts of production, of Randagiu Sardu, Mama Marjas, and Claudia Aru, we aim to demonstrate how these diverse and eclectic artists consciously reinterpret and celebrate their marginality. We argue that this self-conscious celebration of marginality is carried out through a cultural politics based on diversity, multilingualism (including the deliberate use of local southern dialects and languages), and the transcendence of dominant and fixed notions of gender and cultural identity.

From Raggamuffin to Rappamuffin: Randagiu Sardu (the Stray Sardinian)

Carlo Concu, aka Randagiu Sardu, is a Sardinian raggamuffin rap artist. In collaboration with Quilo and Micio P from Sa Razza/Malos Cantores, he released his first single and video clip, "S'arrespiru" (The Breath, Nootempo) in 2008. Between 2008 and 2012, he released the albums *Io Randagiu*

Sardu (I, Stray Sardinian, Nootempo, 2008), *Sighimì* (Follow Me, Nootempo, 2009), *Rappamuffin de Sardigna* (Nootempo, 2011), and the single "Danza Noa" (Our Dance, Nootempo, 2010), and, in 2015 and 2016, he released the singles "Country man" (Nootempo) and "Xelu" (Frost, Nootempo). The latter tracks are included in the 2016 collection entitled *Randagiu Sardu: 12 Original Hitz* (Nootempo).

Fiercely independent, Randagiu Sardu has released all of his albums and singles with the production company Nootempo, founded by Quilo in 2008. As discussed in Chap. 6, Nootempo is a "no-brand, media factory" committed to the notion of free art and creative commons. Artists associated with Nootempo collaborate with each other and are not necessarily invested in achieving popularity for the sake of becoming wealthy and famous (see http://www.nootempo.net/). Instead, as Randagiu states, they are the "underclass"; they are those "who stay at the margins of the music business because they are doing something different. It is part of the game. It is a choice" (Personal interview). Thus, making music for Randagiu Sardu is "a mission" (Personal interview).

Invested with a mission, Randagiu creates music of social protest inspired by the melodies and rhythms of reggae and the militant lyricism of rap. As he recounts, his fascination with reggae began with Bob Marley and with "this kind of music that sang of protest without violence," but the yearning to voice his critique against the exploitation of Sardinia also led him to US rap music, particularly the music of the 1980s (Personal interview). Hence, the anti-colonial sentiments of reggae allowed him to express his pride in, and affection for, Sardinia, which—as a proponent of Sardinian autonomy from Italy—he defines as his nation, while rap provided him with powerful and passionate examples of protest against inequality, racism, and marginalization. Sa Razza and others involved in the Sardinian scene offered Randagiu models that he could follow, particularly in relation to his choice to rap in his native language, the southern variation of Sardinian called *Campidanese*. Inspired by what he calls his "encounter" with Quilo, and creating a fusion between rap and raggamuffin, Randagiu Sardu has developed a distinctive and hybrid music style, which he calls rappamuffin. However, his musical approach is broader than this and exhibits influences from roots and dub reggae and also elements of folk and country. His lyrics, mostly written in Sardinian (*Campidanese*), focus on life on the island, including reflections on the pollution and degradation of the environment, and deal with Sardinian history, culture, and politics.

196 S. SCARPARO AND M. S. STEVENSON

Randagiu Sardu achieved immediate and widespread popularity in Sardinia with the release of his first album in 2008, produced in collaboration with Quilo, and since then, the two artists often perform together, playing in the main squares of small country towns across Sardinia as well as in clubs and dancehall parties. Randagiu Sardu's video clips, available on YouTube, have attracted well over one million views in total, an especially impressive number in light of the independent and marginal context in which his music is produced. Translations of his most popular tracks in Italian and English, uploaded by his loyal listeners, can also be found online.[1] Moreover, T-shirts and shorts with the Randagiu Sardu logo are available for sale through his Facebook account.

The track "Fibai e Tessi" (Spinning and Weaving), from his 2011 album *Rappamuffin de Sardigna*, showcases Randagiu's signature blend of raggamuffin and rap while also exemplifying the sharp irony and self-reflexive playfulness which distinguish most of his lyrics and video clips. The video clip (directed by Roberto Pili) and the lyrics of "Fibai e Tessi" are comic and burlesque in tone. Set in the countryside, where Randagiu lives and works as a farmer, the video opens with lateral and frontal close-up shots of a donkey. It then cuts to a medium shot of Randagiu Sardu as he introduces himself and the track sporting streetwear, sunglasses, and bandana while holding a large bottle of the iconic Sardinian beer, Ichnusa. A stripped-back version of the reggae-hip hop rhythm, produced by Ruido (ex-Sa Razza), comprises electronic keyboards on the offbeat and bass guitar and bass drum on the downbeats, with electric guitar riffs at the end of each four-bar segment. Standing next to Randagiu Sardu, but also slightly behind him, is Quilo dressed in a flowery shirt and a comical black curly wig. He makes histrionic gestures which could ironically reference either the horned hand signs of the Latin Kings gang from the US, of rock fans, or of the Italian *le corna* sign (a sign Italians use to avert bad luck).

The pair claim belonging to Sardinia and as the camera cuts to a frontal, medium shot of Randagiu holding a puppy dog and patting a donkey, he introduces himself proudly as Randagiu Sardu. The subsequent shot features a wide-angle lens of a slightly distorted donkey as it looks straight into the camera. The wide-angle lens of this shot adds symbolic, but also comic, significance to the donkey, making it larger than life and ludicrous

---

[1] See the following websites: http://lyricstranslate.com/it/randagiu-sardu-lyrics.html; http://www.raptxt.it/testi/randagiu_sardu/sarrespiru_13670.html; http://www.cagliari-artmagazine.it/randagiu-sardu-countryman-omini-de-sattu.

at once. In the sequence that follows, we see Randagiu Sardu sitting next to two farmers, wearing a T-shirt with the slogan "No Radar" and declaring that he is playing raggamuffin for Sardinians. The two farmers look at him with a mixture of pride and bewilderment as the camera cuts to a medium shot of Randagiu walking by his donkey and repeating his commitment to raggamuffin for Sardinians.

These sequences playfully establish Randagiu Sardu's connection to the Sardinian countryside and to the farm, while also equating him to a donkey, as conveyed through the graphic match between alternating shots of the animal and of Randagiu Sardu looking into the camera. Significantly, along with being linked to farm work and rural lifestyles, the donkey is traditionally associated with stubbornness, a feature often attributed to Sardinians.[2] Thus, on the one hand, by creating a visual link between Randagiu Sardu and the donkey, the video clip imbues the former with the characteristic of the latter, while, on the other hand, it makes fun of the claim to Sardinian authenticity that the correlation with the donkey presumably confers upon the rapper. The parody evoked by the association of Randagiu Sardu with the donkey, moreover, invites the viewer to question cultural stereotypes that are often implicit to notions of authenticity.

Accordingly, the lyrics of the following lines, delivered in his unique rappamuffin style, which combines the rhyming patterns and vocal inflections of raggamuffin with those of rap, over a rollicking reggae-hip hop rhythm, articulate a pointed critique of Sardinians, with their superstitions, their practice of littering the landscape with rubbish, only to blame tourists, and their proverbial obstinacy. Despairing of the "misenia de custa terra" (misery of this land), Randagiu declares:

> no nci at essi meda axia ma seus preus de cotzia.
> Apu scipiu ca su mundu spàciat de siguru
> candu spàciant is traballus me in sa 131
> Apu scipiu ca at a spaciai po fintzas sa birra
> candu nci eus a bogai u pagheddu 'e merda de Quirra.
> Est totu a postu: a chini cantat inglesu o tedescu
> chi teneis a custa terra cantai in sadru prus a prestu.
> Su nucleari arribat, est siguru ca ge arribat
> e seus propriu nosu a ddi fai sattai s'arrastu?

---

[2] The characterization of Sardinians as marked by a wilful and stubborn nature has its origins in literature and has become a widely accepted categorization (Urban 2013, p. 423).

> (maybe there aren't many grapes but there are plenty of stubborn idiots
> I've heard that the world will certainly end
> when the works on the road 131 will end.
> I've heard that even the beer will end
> when we'll get rid of a bit of shit in Quirra.
> But it's all okay: someone sings in English or in German
> If you care for this land you should sing in Sardinian at once.
> The nuclear waste will arrive, no doubt it will arrive,
> and are we going to be capable of stopping it from coming here?)

Blaming Sardinians for their inertia, Randagiu Sardu ironically comments on the lack of serviceable infrastructure, hence the reference to the perennial roadworks affecting the road 131, the main highway in Sardinia which runs across the whole island, the environmental degradation caused by the biggest military polygon of Italy and Europe based in the Sardinian district of Quirra,[3] and the impending dumping of nuclear waste from the mainland being planned by the Italian government. The rhetorical question at the end "e seus propriu nosu a ddi fai sattai s'arrastu?" (and are we going to be capable of stopping it from coming here?) suggests that Randagiu's protest is directed to his fellow Sardinians, inviting them to take action, rather than assume victimhood and wait for others to come to the rescue. The second-person address of the imperative in the line "chi teneis a custa terra cantai in sadru prus a prestu" (If you care for this land you must sing in Sardinian at once) reinforces the role that he attributes to language and to rapping in Sardinian as vehicles for developing cultural and social awareness. The urgency of the delivery as well as the message of the lyrics are set in juxtaposition with the caricature of Quilo who dances ironically and in a clown-like manner while wearing a wig and flowery shirt. As such, Quilo's comedic persona introduces an element of playful self-criticism, inviting Randagiu Sardu to take himself less seriously in his self-appointed role as social conscience of the island.

In addition to presenting himself as the social conscience of the island, with the hip hop ballad "Sa Battalla" (The Battle, from the 2009 album

---

[3] This area is occupied by an experimental polygon for ballistic missiles and by a training base commanded by the Italian Air Force and at the disposal of NATO. As Zucchetti explains, "the Quirra zone has come to the attention of the Italian media due to the so-called 'Quirra syndrome'" (2006, p. 83). Many believe that the military use of depleted uranium is causing higher-than-normal incidences of cancer and genetic defects in new born infants (Zucchetti 2006, p. 83).

Sighimi), Randagiu Sardu takes on the role of historian. The ballad tells the story of the Battle of Sanluri, in which, as discussed in Chap. 6, on June 30, 1409, the Sardinian *giudicati* lost against the Spanish Crown of Aragon. Given that Sardinian history is, by and large, not studied in depth within the island's school curriculum, and is not included in the standard Italian school curriculum, with "Sa Battalla," Randagiu Sardu attempts to recount to his fellow Sardinians an event which he considers to be of great importance to them. According to Randagiu Sardu, in fact, the Battle of Sanluri counts as one of the most important battles fought by Sardinians in their struggle to defend their independence, and as such, the battle has to be understood as a significant event in the history of the island (Personal interview).[4]

Echoing its medieval setting, the musical backing of "Sa Battalla" evokes medieval resonances by mixing the hip hop beat with nostalgic flute and mandolin notes. The ballad starts with the chorus, chanted by Randagiu Sardu and Quilo, as they state:

> Arregoda sa battalla, rimas forgiadas in su fogu 'e sa muralla
> Bintimilla sardus scioberant morrendi
> Vidas chi bivint in sa morti cumbattendi, e intzandus
> Arregoda sa battalla rimas forgiadas in su fogu 'e sa muralla
> Po sa libertadi 'e custa terra seus bivendi
> Oi comenti un'orta seus sempri cumbattendi, e intzandu

> (Remember the battle, rhymes forged in the fires of the fortification
> Twenty thousand Sardinians choose to die
> Lives who live through death by fighting, and then
> Remember the battle, rhymes forged in the fires of the fortification
> We are living for the freedom of this land
> Today like in the past we are always fighting, and then)

The repetition of the second-person address of the imperative *arregoda* (remember) highlights the didactic intent of the ballad, as Randagiu and Quilo take upon themselves the task of recounting the events that took

---

[4] Since the early 2000s, every two years at the end of June, the Sanluri city council stages a re-enactment of the battle that took place in 1409 alongside other cultural events such as exhibitions, conferences, and concerts. Although the aim of the city council is to remember and to celebrate the significance of the battle for the history of Sardinia, the celebration is also designed to attract tourists to the area.

place on the day of the battle. The reference to rhyming emphasizes the role of rap music in remembering the past but also the role that it plays in fighting for *libertadi* (freedom) in the present. In this context, the word *libertadi* implies freedom from Italian control but also refers to the cultural and intellectual freedom that comes from knowledge and consciousness of self. Such an understanding is reinforced towards the end of the ballad, in the last lines prior to the final chorus, which is repeated twice. In these lines, Randagiu Sardu and Quilo declare that:

E dogna cussentzia sindi scidat e pesat
liggint sa storia chi no est stettia mai cumpresa
Custa die no est festa ma po mei est tristesa
E imoi tocat a nosu a dda contai sa giovunesa

(And the consciousness of all wakes up and rises
They read the history that has never been understood
Today is not a holiday for me but a day of mourning
And it's our duty now to tell the story to the youth.)

With his 2015 single, "Country Man," Randagiu Sardu returns to the theme of life as a farmer. Like "Fibai e Tessi," the video clip, also directed by Roberto Pili and produced by Nootempo, is set in a rural context. As Randagiu Sardu comments, "I am what I sing. It is unlikely that I sing amidst beautiful women and wealth when my life is a completely different reality. It is a life marked by work on the land, and life in a country town" (Personal interview). Consequently, with musical backing that starts with acoustic country guitar accompanied by bluesy harmonica notes, "Country Man" opens with such a description of himself: "I am a country man, omin'e sattu seu." Appropriate to its themes and setting, "Country Man" experiments with a country blues-inflected version of Randagiu's familiar rappamuffin style. In order to create this musical mood, the music incorporates the abovementioned acoustic guitar and harmonica (played by Randagiu), with percussion (also played by Randagiu), with live bass and light drum machine backing. Combined with Randagiu's melodic singjay style of vocal delivery, the overall effect is a cheerful feel which ties into, and contrasts with, the rural themes of the lyrics and images.

Visually, the video clip accentuates this bright musical mood through a combination of stylized, sharply defined, high-key lighting, and humorous mise-en-scène. The high-key lighting, typical of comedies and musicals, and amplified by green and blue filters, intensifies the bucolic setting of the video clip. Shots of Randagiu Sardu handling farming tools, such as the plough, and standing on the back of a moving tractor, while he plays the harmonica, raps, and dances, amalgamate his musical and working personae and roles of farmer and hip hop/raggamuffin artist. This amalgamation of these farming and rapping personae is emphasized by his substitution of US urban hip hop attire, such as the basketball cap and T-shirt, with the wide-brimmed straw hat and checkered shirt associated with farmers and the rural lifestyle. Older farmers with weathered faces, younger men and women dressed in farm clothes, a scarecrow, and a fellow musician playing the guitar joyously dance and sing along to the chorus with Randagiu Sardu.

Nonetheless, the visual playfulness of the setting contrasts with the lyrics' account of Randagiu Sardu's gruelling work on the land, as he states:

> I'm a countryman omin'e sattu seu
> Potta ua birra ca seu giai scallau
> I'm a countryman omin'e sattu seu
> Ca su biu innoi d'eusu giai spacciau
> Babbaugas loccas babarroccias
> Ki non ddi ciccas esti siguru ca non ddi papas
> Esti spacciau su tempu de su sparau
> Esti tempu de poi occhiellus a totu die incrubau
> Fammi fai su preu a sa fresa
> Atru ca ci cabai a mari
> Aberri su siffoi ca deu abarru innoi
> Ca sa carroga esti giai spizzuendi su meboi e intza
> Storni maledetti

> (I'm a countryman I'm a countryman
> I bring beer because I'm already exhausted
> I'm a countryman I am a countryman
> Because here we have already finished the wine
> You won't eat snails unless you look for them
> The time of the asparagus is over
> It's time to put on eyelets bowing down the whole day
> Let me get to the mill
> Instead of going to the beach
> Open the siphon that I have to stay here
> Because the crow is already picking at the melon
> Cursed starlings)

Ge seus a frori oi ca esti suendi bentu e sobi
Esti pappendumi sa musca non mi parrit sa di giusta ca s'obia esti
pedrendi su frori
E mi toccat a d'acquai
Ca si toccat a trummentai
E in s'interi ki seis ascuttendi
C'esti sa marra in cussa matta e sa xibudda de marrai e intza

(It is hard today that the wind is blowing from the east
Flies are attacking me and it's not a good day and the olives are
losing their flowers
And I've got to water them
I've got to sweat
There's the hoe resting on that tree
And the onion to pick be damned)

Pointedly, as the music grows silent, the video clip ends with Randagiu Sardu kicking to the floor a "For Sale" sign for Sardinia and walking away carrying a hoe on his back. For Randagiu Sardu, hard work on *his* land is by far the best option.

THE ITALIAN QUEEN OF REGGAE: MAMA MARJAS

While Randagiu Sardu in Sardinia exemplifies the continuing intergenerational legacy of pioneering groups, such as Sa Razza, as demonstrated through his close collaboration with Quilo and other members of this crew, Mama Marjas, aka Maria Germinaro, epitomizes the continuing significance of the Apulian scene within Italy's diversified reggae, raggamuffin, and hip hop milieu. Based in the Apulian coastal city of Taranto, Mama Marjas has become one of the most popular and respected artists in Italy's contemporary independent reggae scene. She has been called a "Diva Raggamuffin" (Fontana 2010, p. 89) and has been described as a *guerriera* (fighter), with a *personalità grintosa e forte tipica della meridionale doc* (gritty and strong personality typical of a true southern woman) (Conti 2015, p. 3). The online magazine *reggae.today* pronounced her a "leading representative of the Italian reggae scene," attracting remarkable attention from the musical media (http://reggae.today). More recently, she has been crowned the "Italian queen of reggae" (Conti 2015, p. 3).

From the age of 6 to 18, she sang with her parents' band at weddings and parties, thus becoming well versed in a broad and eclectic variety of music genres. This experience probably explains the notable sonic melting pot that distinguishes Mama Marjas' music style, ranging from roots reggae, dancehall, reggaetón, and Caribbean soca to kuduro, hip hop, blues, and soul music. Her transcultural approach to musical and vocal styles is reflected also in her multilingualism, as her songs include Italian, Spanish, Apulian dialects, Jamaican Patois, and English. Moreover, her multilingual and stylistically wide-ranging approach to music reflects an openness to diversity and anti-racist politics. Her music deals with issues of marginalization connected to the South, women and migrants, and the pervasive corruption that defines local and national Italian politics. Mama Marjas' representation of womanhood and femininity in her music is also subversive, as her vocal delivery and bodily performance blur the boundaries between conventional and dominant notions of masculinity and femininity and her dance styles openly acknowledge and promote African influences. The music of Mama Marjas is also explicitly political in terms of its contexts of production and performance, as she works with independent music labels and is a regular performer at *centri sociali* and at large-scale 1st of May concerts.

She began her reggae career as MC for the Apulian sound system Kianka Town. As a soloist, she has released four albums, *B-Lady* (2009), *90* (2011), *We Ladies* (2012, with Michela Giannini, aka Miss Mykela, and recorded and mixed by the eminent English reggae/dub producer Adrian Sherwood), and *Mama* (2015). Her albums are produced by Love University Records, the independent label from Taranto which was founded by Italian raggamuffin-hip hop pioneer from the posse era, Francesco "Don Ciccio" Grassi, and which she joined after the release of her first album, *B-Lady*.

In relation to Love University, she states: "Don Ciccio and I have the Love University label because we want to remain independent and as independent artists we want to produce high quality music. We want this music to be successful entirely because of its quality" (in Conti 2015, p. 8). Other female artists produced by Love University include Francisca, Nikaleo, and Miss Mykela. Echoing Mama Marjas, Miss Mykela comments on the cooperative approach of Love University Records, defining the label as a shared project, resembling a family. As she states: "there are many of us. Many young women and we strive to do our best, to collaborate with each other, to work harmoniously and not in competition with each other, without envy. It is truly wonderful. We are the living example of how women working together can achieve so much" (see http://www.

gingergeneration.it/n/mama-marjas-e-miss-mykela-presentano-we-ladies-lintervista-97196-n.htm).

Mama Marjas is an assiduous live performer, with over 400 live performances since 2009. Demonstrating her versatility and popularity, in 2015 she was cast as the main character in the musical *Carmen secondo l'Orchestra di Piazza Vittorio*, produced by the Accademia Filarmonica Romana, Vagabundos, and Teatro Olimpico. Her promotional tours abroad, which have taken her to England, the US, and the Sziget festival in Budapest, have been very successful, as are her "sold-out dates in the best Italian clubs and festivals" (http://reggae.today). Her popular 2016 tour, "Mamatour," spanned 35 major cities across Italy, from Bolzano (in the north-eastern region of South Tyrol) to Trapani (in the west coast of Sicily). Mama Marjas is also highly collaborative. In addition to working with fellow Apulian, Miss Mykela, and with the English producer Adrian Sherwood, she has collaborated with internationally recognized Italian-Jamaican reggae artist Alborosie and twice with the historical Neapolitan group 99 Posse, which we discuss in Chap. 5. Her collaborations with southern artists also include the Calabrian hip hop veteran, Lugi, originally from the historical South Posse; Neapolitan rapper Clementino; Sicilian reggae-hip hop collective, Shakalab; and the pioneering reggae group from Torino, Africa Unite (see http://www.mamamarjas.com).

In a 2015 interview with Eugenia Conti, to a question about being a female artist and also an artist from the South, she replied:

> It means having a lot of determination, strength, courage and love for yourself because they will always try to destroy your ambitions. For women it is always difficult to emerge in all fields. You have to prove you are three times better than others to receive half the recognition that a man will receive, even if only in terms of recognition and visibility. Starting off from the South is a further difficulty because we live in a context where it is hard to lead our lives with dignity and honesty. (Conti 2015, p. 3)

As a southern Italian female artist, Mama Marjas' advocacy for the welfare of women is a constant feature of all of her albums. Notably, "Bless the Ladies," one of the most popular tracks of her first album, *B-Lady*, deals explicitly with domestic and sexual violence perpetrated on women around the world and more specifically in Italy's South and the world's global Souths. The track is sung and toasted in a unique combination of

Patois, Italian, and a mixture of Apulian dialects over a vintage sounding roots reggae rhythm. The chorus, which is sung in English and Patois and combines the female vocal register typical of reggae and soul music with gruffer raggamuffin-style delivery, demands that women be loved and respected, stating:

> Make what I do
> When listen this tune my Man scream
> Bless the Ladies
> There's the mother of the future
> Give thanks to the creator and sing
> Bless the Ladies
> Make what I do
> When listen this tune you know the message is
> Bless the Ladies
> Me-I represent the women all over di plan so Me-I chant
> Bless the Ladies

The lyrics "Me-I represent the women all over di plan so Me-I chant, Bless the Ladies" evoke Mama Marjas' self-appointed role as spokesperson chanting (speaking) on behalf of women. Pointing out that she is one of the women on behalf of whom she wishes to speak, the "Me-I represent the women" establishes her role as an advocate for women with the authority to comment on their exploitation. In turn, by claiming the power to chant *as* a woman through the words "Me-I represent the women all over di plan so Me-I chant," she asserts women's empowerment and also calls for women to empower themselves. Specifically, the reference to "so Me-I chant" establishes a connection between the message that women be loved and respected with reggae's oral tradition of toasting/chanting, that is, the Jamaican equivalent of rapping. In so doing, she claims authority as a woman and also as a reggae artist.

Accordingly, in the video clip of "Bless the Ladies" (available on YouTube), Mama Marjas is often framed by low-angle shots, investing her with authority and power, as she looks directly into the camera. The clip alternates between three different personae—anarcho-punk reggae deejay accompanied by multicultural female-only performers, solo dancing hip hop B-girl, and singing stage performer—and three different locations, abandoned multistorey buildings, in what appears to be a typical neighbourhood on the fringes of a southern Italian urban centre, a graffitied wall, and a stage. The grainy feel of the clip, created through the use of

206 S. SCARPARO AND M. S. STEVENSON

dark and grey lighting, reinforces the gravity of the message concerning the abuse and exploitation of women, while also presenting the women on the video clip as devoid of the trappings of hypersexualized and soft femininity typical of music videos. Thus, Mama Marjas and the women who accompany her in the video clip demand to be taken seriously as resilient, dignified, and strong women.

The demand to be taken seriously as women and as artists underscores her second album, *We Ladies*. Produced and performed in collaboration with fellow artist Miss Mykela, *We Ladies* combines London-style reggae roots with Italian melodies. It deals primarily with women's lives and friendships between women in the context of the South. In conversation with Nicola Signorile, Mama Marjas explains the forward female-respect manifesto of the album in these terms: "the concept we want to clarify is that we finally demand our place in music. Specifically, we claim a place in reggae, but we do not ask for approval because we are women. We want to be taken seriously as artists and as women" (Signorile 2012, n.pag.). Moreover, Miss Mykela confirms that the central concern of the album is to tell stories about women from diverse perspectives and from the point of view of two best friends (http://www.gingergeneration.it/n/mama-marjas-e-miss-mykela-presentano-we-ladies-lintervista-97196-n.htm). Thus, even though the album includes tracks such as "Ancora" (So Far), which seemingly focuses on heterosexual love and heartache, the album maintains an emphasis on female friendship and on relationships between women.

Sung by Mama Marjas and Miss Mykela over a reggae rhythm incorporating elements of rocksteady and lovers rock, "Ancora" (So Far) is a love song dealing with a woman's heartbreak due to her lover's deceit. The video clip (available on YouTube), however, invests the song with an additional layer of meaning beyond that of the themes of the typical love song. In the clip, Mama Marjas and Miss Mykela sing in a 1920s cabaret setting with matching gowns and accessories. They interact with each other in flirtatious, loving, and playful ways through both the lyrics and their movements on stage. They sing in contrasting voices, with Miss Mykela taking on her recognizable sassy soulful female register and Mama Marjas adopting at various stages both a singjay style, blending toasting and singing, and a baritone vocal register. The camera cuts between a mixture of close-up, medium, and long shots of the performers, with their all-male band in the background, and shots of male-female couples seated in the audience.

Significantly, the evident harmony between the two performers is contrasted with the obvious discord between the couples in the audience. Whereas the lyrics of the first verse, sung by Miss Mykela, express an affirmation of female desire in relation to her partner, the women in the audience all exhibit a combination of anger, frustration, fear, and boredom in their interactions with their male partners. As Mama Marjas joins Miss Mykela in her singjay style, the narrator of the song starts to question the effect that her lover has on her and increasingly complains of his undue influence and control over her: "Io non posso che cedere" (I have no choice but to give in). As if commenting on these lyrics, the camera cuts to the seated couples showing, in turn, a woman looking mistrustfully at her companion and, more disturbingly, another woman passively receiving what are clearly unwanted and forceful sexual advances from her partner. Moreover, as Mama Marjas declares: "Ti mette fra le dieci bambole che non gli piacciono più" (He places you amongst the ten dolls he no longer likes), the camera cuts to a shot/reverse shot sequence of a man talking on his mobile phone as his female partner expresses disappointment due to his lack of attention.

By contrast, Mama Marjas and Miss Mykela support each other on stage, singing and dancing together. As the song continues, the growing connection between the two performers contrasts with the increasing hostility between the couples in the audience, culminating in harrowing close-up shots of each of the women shedding tears before all standing up and physically confronting their partners. With escalating conflict initiated by the women, tables are overturned, faces are slapped, and objects are thrown. This mounting conflict, however, does not perturb the singers. On the contrary, it appears that their performance is designed to inspire the women in the audience to reflect on their predicament, claim agency, and act accordingly. Meaningfully, the friendship between the two women on stage is a catalyst for self-understanding and agency among the women in the audience. Hence, departing from established conventions, this seemingly traditional love song ascribes power to female friendships and claims agency for the female musicians.

In turn, the role that Mama Marjas and Miss Mykela ascribe to themselves as female musicians capable of inspiring women amongst their audience recalls the influential role that other female musicians have had on them. Fittingly, Mama Marjas has emphasized her admiration for those she calls the "donne del reggae" (the women of reggae), citing Judy Mowatt, Marcia Griffiths, and Rita Marley as veritable role models. She has also credited R&B singer Mary Jane Blige with being her singing model. Among her Italian role models, she references Raffaella Carrà for her trailblazing performances and ability to combine diverse styles of singing with uninhibited dancing and elaborate choreography (Interview with Gigi Piccolo in *reggae.today*, published on YouTube on October 20, 2014).

Taking full charge of her musical direction, Mama Marjas wrote both the lyrics and the music for her latest 12-track concept album, *Mama*. Commenting on the central concept of the album, she explains that the "thread of the record is the notion of Mama Africa understood as the originator of, and primary influence on, music" (Conti 2015, p. 7). As discussed in previous chapters, this conceptualization of the key role of Africa, and of the African diaspora, in relation to the evolution of blues, R&B, ska, rocksteady, hip hop, dancehall, kwaito, reggaetón, and all that goes under the label of "black music" is a widely accepted belief (Dawson 2007; Rommen 2013; Niaah 2010). Similarly, Mama Marjas' comments about the role of Africa mirror the widespread assumptions discussed elsewhere in this book that the evolution of reggae in Jamaica illustrates the "cross-fertilising process" of a long tradition of "African diasporic hybridity and bricolage" (Cooper 2004, p. 234). Moreover, in line with the British context (see Dawson 2007), Mama Marjas' reference to Africa and so-called black music functions as a system of conscious affiliation based on political solidarity. For Mama Marjas, in fact, reggae music, and more broadly what she calls "street music," is not a business. Rather it is inextricably bound to a political message. As she states, her "mission is to try to show people what they cannot see," not because she is "better than them," but because she is *one* of them: "a young woman with a great deal of musical knowledge who is determined to use music to interpret the shared struggles of daily life" (Interview with Gigi Piccolo in *reggae.today*, published on YouTube on October 20, 2014).

Drawing on the artist's familiarity with diverse music genres, Mama Marjas' *Mama* is a fusion of Latin American, Caribbean, and African-American rhythms, sung predominantly in Italian. Through her characteristic experimentation, Mama Marjas combines reggae with other musical genres that are largely unrecognized or poorly represented in Italy, such as Caribbean soca and dembow. The themes of the album include women's everyday lives and the ways in which they are commonly represented in social media, consumerism, and urban degradation. Ultimately, the album proposes a politics of enjoyment built through community and solidarity in spite of, and in reaction to, the difficulties of everyday life. As happens with music practices that have migrated from ghetto streets to the world stage, "the existence of such enjoyment assaults and mocks oppression, and those who construct and maintain it" (Niaah 2010, p. 190).

Track number ten of the *Mama* album, "Poco Poco" (A Little a Little), is a powerful illustration of protest through enjoyment. Written in collaboration with Don Ciccio, the track is a poignant and playful critique of contemporary consumer society which is dominated by an excessive and narcissistic use of social media. As such, the lyrics reference the prevailing obsession with technology-driven self-promotion, as demonstrated through constant posting on social media platforms of selfies and the superficial and banal documentation of the minutiae of life. The lyrics of "Poco Poco" critique the "culture of the selfie" by linking it to consumerism more broadly, whereas its music is a southern Italian take on the Caribbean genre of dembow. Given that this musical style originated in Jamaican dancehall music and then inspired the rise of reggaetón in the Spanish-speaking Caribbean, its use in this track establishes a southern Italian transcultural and transnational connection with diasporic Afro-Caribbean forms of expression.[5]

The video clip of "Poco Poco" is shot on location in Taranto, including gritty streetscapes, such as public housing blocks, graffitied walls, and run-down historic centres. In the video clip, Mama Marjas and her fellow dancers, comprising Italian dancehall queen Alevanille, children, a pregnant woman, and an array of bright and eccentric male and female characters, grind and gyrate to the music in a kitsch reference to Jamaican dancehall and reggaetón. Fast-paced editing interweaves multidirectional shots of sexualized female dance moves and body parts, which evoke

---

[5] As Sonjah Stanley Niaah explains, reggaetón is "known as a pan-Latino culture that originated from and represents inner-city Latino youth" (2010, p. 185). It is "symbiotically related to hip hop and reggae" and was known as "Spanish reggae" (2010, p. 185). Significantly, its "relationship to a discourse of freedom is seen through the articulation of survival and independence by young Latinos and Latinas" across diverse locations within the US and in countries such as Cuba, Colombia, and Chile (2010, p. 185). According to Niaah, Jamaican migrants to Panama "took their music with them and Panamanians started recording and performing 'Spanish reggae' in the 1970s. Later in the 1980s and 1990s, Panamanian artists updated their music with the latest dancehall reggae rhythms, in many cases maintaining the attitude and stories being told. This music migrated with the movement of Latinos to metropolitan centres such as New York, where the migrants and their music encountered Puerto Rican rappers, and a new musical relationship was born" (2010, p. 185). This music included the blending of rapping with Jamaican deejay style (2010, p. 186).

dancehall culture's "flamboyant performing of sexuality" (Cooper 2004, p. 3). Carolyn Cooper identifies subversion as a "quintessential feature of the promiscuous culture of the dancehall" (2004, p. 3). As with dancehall, reggaetón has been criticized for its seemingly excessive sexual content, expressed through descriptions of "sexual acts, sexual desire, bodily fluids and female body parts" (Niaah 2010, p. 187). In the words of Sarah Bentley, "some couples face each other, arms locked around the waist, banging their crotches together hard, while for others the guy stands behind the girl, pushing it up against her as she gyrates her *culo* [butt]" (2005, p. 44). Moreover, solo female dancers "shake their butt cheeks and dip their knee" as solo male dancers "dip, pull suggestive faces and dance as if riding an imaginary horse" (Bentley 2005, p. 44).

Accordingly, the video clip of "Poco Poco" references all of these dance moves. However, by investing these moves with playful irony, the clip foregrounds the pervasive sexualization of women in music videos, and in popular culture more generally, while also emphasizing the women's enjoyment in reclaiming their sexuality on their own terms through localized versions of Afro-Caribbean music and dance. This localized subversion of stereotyped sexuality is conveyed, for instance, through the opening extreme close-up of Mama Marjas sucking a raw mussel instead of the familiar prop of the ice cream or banana commonly found in music videos. Moreover, the video clip's inclusion of the sexualized dance moves typical of dancehall and reggaetón evokes shared experiences of marginalized identities, as "local politics and communities occupy national and transnational geographies, at the same time as they engage in dialogue with each other through performance" (Niaah 2010, p. 189).

Similarly, visual representations of Taranto's poor neighbourhoods in the video clips from the album *Mama* recall the representations of the ghettos, townships, or barrios of disadvantaged urban centres across the globe. In this context, Taranto becomes part of the transnational networks through which ghetto citizens around the world maintain links of solidarity built around music. Track number three of *Mama*, "La Gente" (People), exemplifies this dialogic process. The track consists of a percussive musical synthesis which combines elements of Cuban and Central and South American music with hip hop, ragamuffin, and reggaetón. In the video clip (available on YouTube), Mama Marjas materializes on-screen to the sound of syncopated scratching. Reminiscent of a spectre, she is dressed as *la Calavera Catrina*, the elegant female skeleton that has come to symbolize the Mexican Day of the Dead. For the remainder of the video clip, she meanders through the polluted landscape of Taranto, a town which is "dominated by smoking chimneys" and whose old centre "is a half-abandoned collection of bricked up and crumbling palazzi" (Kington 2012).

Founded as a Greek colony in 706 BC, and with a population of more than 200,000 people, Taranto is currently the third-largest continental city of southern Italy. It is also a significant commercial and military port and home to steel foundries, oil refineries, and chemical and food-processing industries that have attracted increasing criticism for their harmful impact on the town. In particular, the steelworks owned by the Ilva Groups have attracted growing public concern over the toxic emissions that many believe are causing increased levels of cancer and respiratory illnesses among the inhabitants of Taranto, especially those living in the vicinity of the foundry ("Ilva" 2016). According to the European Pollutant Emission Register (EPER), in 2002 "estimated emissions" of dioxin from the Ilva plant in Taranto accounted for approximately 30 per cent of Italy's total reported emissions. The emissions increased to 83 per cent of the country's total reported emissions in 2004 (http://www.europarl.europa.eu).

In 2012, the Ilva steelworks were described as "an environmental disaster" and were ordered to shut down (Kington 2012). However, fearing job losses the labour unions protested against the closure, securing the backing of the government, with the health minister actively criticizing the magistrate who had ordered the closure of the polluting furnaces. Writing for *The Guardian* in 2012, Tom Kington commented that "pollution is part of local life" in Taranto: "Everyday residents sweep their balcony clean of the red mineral dust blowing in from Ilva's mountainous deposits and the black soot from its chimneys, which regularly clog storm drains" (2012, n.pag.). The plant was placed under special administration in 2013, and in 2016 the European Union initiated an inquiry into the Italian government's decision to grant almost two billion euro to assist the struggling Ilva steelworks, which were still deemed to be one of Europe's most polluting industrial plants (Kemp 2016). Despite its fraught history of noncompliance with environmental standards, the Ilva steelworks employed approximately 14,000 workers, and many locals opposed its closure fearing the consequences that the job losses would have on a town already afflicted by high levels of unemployment (https://phys.org/news/2016-01-eu-probe-italian-aid-polluting.html).

The spectre of Mama Marjas dressed as *la Calavera Catrina* alludes to such situations, evoking the death and devastation afflicting Taranto. With smoking chimneys, car traffic, and desolate landscapes in the background, Mama Marjas/*Calavera Catrina* declares:

> La gente moderna
> La gente pretende
> La gente che parla ma poi non sa niente
> La gente mente
> La gente non sente
> La gente sbaglia ma poi non lo ammette
> La gente si pente
> Fa finta di niente
> La gente si vanta
> La gente si arrende
> La gente dimentica assai facilmente
> E cambia le idee come cambia le tende
>
> (Modern people
> People pretend
> People talk but know nothing
> People lie
> People don't hear
> People are wrong but don't admit it
> People have regrets
> But pretend everything is fine
> People boast
> People give up
> People forget very easily
> And change their minds as if they were curtains)

These lines are followed by the repetition of "la gente" (people), pronounced as the Spanish word, and accompanied visually by a sequence of close-up shots of men and women of different ages and backgrounds. In subsequent verses, Mama Marjas/*Calavera Catrina* laments further that so-called normal people are superficial, they can hurt others without "thinking about the consequences" of their actions, and they can also be truthful only when "convenient" to them, having lost their desire to come together as a community for the sake of acquiring power as individuals: "La gente è maligna / non sta più insieme / si isola e parte alla conquista del potere" (People are bad / they can't stick together / they isolate themselves and go chasing power). Both the lyrics of the track and the images of the video clip suggest discomfort and pessimism. Indeed, through "La Gente," Mama Marjas expresses anger and resignation in light of Taranto's overt incapacity to react against its own devastation and exploitation. Yet the track also conveys a desire for connections enacted through music and culture between marginalized southern Italians and fellow Latinos across transnational, global Souths. To this end, the blending of Latin American and Caribbean music styles, the repetition of the Spanish word for "people," and the appropriation of the symbol of the Mexican Day of the Dead evoke the artist's yearning for political solidarity between Latinos across the continents. This message of political solidarity across and through connective marginalities remains the driving impetus behind Mama Marjas' music.

JIMINY THE TALKING CRICKET: CLAUDIA ARU

The manifesto of music as message is central to many who belong to the diverse network of independent and grassroots artists active today in southern Italy and particularly in the regions of Apulia and Sardinia which are the focus of this book. While reggae, raggamuffin, and rap, broadly intended, have been the musical genres of choice for many operating in these contexts, other transnational fusions have emerged within these marginal musical milieus. The eclectic singer and songwriter from Sardinia, Claudia Aru, provides an example of the ways in which these transnational fusions are used in order to articulate a political message centred on localized cultural issues. For Aru, self-production is also a political act. Aru, in fact, has no agents and no label. She relies on word of mouth and social media to reach her audiences and on creative commons to protect the copyrights of her music. She refuses to belong to a label because she believes that labels tend to build an artistic persona according to their own interests. As she states: "they do not want you, they want something else. Instead, by remaining independent and by self-producing my music, I am in charge of myself. I dress as I want, I say what I want to say, I make my own decisions" (Personal interview). Thus, with her all-inclusive approach to the production, distribution, and marketing of her music, Aru exemplifies the tension between self-production and cultural and political autonomy that, according to Fanelli, characterizes the history of Italian social and political song, from singer-songwriters to posses (Fanelli 2015, n.pag.).

After studies in Barcelona, New York, and Rome, Aru returned to live in Sardinia and founded with producer Francesco Medda (aka Arrogalla) the dub electro-folk duo Bentesoi. Bentesoi produced two experimental albums sung in English, Sardinian, Turkish, and Catalan with the independent collective factory Nootempo: *Tripland* (2008) and *Folk You!* (2010). These albums boast collaborations with a range of international and Sardinian artists, including Sa Razza and Randagiu Sardu. In 2012, Aru released her first solo album with Nootempo, *Aici* (Like This), which like her previous collaborative works blend diverse genres, including blues, country, rock bolero, gospel, and swing. As with Mama Marjas' work, Aru's musical diversity is accompanied by linguistic diversity ranging from Italian, Spanish, English, to Sardinian, which, nonetheless, remains the central language of her albums. Aru released her second album, *A giru a giru* (Around Around) in 2013 (Nootempo), and her latest album, *Momoti* (Bogeyman, Matriota), in 2015. The self-produced *Momoti* blends funk, progressive rock, and alternative blues with hints of samba, swing, and Balkan music. The album also combines political and humorous texts in Sardinian, creating a progressive cultural vision of Sardinia where music and language merge to establish a glocal and transcultural identity (see http://www.cagliariartmagazine.it/claudia-aru-faccio-lartista-non-per-voti-ma-per-missione/). In 2017, Aru released a 17-track collection of her previous songs titled *Collection* (Nootempo).

As demonstrated by her prize-winning performance at the 2015 Andrea Parodi world music award, the eclecticism of Aru's music falls under the loose definition of world music. Significantly, in her Facebook site, Aru describes herself as a "Sardinian, world music singer-songwriter who combines jazz, blues, country, swing manouche and gospel." This categorization of herself as Sardinian and of her music style as world music is noteworthy for two reasons. First, it underscores Aru's position outside the mainstream, and second, it establishes a dialogic relationship between her localized identity as a Sardinian woman and her belonging to a worldwide tradition of transnational music steeped in "Black Atlantic" musical forms. Indeed, even before the term world music became popular in the 1980s to encompass non-Western musical genres "outside the mainstream categories of commercial popular and classical music" (Niaah 2010, p. 177), a melting pot of what Niaah has defined as "Black Atlantic cross-fertilization" was already producing much of the music that is now categorized under this label. Hence, music styles such as reggae, R&B, blues, and hip hop precede the use of the term world music, a term that, "in any case, is contested by the very existence and proliferation of Black Atlantic musical forms far beyond the popularity of the 'mainstream' musics they are defined in opposition to" (Niaah 2010, p. 177).[6]

For Aru, moreover, music is a means rather than an end in itself. As she states, "in my vision, music becomes the means to the end, which for me is the message I want to convey. Hence, I do not choose a genre but rather I choose a message" (Personal interview). As with Mama Marjas, Aru's message focuses on women's daily lives, domestic violence, discrimination, and marginalization. Like Randagiu Sardu, she sings primarily in Sardinian *Campidanese* and writes lyrics about Sardinian history and politics. She describes her choice to sing in Sardinian as "a political act" that seeks to reclaim a language too often relegated to minor roles and to traditional folk music (Personal interview). Aru maintains an active presence on social media through Facebook and YouTube and is often invited to play and perform at local Sardinian festivals and in village squares. She is also popular with local media, appearing as a guest performer in much-loved Sardinian TV programmes, such as *I due di Via Venturi* (on Sardegna 1 TV channel). With financial support from the Sardinian regional government, in 2016 and 2017, she performed at Italian cultural institutes in Japan and in Belgium. Despite attracting loyal fans, her outspoken advocacy for gender equality, support for LGBTIQ, and respect for migrants have attracted criticism and online bullying.

The 2014 single "Vergogna Bregungia" (Shame) epitomizes her unique combination of irony and social critique. The song with accompanying video clip (directed by Roberto Pili and available on YouTube) was composed following Aru's invitation to act as godmother for the 2014 Sardegna Pride festival. Inviting listeners to challenge the casual, yet harmful, discrimination experienced by the LGBTIQ community in daily life through common parlance, the lyrics consist of a mixture of Italian, Sardinian, and some English commonplace sayings about gays and lesbians. To this end, starting with a close-up shot of lips that open and close, evoking mindless talking, the camera cuts to a split screen of a frontal mid

---

[6] It is generally assumed that the term world music was coined in the 1960s by the musicologist Robert E. Brown to replace the term "ethnomusicology." It has since been often used to refer to music genres that include hybrid fusions of Western popular music with non-Western or so-called ethnic music. A discussion of the complexities associated with any attempt to define and challenge the appropriateness of labels such as world music is beyond the scope of this book. For a discussion of the definitions and the many uses of this term, see Bruno Nettl 2013, pp. 23–54.

shot of Aru stating: "Va bene lui è gay ma non si vede tanto" (Yes, he is gay but you can't really tell from his looks), and with a conspiratorial stance declaring "Non middu narrasa sembrava uno normale" (I don't believe it, he looked normal) with black and white images of demonstrators marching on the streets and clashing with police. Subsequent shots return to close-up images of Aru's open mouth as she gives voice to the often-heard male wish to have sex with two women at once, thus critiquing the belittling of lesbian relations in the service of heterosexual male desire.

These images are followed by the camera's return to split-screen shots of Aru and to images of clashes between demonstrators and police. In these shots, the grainy, documentary look of the images featuring the demonstrators and the police contrasts with the bright lighting of the images featuring Aru. Sporting red lipstick, slick make-up, colourful clothes, tattoos, and bare shoulders, the singer playfully declares that "Il vero uomo ha i peli e puzza da bestia" (Real men are hairy and stink like animals), whereas "loro sono trendy e cool e usano il sapone" (them, are trendy and cool and use soaps), "sono molto gentili" (are very polite), and "hanno un animo sensibile" (are very sensitive souls). The contrast between the stereotypes of gentleness and sensitivity ascribed to "them," that is, those who are set in opposition to "us" and to "real men," is clearly challenged by the images of the demonstrators facing up to heavily armed police. This juxtaposition between the tongue-in-cheek repetition of seemingly benign platitudes with the dangerous violence implicit in the confrontations between demonstrators and police invites viewers to reflect on the role of language in propagating discrimination and violence. In so doing, everyone is called to question their own, often unwittingly repeated, use of clichés that implicate us all in the perpetuation of prejudice and intolerance.

Subsequent lyrics continue to list commonplace views, such as "questa nuova libertà da alla testa e fa si che donne e bambini non abbiano più esempi" (this new freedom has gone to our heads and has deprived women and children of appropriate role models), followed by close-up shots of Aru denouncing "questa società ipocrita che continua a celare la propria identità" (this hypocritical society that continues to disguise its own identity) and stating in English: "shut up now and open your fucking mind." The refrain "vergogna" (shame in Italian), "bregungia" (shame in Sardinian), "mai mai più shame" (never, never again, shame), expressed by close-up shots of Aru's lips, renders explicit the message of the song.

Like Randagiu Sardu and Mama Marjas, Aru has also written texts about the degradation of the environment. The track "Lillica Babajola" (Ladybird Lillica) from her first solo album *Aici* for which she wrote both lyrics and music critiques Sardinians' widespread habit of littering the countryside with all manner of rubbish. The video clip (directed by Roberto Pili and available on YouTube) adds further elements of irony and humour, while also emphasizing the links between corrupt politicians and illegal waste disposal. Set in the countryside, the video clip begins with extreme close-up shots of Aru dancing and looking directly into the camera. In these shots, Aru sports her characteristic red lipstick, impeccable make-up, and a red rose on her raven black hair. In subsequent shots, she turns into a sort of superhero dressed as a ladybird, spying on a corrupt mayor who is clearly making deals with a shady character dressed in a suit and carrying a briefcase. A point-of-view shot from Aru/ladybird superhero, witnessing the deal from behind a bush, cuts to a low-angle shot of the two men, giving prominence to the briefcase, presumably stuffed with money, as it exchanges hands from the suited man to the politician. Subsequent long shots focus on rubbish scattered around the landscape as the lyrics, all in Sardinian and in the first-person point of view, state:

> Fia in su sartu
> Circhendi codrobinu
> Po circai de mi pasiai
> Intra is murdegus seu andada a circai
> Ma podia sceti agatai
> Codrobinu pero' fatu de àliga
> Ojamumia su nervosu ca mi pigat
> Ma podit essi ca est totu schifosu
> Chi no ti bia maladitu putzinosu

> (I was in the country
> looking for mushrooms
> trying to rest
> I went behind the rockrose
> But all I could find
> Mushrooms but made of rubbish
> Mamma mia, how angry I am
> How disgusting can you be
> I hope not to see you dammed filthy bastard)

218   S. SCARPARO AND M. S. STEVENSON

Anger against the corrupt system which allows for the destruction of the common good, as expressed by these lyrics, is set in contrast with the laughter that is generated by the appearance of the ladybird/superhero. While declaring that "Nc'est sa genti ca no tenit sa cuscientzia bivit sa vida in sa prus lègia innioràntzia" (There are many who don't have any awareness of the situation and live in complete ignorance), "no scit biri su chi tenant acanta de su logu 'e totus si ndi frigant" (cannot see what there is around them and they don't care), the ladybird/superhero runs towards the politician and his friend and like an old-fashioned teacher takes them by the ears and drags them away as if they were two naughty children.

In the refrain, a serious Aru, by contrast, looks straight into the camera and, adopting an aggressive stance, warns the listener that the road should not be viewed as a rubbish bin. In subsequent scenes, the ladybird/superhero, introducing herself as Lillica, laments the destruction of her home, stating: "Bivu innoi custu ast su miu bixinau" (I live here, this is my neighbourhood) "castia cumenti mi dd'an imbruttiu" (look what they've done to it). Attempting to clean the "bu'tillas, imbidris, su frigoriferu, sa bacteria se sa machina" (bottles, glass, an abandoned fridge, a car battery), the ladybird/superhero finds others who casually leave their rubbish bags and throw their rubbish from their car windows. She gets them all out of their cars, drags them by their ears, and forces them to sit down. Like schoolchildren, they listen to her as she stands in front of a blackboard and teaches them about respect for the environment and the common good.

The humour of these scenes, accentuated by bright lighting and quick editing, underscores the seriousness of the lyrics, which call for collective responsibility, denouncing indifference and ignorance as equally responsible for widespread social and political corruption. The hilarious reference to Aru as ladybird/superhero turned school teacher functions as a self-referential reminder of the role of music as "edutainment," which, as discussed in previous chapters, had been central to the posses and their predecessors such as Different Stylee and which continues to distinguish self-produced music in southern Italy today.

Aru's latest album, *Momoti*, confirms this approach. The album consists of 12 tracks that deal with diverse themes ranging from personal feelings, such as fear in the case of the title track "Momoti," to Sardinian history, language, and customs, as well as social issues such as domestic violence. Many of these themes are presented through various female characters recognizable by Sardinian audiences as familiar types: *Sa Coga* (the witch) who has the power to dispel the evil eye, *Zia Peppina* (Aunty Peppina) who likes to feed her relatives until they burst, *Zia Chicchina* (Aunty Chicchina) who knows everything about everyone, *Zia Francisca* (Aunty Francisca) who spends most of her time in church, and, finally, *Marta* (Martha) who is killed by her husband. Sardinian history features in the track "Su Giganti" (The Giant). Told from the point of view of the stone giant, the track celebrates the significance of the Giants of Mont'e Prama, ancient stone sculptures found in central western Sardinia in the 1970s and believed to be amongst the oldest anthropomorphic sculptures of the Mediterranean, dating back to the seventh century BC (see Dyson and Rowland 2007, pp. 94–96). The giant in the song laments the fact that, by and large, Sardinians have failed to capitalize on the stone sculptures' historical and cultural significance, which attest to the island's ancient role as key player in the Mediterranean region.

The characters featured in *Momoti* form the basis of Aru's most recent show, "Cantus e Chistionis" (Songs and Disquisitions). In the show, the singer turns into a theatre performer as she introduces her characters to the audience and uses props and body language to personify them on stage while singing the relevant song featuring each character. Invariably, audiences respond with rapturous laughter to this show. Specifically, they laugh at the ways in which Aru introduces her characters and her songs by mimicking Sardinians' commonly used expressions when speaking in Italian. Audiences laugh at these expressions because, rather than being Italian sayings, they are, in fact, literal translations of Sardinian phrases. Aru's show invites reflection on the reasons why audiences laugh when hearing their own idioms and watching performances of their culture on stage. On the one hand, by laughing about those characters and their language, audiences laugh self-referentially, as they recognize themselves or people they know in those caricatures. On the other hand, the laughter points to a more complex dynamic. As Aru suggests, the laughter allows her Sardinian audiences to distance themselves from their culture, while at the same time feeling nostalgic for it (Personal interview). The mix of laughter and grief derives from the Sardinian audience's conflicted attachment to a culture which they cannot fully own because they feel uncomfortable with and are ashamed of being identified with it. Accordingly, Aru identifies the complex ambivalence experienced by Sardinians in relation to their language and culture as a legacy of colonialism. As she maintains: "because by believing that, as we have been told for so long, we are short, ugly, hairy and uncultured, we lost the connection to our own culture and, in turn, have distanced ourselves from our language. Thus, we are a few brave artists making the choice to sing in Sardinian" (Personal interview). For these reasons, Aru uses music as a means to communicate about, and raise awareness of, social and political issues concerning Sardinia and the world more broadly. Invested with this mission, she defines herself less as a singer-songwriter and more like Jiminy, Pinocchio's talking cricket and his conscience (Personal interview).

In conclusion, all three of the artists discussed in this chapter view music as a mission. Their approach to self-production, their linguistic choices, and their resistance against conforming to clear-cut musical genres are a legacy of the antagonistic scenes of the 1980s and 1990s, widely referred to as the posse era. During this time, musically diverse groups, including those which did not explicitly fit into the stylistic categories of reggae or rap, were considered to be a part of a broad movement that was both experimental and political. This combination of experimentation and politics led to the fusion of diverse music genres which, as discussed, stemmed from a desire to form transnational connective marginalities with disenfranchised peoples across the world through localized interpretations and adaptations of musical styles generally associated with protest, the ghetto, and black and Latino identities. The new millennium, in turn, has seen the internet and social media secure an expressive space for new subjects who have traditionally been doubly marginalized, such as women and artists from the island of Sardinia.

WORKS CITED

Aru, Claudia. 2016. Personal Interview. December 6.

Bentley, Sarah. 2005. Reggaeton in Puerto Rico: Three Worlds Collide. *Riddim* 1 (42): 42–47. Print.

Conti, Eugenia. 2015. Mama Marjas, la guerriera che canta le battaglie di Taranto. *Identita insorgenti*, May 6. http://www.identitainsorgenti.com. Accessed 13 Sep 2017.

Cooper, Carolyn. 2004. *Sound Clash: Jamaican Dancehall Culture at Large*. New York: Palgrave Macmillan. Print.

Dawson, Ashley. 2007. *Mongrel Nation: Diasporic Culture and the Making of Postcolonial Britain*. Ann Arbor: University Press of Michigan. Print.

Dyson, Stephen L., and Robert J. Rowland Jr. 2007. *Archaeology and History in Sardinia from the Stone Age to the Middle Ages: Shepherds, Sailors, and Conquerors*. Philadelphia: University of Pennsylvania Press. Print.

Fanelli, Antonio. 2015. Il canto sociale dai Dischi del sole alle posse. http://www. treccani.it/enciclopedia/il-canto-sociale-dai-dischi-del-sole-alle-posse_%28L%27Italia-e-le-sue-Regioni%29/. Accessed 12 Sep 2017.

Fontana, Ludovico. 2010. Mama Marjas Diva Raggamuffin. *Musica*, December 17: 89–92. Print.

Ilva, I dati su malattie e inquinamento 'Taranto non supera Roma.' 2016. *La Gazzetta del Mezzogiorno*, December 7. http://www.lagazzettadelmezzogiorno.it/news/home/834791/ilva-i-dati-su-malattie-e-inquinamento-taranto-non-supera-roma.html. Accessed 10 Mar 2018.

Kemp, Danny. 2016. EU Opens Probe into Italian Aid for Polluting Ilva Steelworks. *Phys.org*, January 20. https://phys.org/news/2016-01-eu-probe-italian-aid-polluting.html. Accessed 10 Mar 2018.

Kington, Tom. 2012. Italian Town Fighting for Its Life Over Polluting Ilva Steelworks. *The Guardian*, August 17. https://www.theguardian.com/world/2012/aug/17/italy-ilva-steelworks-cancer-pollution. Accessed 20 Sep 2017.

Mama Marjas. 2014. Intervista con Mama Marjas—Reggae. Today. *YouTube*, October 20: 10. https://youtu.be/mTSwuQAeyeQ. Accessed 10 Mar 2018.

Nettl, Bruno. 2013. On World Music as a Concept in the History of Music Scholarship. In *The Cambridge History of World Music*, ed. Philip V. Bohlman, 23–54. Cambridge: Cambridge University Press. Print.

Niaah, Sonjah Stanley. 2010. *Dancehall: From Slave Ship to Ghetto*. Ottawa: University of Ottawa Press. Print.

Nowak, Raphael. 2016. *Consuming Music in the Digital Age: Technologies, Roles and Everyday Life*. London and New York: Palgrave Macmillan. Print.

Randagiu Sardu. 2011. Fibai e Tessi | Randagiu Sardu | nootempo NOOT006— Official Single Sardegna. *YouTube*, July 13. https://youtu.be/5I7dsumikt0. Accessed 10 Mar 2018.

———. 2016. Personal Interview. December 14.

Rommen, Timothy. 2013. Landscapes of Diaspora. In *The Cambridge History of World Music*, ed. Philip V. Bohlman, 557–583. Cambridge: Cambridge University Press. Print.

Signorile, Nicola. 2012. Quando il reggae e femmina. Parlano Mam Marjas e Miss Mykela. *Corriere Del Mezzogiorno*, June 12. http://corrieredelmezzogiorno.corriere.it/napoli/notizie/spettacoli/2012/12-giugno-2012/quando-reggae-femminaparlano-mama-marjas-miss-mykela-201569189504.shtml. Accessed 15 Sep 2017.

Urban, Maria Bonaria. 2013. *Sardinia on Screen: The Construction of the Sardinian Character in Italian Cinema*. Amsterdam: Rodopi. Print.

Zucchetti, Massimo. 2006. Environmental Pollution and Health Effects in the Quirra Area, Sardinia Island (Italy) and the Depleted Uranium Case. *Journal of Environmental Protection and Ecology* 7 (1): 82–92. Print.

Discography

Aru, Claudia. 2012. *Aici*. Nootempo. CD.
———. 2013. *A giru a giru*. Nootempo. CD.
———. 2015a. *Momoti*. Bogeyman, Matriota. CD.
———. 2015b. Momoti. *Momoti*. Bogeyman, Matriota. CD.
———. 2017. *Collection*. Nootempo. CD.
Bentesoi. 2008. *Tripland*. Nootempo. CD.
———. 2010. *Folk You!* Nootempo. CD.
Mama Marjas. n.d. Poco Poco. *Mama*. Love University. CD.
———. 2009. *B-Lady*. Love University. CD.
———. 2011. *90*. Love University. CD.
———. 2015. *Mama*. Love University. CD.
Mama Marjas and Miss Mykela. 2012a. Ancora. *We Ladies*. Love University. CD.
———. 2012b. *We Ladies*. Love University. CD.
Randagiu Sardu. 2008. *Io Randagiu Sardu*. Nootempo. CD.
———. 2009a. Sa Battalla. *Sighimi*. Nootempo. CD.
———. 2009b. S'arrespiru. *Sighimi*. Nootempo. CD.
———. 2009c. *Sighimi*. Nootempo. CD.
———. 2010. Danza Noa. Nootempo. CD.
———. 2011a. Fibai e Tessi. *Rappamuffin de Sardigna*. Nootempo. CD.
———. 2011b. *Rappamuffin de Sardigna*. Nootempo. CD.
———. 2015. Country Man. Nootempo. CD.
———. 2016a. *Randagiu Sardu: 12 Original Hitz*. Nootempo. CD.
———. 2016b. Xelu. Nootempo. Single.

CHAPTER 8

Conclusion

In 2011, 31 years after Bob Marley's concert at San Siro Stadium, the Italian-born and naturalized Jamaican, Alborosie (Alberto D'Ascola), became the first white person to win the prestigious Music of Black Origin (MOBO) award for Best Reggae Act. Although beyond the scope of this book, Alborosie's artistic and cultural evolution helps our understanding of the rhizomatic nature of Italian reggae music, particularly in relation to language, and identity. D'Ascola was born in 1977 in Marsala—where Garibaldi and his troops had landed in 1860 to conquer the South—of mixed Sicilian, Calabrian, and Apulian parentage, before migrating to the North with his family as a youth. In 1992, he co-founded and became the lead singer for the Bergamo-based reggae band, Reggae National Tickets, adopting the alias Stena. Riding the wave of the posse movement, and being inspired by previously discussed Italian groups, such as Africa Unite and 99 Posse, Reggae National Tickets released their first demo tape, *Metropoli Selvaggia* (Savage Metropolis), in 1994. They were subsequently signed by the multinational BMG and EMI labels and produced 5 albums between 1996 and 2000, which sold more than 200,000 records (*ALBOROSIE*). Demonstrating their indebtedness to the posse era, almost all of the group's songs were sung in Italian. Reggae National Tickets became the first Italian reggae band to be invited to play at Jamaica's important Sunsplash and Sumfest reggae festivals, before disbanding in 2000.

© The Author(s) 2018
S. Scarparo, M. S. Stevenson, *Reggae and Hip Hop in Southern Italy*, Pop Music, Culture and Identity,
https://doi.org/10.1007/978-3-319-96505-5_8

223

The Italian phase of D'Ascola's reggae career set him up for his remarkable musical and cultural transformation after migrating to Jamaica in 2001 in search of reggae's roots. He began unpaid work as a sound engineer at Port Antonio's Geejam Studios, learning Jamaican Patois and immersing himself in Jamaican and Rastafarian culture. Employing his newfound production skills and his proficiency in guitar, bass, drums, and keyboard, he began to produce *riddims* for other Jamaican vocalists, before founding the independent Forward Recordings label with Jon Baker and undertaking a solo career.

In 2003, under the moniker Alborosie, he self-produced his first Jamaican single, "Dash Me Away" (Forward Recordings), which was sung in Patois and showcased a decidedly gruffer and deeper vocal timbre. Along with his newfound Jamaican vocal and linguistic qualities, D'Ascola's new *nom d'art* symbolized his personal cultural transformation, combining the first two letters of his Italian name, "Al," with the pejorative Patois term, *borosie*, with which he had been labelled when he first arrived in Jamaica (Marchetti 2008, n.pag.).

Alborosie has explained the ease of his cultural transformation in terms of his southern roots: "I lived in Sicily so I have actually maybe like 150 miles [sic] from Tunisia in North Africa. That is why Africa is my thing.... The fact that I come from the South of Italy I really come from the African culture, so it was actually very easy for me to learn the *ting* [Patois for 'thing' italics added], and to get the real vibe" (in Ketola 2010, n.pag.). The syncretic and global quality of Alborosie's cultural identity is further reinforced by his personal description of his spirituality as "a little bit of Hindu, a little bit of Christianity, a little bit of Catholic, a little bit of Rasta" (in Rudis 2010, n.pag.).

Despite his tendency to deal with political, social, and spiritual issues from a Jamaican and global perspective, in 2009 Alborosie demonstrated his indebtedness to the political tradition of 1980s and 1990s Italian reggae by releasing "Mr President," which denounced the alleged corruption of Silvio Berlusconi (then Italy's *Presidente del Consiglio*). At the same time, however, "Mr President" provided a powerful example of the extent of Italian reggae's evolution, incorporating Rastafarian terminology and heavy Patois over vintage Jamaican instrumentation.

In many respects, "Mr President" exhibits a direct line of continuity with Different Stylee's 1986 production, "Mr Babylon," discussed in Chap. 3, which critiqued the Berlusconian neoliberal capitalism of the 1980s by incorporating Rastafarian metaphors and Patois nuances with a

CONCLUSION   225

heavy roots-dub style instrumentation inspired by British and Jamaican reggae. Similar to "Mr Babylon," "Mr President" uses the metaphor of Babylon to denounce materialism and greed. However, while the Jamaican production values, heavy Patois, and Rastafarian tropes showcased by "Mr President" appear to mark it as unmistakably Jamaican in origin, Alborosie's "made in Jamaica" production in fact involves a more explicitly local reading of Italian politics and nationalism than did "Mr Babylon":

> Watch out Babylonian Mafia maccheroni,
> Fyah pon di one deh name Silvio Berlusconi,
> Lucifer rolling out inna one blue Lamborghini,
> Fyah pon di one deh name Benito Mussolini,
> Mi bun di fyah from Rome to Milan,
> Twelve Tribes of Israel[1] bun dung Vatican,
> President Berlusconi why yuh pushing us back?,
> Your lies dem dun long time but ya mouth still a talk,
> Silvio mi haffi send yuh one big Bomboklaaat.[2]

Furthermore, in the tradition of Italian reggae from the 1980s and 1990s, the lyrics speak on behalf of a marginalized youth demographic— "Mek di youth dem express demself / … Invest inna di youth dem / Believe in all a di youth dem / Stop pressure dung di youth dem"—and openly denounce racist nationalism—"I don't want to live in a one Fascist society / Mi nah go be a part of a Nazi democracy."[3]

In 2011, Alborosie teamed up with the eclectic Apulian rapper, Caparezza, to produce another anti-Berlusconi song, ironically titled "Legalize the Premier," which they performed together at the annual workers' concert in Rome on the first of May. Further demonstrating Alborosie's connection to Italian reggae's past and present, in 2014 he appeared on 99 Posse's remake of the seminal track, "Curre Curre

---

[1] The Twelve Tribes of Israel is a Rastafarian group based in Kingston, which was formed in 1968 and based on the 12 astrological zodiac signs; Bob Marley was an adherent.

[2] "Watch out Babylonian Mafia macaroni / Fire upon the one named Silvio Berlusconi / … Lucifer rolling out in a blue Lamborghini / Fire upon the one named Benito Mussolini / … I burn fire from Rome to Milan / Twelve Tribes of Israel burn down Vatican / … President Berlusconi why are you pushing us back? / Those lies of yours got tired long ago but you're still talking / Silvio I'm going to have to tell you to get fucked."

[3] "Let the youth express themselves / … Invest in the youth / Believe in all of the youth / Stop pressuring the youth / … I don't want to live in a Fascist society / I won't be part of a Nazi democracy."

Guaglió," discussed in Chap. 6, where he toasts a verse in Patois alongside the *napoletano* of 'O Zulù and the *tarantino* of Mama Marjas.

Whereas sporadic early Italian imitations of Jamaican popular music entirely disregarded its important sociocultural roots, Alborosie is thoroughly immersed in the sociocultural realities of Jamaica and produces a brand of reggae which, at least in terms of its aesthetic qualities, is remarkably Jamaican. Alborosie's music thus embodies the potential for Italian reggae to problematize fixed and exclusionary understandings of culture and identity and to establish broad alliances based on transcultural connective marginalities. This dynamic is a direct consequence of the various phases of reggae's cultural flows explored throughout this book.

We argued that since the 1980s in Italy reggae and reggae-inflected hip hop have resonated strongly with the perceived cultural, linguistic, social, and political marginalization experienced by many Italians, particularly in the southern regions of the country. Hence, reggae, interpreted as modern black music that originated at the margins of the empire, has appealed mainly to independent artists and groups who were searching for alternatives to the Italian tradition of political song of the late 1960s and the word-centric production of singer-songwriters typical of Italian protest music. By infusing reggae and reggae-inflected hip hop with local elements, such as multiple local languages and linguistic codes, southern Italian artists have created transversal and transnational alliances with other marginalized subjectivities along ethnic, cultural, and political lines. As such, reggae and later reggae-inflected hip hop have also provided means to promote transcultural and interlinguistic dialogue within the diverse local contexts that continue to divide Italy along northern and southern regional identities since its unification in 1861.

To this end, in this book we paid particular attention to personal recollections of key Apulian and Sardinian musicians, as well as the contexts of creation, distribution, recording, and playing of their music in the early stages of the adoption of reggae, and some versions of hip hop culture. Hence, we considered issues of self-production and distribution, as well as the political and historical contexts with which the discussed artists and musical groups actively engaged. In light of the complexity of Italian politics and culture, we examined the role of the *centri sociali*, the legacy of the violent and conflicted creation of a unified Italian state, as well as reactions to the rise of media magnate turned politician Silvio Berlusconi and the growth of racist political parties, such as the Northern League. Finally, since the concept of multiple marginalities, along with the connective marginalities framework, was a key element of this book, we focused primarily on independent and marginal artists who produce and distribute their music outside official channels and through the use of social media and the internet.

Ultimately, this musical production represents one of Italy's most significant forms of creative political expression since the 1970s and a means of challenging hegemonic politics and culture. The adoption and adaptation of reggae and reggae-inflected hip hop have provided southern Italian youth with the cultural means through which they have questioned and reinvented the counter-cultural and counter-hegemonic practices of the 1970s.

Beyond the scope and content of our study, Italian reggae and reggae-inflected hip hop culture continued to evolve and expand, remaining a relevant force within autonomous and non-hegemonic contexts. Of particular interest is the proliferation of self-constructed Jamaican-style sound systems throughout the Italian peninsula from approximately 1994, discussed in the 2011 documentary, *Pull it Up: An Italian Story*. Another crucial development was the founding of the Rototom Sunsplash festival in Friuli by the not-for-profit Rototom Cultural Association.

Taking place on a small scale for the first time in 1994, and involving only Italian acts, the festival rapidly grew to become one of Europe's largest and most important cultural events. Not only was Rototom crucial in promoting reggae music by attracting thousands of people from around Italy and the world, and showcasing both Italian *and* international artists, but it also proposed cultural and political debates on topics such as alternative modes of solidarity, Rastafarianism, the prohibition of marijuana, and racism. While the success of Rototom was symbolic of reggae's growing counter-cultural significance in Italy, the fact that it was forced to relocate from Osoppo to the Spanish town of Benicàssim in 2010, due to sustained harassment from local authorities, indicates that reggae culture remains on Italy's cultural margins.[4]

Rototom was central to the emergence and growing international success of the Sardinian group Train to Roots, which is distributed globally by VP Records. Formed in 2004 and inspired primarily by British roots

---

[4] For a comprehensive history of the festival, see the documentary *The Story of the Rototom Crew from 1991*, directed by Tommaso D'Elia and Silvia Bonanni and available online at www.rototomsunsplash.com.

reggae, to date Train to Roots has released five albums, featuring lyrics toasted and sung in a mix of Sardinian, Italian, English, and Jamaican Patois. Their growing international popularity, however, has coincided with a move away from lyrics steeped in social protest towards a more generic message of universal love and respect for all and preference for English and Jamaican Patois over Sardinian and Italian. In this respect, Train to Roots exemplifies a different, more commercially oriented, approach to the processes of transculturation involved in the practice and musical productions of the artists and groups discussed in this book. As such, their example points to the tension, already discussed in relation to international icons such as Bob Marley, between the adoption of reggae as a form of opposition expressed through a focus on local issues in local languages and the desire to perform for, and communicate with, international audiences.

As groups such as Train to Roots enter an international marketplace more focused on mass appeal, the message of reggae in Italy is in danger of losing its potential for localized social and political protest at a time of great need. Within the current global context, which is marked by the increasing movement of migrants and refugees and a concomitant increase in xenophobic ethnic-nationalisms across the European continent and beyond, the examples of the musical practices we discussed in this book provide concrete instances of the potential for intercultural dialogue much needed today. Fittingly, in 2010, Sud Sound System provided a powerful example of their ongoing transcultural tradition from the 1980s and 1990s by releasing a bilingual composition mixing Salentine dialect and English, which featured the collaboration of the internationally recognized Jamaican reggae singer Luciano. Titled "Lampedusa," the lyrics provide direct opposition to the demonization of so-called illegal immigrants, anticipating the polarizing debates and tragic deaths of thousands of migrants who have attempted to make the crossing since then.

This capacity for reggae to open new avenues of intercultural dialogue and exchange with immigrant communities, and thus contribute to new and inclusive understandings of cultural identity, is also manifest in the work of Salento's Afro-reggae crew, Ghetto Eden. The founders of Ghetto Eden were inspired directly by the Salentine reggae of Sud Sound System who produced their albums: *Fuori Città* (Out of the City, 2011) and *Senegalentino* (2014). The title of the second album makes explicit the group's rich mixture of diverse stylistic influences and the ability of the vocalist Diene Khadim to switch adroitly between Salentine dialect, Italian, and Wolof. In recognition of the symbolism of their musical project, Ghetto Eden were nominated as "ambassadors of cultural identity" at the 2013 edition of the Negroamaro festival in Cellino San Marco, Salento, and their music must be understood as the logical evolution of the pioneering work of the groups discussed throughout this book.

At the same time, however, and approximately 20 years after "Legala" (which we discussed in Chap. 5) was produced, in April 2013 the *Lega Nord*'s Mario Borghezio claimed that the newly elected Minister for Integration Cécile Kyenge would impose "tribal conditions" on Italy and help form a "bongo-bongo" administration, adding that Africans had "not produced great genes" (in Kington 2013). In June of the same year, a local councillor for the party called for Kyenge to be raped, while in July, Roberto Calderoli, a former *Lega Nord* minister of Berlusconi's government, compared her to an orangutan before bananas were thrown at her as she made a speech. In addition, in September of the same year, the neo-fascist *Forza Nuova* party dumped three Ku Klux Klan-style mannequins stained with fake blood outside a town hall where Kyenge was due to make a speech.

In the present-day context of Italian and European neoliberalism and austerity, Italian youth are even more marginalized than they were throughout the 1980s and 1990s. In August 2017, unemployment figures for Italians between the ages of 15 and 24 stood at 35.1 per cent (Istat, "Employment"), with a staggering 51.8 per cent in the South (Istat). These statistics are higher than the already-disconcerting averages of 28.7 per cent throughout Italy and 39.7 per cent in the South, between 1980 and 1994 (Istat). In fact, even between 1986 and 1994, the period when Salentine youth marginality inspired Sud Sound System's first phase of musical activity, the average unemployment figure in the South stood at 42.9 per cent (Istat), almost 10 per cent lower than present-day figures.

Furthermore, the anti-democratic tendencies and institutional failings that had inspired such works as "Batti il Tuo Tempo" and "Stop al Panico," which were discussed in Chap. 5, continue to plague Italy. Nonetheless, as demonstrated by the examples of the Sardinians Randagiu Sardu and Claudia Aru, and the Apulian Mama Marjas discussed in Chap. 7, southern Italian artists have continued to respond to these worrying trends through self-produced and politically self-reflexive music. Moreover, ever since Different Stylee's experimentations with what we referred to in Chap. 3 as "reggae world fusion," reggae and reggae-inflected hip hop have continued to evolve into and inspire eclectic music styles, as evident in the work of the artists we discussed in Chap. 7.

This blending of and openness to varied styles allow for the establishment of diverse connections across multiple levels of marginalities determined by geography, the legacy of colonialism, and gender. The latter has become particularly relevant as more women, such as Mama Marjas and Claudia Aru, are achieving greater visibility and creative autonomy, continuing the work of pioneering female artists such as Different Stylee's lead singer and bassist from 1983 to 1992, Rosapaeda (Antonella Di Domenico), who is now an acclaimed solo world music artist. Fittingly, Rosapaeda's sixth, and most recent, album was an aptly named tribute to her former band, *Inna Different Stylee* (2015, Femlay), which was crowd-funded and overseen by the pioneering British reggae legend Dennis Bovell. The album continues the transcultural and multilingual exploration of southern and particularly Apulian and Neapolitan traditions, which Rosapaeda commenced with her fellow members of Different Stylee way back in early 1980s Bari.

According to archaeologist Steven Mithen, when people make music together, they "mould their own minds and bodies into a shared emotional state," merging identities, facilitating cooperation, and effacing the sense of the "Other" (2006, p. 215). As such, music has a potential to inspire and connect human beings. Echoing Mithen's observation, Rosapaeda claims that "reggae's greatest attribute lies in its ductility and inclusiveness. Dub, in particular, can pervade any music and reggae encapsulates the roots we all share. This is the revolutionary power of reggae" (Personal interview). Our study of southern Italian reggae and reggae-inflected hip hop has demonstrated that the socially binding potential of these forms of expression and their capacity to mediate profound transnational connections and alliances place them in a privileged position to challenge economic, cultural, and political marginalization and provide a voice, albeit marginal to mainstream cultural practices, for those who lack institutional power.

WORKS CITED

De Gaetano, Giovanni, dir. 2011. *Pull It Up: An Italian Story*. Nine Lives. Film.

Istat. n.d. Unemployment Rate Dataset. Istituto nazionale di statistica. www.istat. it. Accessed 15 Apr 2014.

Ketola, Justine A. 2010. Alborosie Set to Conquer California. http://zionbound-media.blogspot.com.au/2011/07/alborosie-escape-from-babylon-to.html. Accessed 24 Feb 2014.

CONCLUSION   231

Kington, Tom. 2013. Italy's First Black Minister: I Had Bananas Thrown at Me But I'm Here to Stay. *The Guardian*, September 8. https://www.theguardian. com/world/2013/sep/08/cecile-kyenge-quest-for-tolerance. Accessed 3 Mar 2014.

Marchetti, Simona. 2008. Il reggae partito da Bergamo ha conquistato la Giamaica. *Corriere della Sera*, January 18: n.pag. http://www.corriere.it/spettacoli/08_ gennaio_18/reggae_bergamo_giamaica_d7acc28c-c5d8-11dc-8434-0003ba99c667.shtml. Accessed 5 Jan 2014.

Mithen, Steven J. 2006. *The Singing Neanderthals: The Origins of Music, Language, Mind, and Body*. Cambridge: Harvard University Press. Print.

Rosapaeda. 2017. Personal Interview. October 20.

Rudis, Al. 2010. Italian Reggae Star Puts Down New Roots and Rhythms in Jamaica. *Press-Telegram*, February 17. https://www.presstelegram. com/2010/02/18/italian-reggae-star-puts-down-new-roots-and-rhythms-in-jamaica/. Accessed 19 Mar 2014.

DISCOGRAPHY

99 Posse. 1993. Curre Curre Guaglió. *Curre Curre Guagliò*. Esodo Autoproduzioni. CD.

Alborosie. 2003. Dash Me Away. Forward Recordings. 7-inch.

———. 2009. Mr President. *Escape From Babylon*. Greensleeves. CD.

Different Stylee. 1986. Mr Babylon. *Mini Album Dubwize*. Mole Reggae Diffusion. EP.

Ghetto Eden. 2011. *Fuori Città*. Salento Sound System. CD.

———. 2014. *Senegalentino*. Salento Sound System. CD.

Reggae National Tickets. 1994. *Metropoli Selvaggia*. Self-produced. Demo tape.

Rosapaeda. 2015. *Inna Different Stylee*. Femlay. CD.

Sud Sound System. 2010. Lampedusa. *Ultimamente*. Universal Music. CD.

Torino Posse. 1992. Legala. Vox Pop. 12-inch.

Index[1]

A

Activism, indigenous, 28n7
Aeroplanitaliani, 145
Africa Unite/d, 41, 41n13, 69n25, 70, 72n26, 139, 141, 144, 204, 223
Afro-Caribbean, 10, 21, 23, 34, 59, 60, 94, 97, 209, 210
Afrocentrism, 26
Alborosie, 204, 223–226
Al Darawish, 123
Alevanille, 209
Alla Bua, 123
Almamegretta, 127, 154–157, 154n16
Aloisha, 141
Amata, Renato (DJ R), 107
Americanization, 77, 101
Amore Tossico, 51n9
Anagrumba, 154
Anarchists, 1, 49n6, 62, 132
Anarcho-punk movement, 12, 48, 61, 61n13, 62, 62n14

Anni di piombo (1969–1983), 51, 51n8, 64, 65
Anselmi, William, 10n8, 102
Anti-fascist movement, 29
Anti-militarism, 61
Apache Indian, 4
Appadurai, Arjun, 182
Apulia, 2, 7, 8, 9n7, 13, 77n33, 78, 85n1, 96n13, 97, 105, 165, 194, 213
Area, 23, 33, 39, 50, 62, 71, 72, 104, 131n1, 132, 166, 170, 175, 176, 183n6, 186, 198n3, 199n4
Arezzo, 70
Artists, see Individual entries
Aru, Claudia, 12, 13, 165, 193–220, 229, 230
Assalti Frontali, 146–148, 150
Assante, Ernesto, 128
Aswad, 74
Attack Punk, 61n13
Autogestione, 45, 61, 72, 148, 149

[1] Note: Page numbers followed by 'n' refer to notes.

© The Author(s) 2018
S. Scarparo, M. S. Stevenson, *Reggae and Hip Hop in Southern Italy*, Pop Music, Culture and Identity,
https://doi.org/10.1007/978-3-319-96505-5

233

234 INDEX

Autoproduzione, 45, 61, 72, 148, 149
Autoriduzione, 30, 32, 38
Avanzi, 118, 147, 147n10

B

Babylon, 35, 36n11, 70, 71, 73, 75,
  91, 92, 225
Balentia, 170n1
Ballads, anarchist, 1
Banco Ambrosiano, 137
Band, Ludus Dub, 138
Bari, 11, 41, 45–80, 85, 90–94, 100,
  106, 123, 130, 141, 230
Bari Posse, 129, 145
Bass Culture, 48n3
Beastie Boys, 164
Beeley, Vanessa, 184, 184n8
Belafonte, Harry, 21, 22
Bennato, Edoardo, 33
Bennett, Andy, 45, 46, 48, 184n7
Bentesoi, 165, 214
Bentley, Sarah, 210
Berlusconi, Silvio, 4, 5, 67n22, 76,
  76n31, 77, 101, 131, 137, 148,
  150, 224–226, 225n2, 229
Berlusconizzazione, 131
Bertè, Loredana, 40
Bettini, Stefano, *see* Generale, il
  (Bettini, Stefano)
Bhangramuffin, 4
Big Youth, 35
Bisca, 149
Black Panther Party, 133
Black Uhuru, 74n28
Blackwell, Chris, *see* Island Records
Blige, Mary Jane, 208
Blues, 33, 37, 155, 203, 208, 214
Bobo Boggio, 141
Boney M, 29
Boogie Down Productions, 107, 111
Boone, Pat, 22
Borghezio, Mario, 229

Borsellino, Paolo, 146
Bossi, Umberto, 138–141, 143, 157
Bovell, Dennis, 90, 91n8, 230
Branson, Richard, 27
Briggy Bronson, 70, 93, 93n11, 140,
  144, 148
Brown, Robert E., 215n6
Burning Spear, 91n8
Byzantine Empire, 166

C

Cagliari, Claudio, 51n9, 166, 170n1,
  182, 182n3, 185, 186
Caldarulo, Nico, 45n1, 90, 123
Calderoli, Roberto, 229
Calura, 104, 118
Caminiti, Attilio, 132
Campbell, Clive "Kool Herc," 20, 89
Campo, Alberto, 10n8, 61, 86, 99,
  145, 151, 153, 155
Cantu a tenore, 183n6
Canzone d'autore, 33, 41, 128
Canzoniere del Lazio, 33
Caparezza, 164, 225
Capitalism, 37, 61, 73, 76, 131, 134,
  224
Capone, Federico, 9n7, 87, 102, 105,
  106, 108, 117
*Carmen secondo L'Orchestra di Piazza
  Vittorio*, 204
Carrà, Raffaella, 25, 26, 39, 208
Carrie D, 145
Casino Royale, 141, 145, 171
Castaldo, Gino, 4, 41, 128, 130
Castro X, 132
Catholicism, 57
Centri sociali organizzati autogestiti
  (CSOA), 10, 48, 58, 106
Century Vox Records, 108n23, 110,
  117, 118, 147, 148, 150, 164
Chernobyl, 75, 91, 132n2
Cherry, Don, 33

INDEX 235

Christian Democrats, 98n15, 113n24,
  137, 152
Cinevox/Cinenova, 164
Clapton, Eric, 29
Clash, 4, 31n8, 36, 37, 58, 59n12, 64,
  65, 95, 96, 216
Clementino, 204
Cliff, Jimmy, 27, 40
Colazzo, Salvatore, 102
Colonialism, 6, 18, 20, 56, 73, 121,
  150, 219, 230
Commercialization, 3, 5, 28, 72, 128,
  148
Communism, Italian, 136
Concu, Carlo, *see* Randagiu Sardu
Consumerism, 37, 75, 77, 101,
  183n5, 208, 209
Conte, Antonio 'DJ War,' 85n2, 105,
  106, 106n21
Conti, Eugenia, 202–204, 208
Cooper, Carolyn, 208, 210
Cordata per l'autorganizzazione, 149,
  150
Corruption, 110, 112, 113, 113n24,
  122, 134, 135, 137, 138, 146,
  203, 218, 224
Cor Veleno, 164
Counter-culture, 5, 11, 18, 29–31, 37,
  41, 50, 60, 127
Count Machuki, 35
Craxi, Bettino, 76, 76n31, 135, 137
CRC Posse, 170n1
Creolization, 17, 18
Cuore, 144
Cypress Hill, 180

D
Daddy Freddy, 107, 182n2
Dance, 3, 9n7, 19, 20, 23, 26, 64,
  77n33, 95n12, 100, 102, 114,
  147, 198, 201, 203, 209, 210

Daniele, Pino, 155, 155n17
Dante D'Ascola, Alberto, *see*
  Alborosie
Dawson, Ashley, 10n8, 21n1, 36–38,
  63n16, 153, 155, 208
De Gaetano, Giovanni, 9n7
De Gregori, Francesco, 33
De Martino, Ernesto, 95n12
De Pascali, Pierluigi (GgD), 85n2,
  106
Deindustrialization, 5, 63, 66
Deleuze, Gilles, 3, 89
Della Mea, Ivan, 31, 31n8
Dembow, 208, 209
Democrazia Proletaria, 62
Denaro, Massimiliano, 130, 131
Devastatin' Posse, 145
Dialogue
  interlinguistic, 4, 97, 226
  inter/transcultural, 4, 97, 226
Di Capri, Peppino, 23, 26
Di Domenico, Antonella, *see*
  Rosapaeda (Di Domenico,
  Antonella)
Different Stylee, 9, 12, 45, 45n1, 48,
  48n2, 50n7, 54, 59, 60, 62–64,
  62n15, 69, 71–80, 90, 91, 94,
  95, 155, 187, 194, 218, 224,
  229, 230
Dischi Ricordi, 40, 50
DJ Gruff (Sandro Orrù), 108,
  108n23, 171
DJ Kote Giacalone, *see* Giacalone,
  D.J. Kote
DJ Nike, 184, 186
Donadio, Francesco, 58, 101
Dub, 10, 10n8, 11, 34–37, 36n11,
  45, 63, 63n16, 64, 64n17,
  64n18, 72, 74–77, 90, 91n8,
  107, 122, 140, 154–156, 203,
  214
Dunbar, Sly, 74

236 INDEX

E

Emigration, 1, 121, 144, 184
Environmentalism, 61
Epifani, Mattia, 9n7, 38, 48n2, 56,
   62, 63, 67
Ethiopia, 23n2, 57
Etruscans, 166
European Pollutant Emission Register
   (EPER), 211
European Union, 211
Exploitation, 3, 6, 7, 53, 57, 68, 75,
   95, 96, 102, 105, 144, 151–153,
   168, 176, 195, 205, 206, 213
Extracomunitari, 139

F

Fabiana, 122
Fabio, Terron, 85n2
Facebook, 68n23, 193, 196, 214, 215
Fanzines
   Ital Reggae, 67, 67n23, 69
   Ital Soul, 67, 68n23, 70, 90
   Nuove dal Fronte, 62n14
   Rebel Soul, 48, 67, 68, 68n23, 70
Fascism, 1, 38, 57, 71, 87, 87n4,
   113n24, 129, 136, 143, 169,
   170, 225, 225n3
Favilli, Sandro, 138
Feminism, 30
Ferrari, Paolone 'Paolone Aka,' 141
Ferraris, Gabriele, 128, 145
Festivals
   Arezzo Wave Festival, 154
   Feste del proletariato, 32
   Negroamaro, 229
   Rototom Sunsplash, 227
   Sumfest, 223
   Tribute to Bob Marley, 68
Finardi, Eugenio, 33
Fiorentino, Vito 'War,' 41, 70, 110
Fiori, Umbérto, 22, 30, 32–34

Fischlin, David, 28
FishEye Sardinia, 165
Folk music, 33, 50, 95, 102–105, 110,
   128, 133, 153, 215
Formentini, Marco, 149
Forte Prenestino, 131, 149
Forza Nuova political party, 229
Francisca, 203
Frankie hi-NRG MC, 145
Fumarola, Pietro, 102, 103, 148

G

Gaetano, Rino, 39
Gangalistics, 165
Garage rock, 22
Garybaldi, 33
Gaudi, Lele, 137n6, 141, 144, 145, 148
Geejam Studios, 224
Geki, 141
Gelli, Lucio, 136, 137
Generale, il (Bettini, Stefano), 9n7,
   53n10, 127, 137–139, 141, 144,
   148
Germinaro, Maria, *see* Mama Marjas
Ghetto Eden, 228, 229
Giacalone, D.J. Kote, 139, 141, 144
Giannini, Micaela, *see* Miss Mykela
Giannotti, Marcello, 58, 101
Ginsborg, Paul, 4n2, 5, 29, 51, 51n8,
   55, 67n22, 73, 76, 113n24, 137,
   139, 151
Giornale de Oritsano, Il, 167
Giudicati, 166, 199
Giungla, La, 48n2, 60–68, 71–80, 90,
   94
   See also *Centri sociali organizzati
      autogestiti* (CSOA)
Gli avventurieri del deserto di mattoni,
   68–69
Glocal, 6, 46, 79, 80, 102, 114, 130,
   142, 214

INDEX 237

Gong, 50
Gori, Cecchi, 150
Gospel music, 214
Gramsci, Antonio, 5, 5n3, 55, 87, 88,
   88n5, 129, 167, 175
Grassi, Francesco 'Don Ciccio,' 203
Griffiths, Marcia, 13, 207
Groups, *see Individual entries*
Gruppo Operaio e Zèzi, 153, 155
Guattari, Félix, 3, 89
Guccini, Francesco, 33
Guerrilla culture, 54, 55
Guru, 164

H
Heavy roots, 34, 35
Hebdige, Dick, 17, 23, 26, 34, 36, 47,
   58n11
Hegemony, 10, 21–23, 28, 39, 55, 57,
   78, 86–88, 88n5, 109, 120, 143,
   148, 149, 152
Hendrix, Jimi, 31
Henzell, Perry, 27
Heroin, 51, 60–62, 65, 66n20, 71,
   95, 96, 99, 110, 113, 135, 154
Hibbert, Toots, 25
Hip hop, *see* Rap
Hybridization, 18, 36, 47, 80, 102,
   107, 182n2
Hymns, socialist, 1

I
Il Grande Ducato Hardcore, 62,
   62n14
Il Nuovo Canzoniere Italiano, 31
Ilva Groups steelworks, 211
Immigrants
   Italy, 21, 56, 58
   UK, 19, 21
Imperialism, 18, 56, 88, 129

Inequality, structural, 55
INK, see Isola nel Kantiere
International Bank for Reconstruction
   & Development, 175
Intifada, Palestinian, 144
Irie, 41
   See also Winnie, Papa
Island Records, 2, 22, 26, 27, 36, 40,
   50, 64
Isola nel Kantiere (INK), 106–109,
   128, 145
Isola Posse All Stars, 108, 108n23,
   128, 145–147
Istituto De Martino, 31
Italian Communist Youth Federation,
   49
Italian jazz-rock, 50
   See also Area; Perigeo
I Tamburellisti di Torrepaduli, 123

J
Jagger, Mick, 39
   See also Rolling Stones
Jah Children Family, 41, 41n14, 69
Jamaica
   music, 21–25, 27, 58
   Patois, 26, 73, 93n11, 97, 99, 114,
      151, 168, 203, 224, 228
J-Ax, 164
Jeans, 79, 79n35
Johnson, Linton Kwesi, 63, 63n16,
   91n8, 122, 141
Jones, Simon, 11n10, 18, 21–26, 28,
   35–37, 59, 77, 99
Jovanotti, 148

K
Katsiaficas, Georgy, 4n2, 29, 49, 51,
   53, 65, 131
Khadim, Diene, 228

238 INDEX

Kianka Town, 203
Kid Frost, 180
Kingston, 20, 23, 24, 55, 91, 96, 98,
225n1
See also Jamaica
Kington, Tom, 19, 211, 229
Kool Moe Dee, 133
Krama Possee, 148
KRS-One, 99, 108, 111, 112, 182n2
Kurtis Blow, 164
Kwaito, 208
Kyenge, Cécile, 229

L
Lady Ninja, 122
Lala, Massimo, 62n15, 64, 68
Lampa Dread, 100, 100n18
Langbauer, Laurie, 93
Language, 12, 87, 88, 97, 167, 168
dialect, Salentine dialect, 12, 87, 88,
97
diglossia, 169
Florentine, 87, 168
indigenous, 88n6
minority; *Campidanese*, 168, 195;
Logudorese, 167; *Sardu*, 167,
168
Patois, 4, 18, 73, 88, 118
political, 8
subaltern idioms, 88
vernacular, 73, 89, 139, 143
West African, 18
La Notte dei Marziani Italiani, 145
La Pantera student movement, 127,
130, 131, 133
Lapassade, Georges, 102–104, 148
Lee, Bunny, 118
Lega Lombarda, 138
Lega Nord, 94, 120, 122, 137–144,
149, 155, 156, 229
Leoncavallo, 61, 110, 134, 135,
135n4, 141, 149

Leone, Sergio, 4, 133
Leoni, Giuseppe, 138
Letts, Don, 26, 26n5, 36
Liberation movements, 4
Liga Veneta, 138
Lion Horse Posse, 110, 145
Li Ucci, 101
Longo, Piero, *see* Militant P (Longo,
Piero)
Lori, 141
Lotta Continua, 49n6
See also Youth movements
Love University Records, 203
Luca Morino, 141
Lucampione, 141
Luciano, 41n14, 228
Lumley, Robert, 4n2, 5, 28–30, 32,
51n8, 58, 60, 66
L'Unità, 148
Lutzu, Marco, 10n8, 163, 168, 170,
170n1, 183, 183n6, 187,
187n10

M
Machuki, Count, 89n7
Mad Sabrina, 122
Mafias
Camorra, 96n13
Sacra Corona Unita, 96, 96n13
Malos Cantores, 164, 194
Mama Marjas, 9, 13, 193–220, 226,
229, 230
'Mamatour,' 204
Manfredi, Tommaso, 9n7, 40, 48n2,
50, 80, 90, 94, 98, 101, 104
Manouche, 214
Mansueto, Enzo, 62, 62n15
Mantagnata, 146
Marginal, 2, 7, 12, 26, 48, 48n2, 50,
57, 58, 72, 73, 109, 132, 133,
146, 163, 166, 170, 171, 196,
213, 227, 230

Marginalization, 2, 8, 36, 40, 57, 60, 63, 109, 141n8, 151, 153, 171, 174, 182, 195, 203, 215, 226, 230
Marilena, 122
Marini, Giovanna, 31, 31n8
Marley, Bob, 2, 4, 5, 11, 22, 24, 27, 28n7, 29, 38, 40, 41, 50, 50n7, 51, 68, 69, 141, 195, 223, 225n1, 228
See also The Wailers
Marley, Rita, 13, 207
Masonic lodge, 67n22, 136
Massilia Sound System (MSS), 103, 104, 122
M'Boye, Ibu, 78, 78n34
MC/selecta, 164
Medda, Francesco (Arrogalla), 214
Mento, 19, 20
Messapians, 102
Mezzogiorno, 8, 167, 175
Micio P, 164, 182, 186, 187, 194
Militant, A., 86, 100, 132, 133, 145, 147
Militant P (Longo, Piero), 9n7, 48n2, 85n2, 90–94, 93n11, 100, 106, 110, 111, 115, 122, 147
Mini Album Dubwize, 72, 77, 90
Miss Mykela, 203, 204, 206, 207
Misty in Roots, 39
Mitchell, Tony, 10n8, 88n6, 127, 128, 148, 158, 181
Mixcloud, 193
Mole Records, 78
Mole Reggae Diffusion, 72
Mole Studio, 90
Mondine, 142
Montevergini, 131
Morricone, Ennio, 133
Movimento, 29, 30, 49, 53, 58
See also Re Nudo
Mowatt, Judy, 13, 207

MSS, see Massilia Sound System
Murazzi del Po, 144, 145
Muro di gomma, 136
Murvin, Junior, 37, 64
Musella, Mario, 155n17, 157
Music of Black Origin awards, 223
Music scene, 10, 17, 45, 46, 50, 132, 145, 153, 154, 188
Music styles, see Individual entries
Mussolini, Benito, 57, 63, 67n22, 225, 225n2
Mustafa MCs and DJ R, 107
Musumeci, Pietro, 136

N
Nabucco, 1
Nandu Popu, 85n2, 100, 122, 149
Naples, 7, 78, 130, 150, 153, 154, 157
Napoli Centrale, 155, 155n17
Napolitano, Giorgio, 136
Nash, Johnny, 29
National Front, France, 103
National popular, 128, 129, 140, 146, 158
NATO, 135, 184, 184n8, 186, 198n3
NCOT, 132
Neapolitan music, 77, 78, 155
Neffa, 108, 108n23
Neoliberalism, see Riflusso
Neopizzica salentina, 101
New urban narratives, 48
Niaah, Sonjah Stanley, 208–210, 209n5, 214, 215
Niceforo, Alfredo, 94
Nigger Kojak, 98
Nikaleo, 203
99 Posse, 13, 127, 146, 147, 149–154, 150n13, 204, 223, 225
Non-garantiti, 55
Nootempo Records, 164

240 INDEX

Northern League, *see* Lega Nord
Notting Hill, 36, 39, 59, 65
Nuclei Armati Rivoluzionari, 136
Nuova canzone politica, 31, 33
Nuova Compagnia di Canto Popolare, 78, 155
Nuovi Briganti, 146, 147
Nuovi cantautori, 33
Nuraghi, 166

O

Occidentale, Paolo 'Sego,' 132
Officina 99, 150, 151, 154
Onda Rossa Posse (ORP), 127, 128, 133, 134
One Love Hi Powa, 100n18, 123, 145, 148, 149
Oppression, 5n3, 7, 18, 24, 87, 98, 104, 165, 209
Organic, 19, 21, 68, 70, 145
ORP, *see* Onda Rossa Posse
Orrù, Sandro, *see* DJ Gruff
Ortiz, Fernando, 4, 17
Osumare, Halifu, 6, 7
'Other,' 56, 91, 94, 97, 100, 108, 138, 139, 153, 230

P

Pacifism, 1
Paninari, 101
Papa Retz, 93
Papa Ricky, 108, 141, 144, 147, 149, 150
Papet Yali, 103
Partito Sardo d'Azione, 167
Pavone, Rita, 22
Perigeo, 50
Peterson, Richard, 45, 46
Petrachi, Antonio, *see* Treble (Antonio Petrachi)
Phoenicians, 166, 176

Pietrangeli, Paolo, 31, 31n8, 133, 134
Pili, Roberto, 182, 182n3, 196, 200, 215, 217
Pinsky, Ludus, 127, 137
Piombo a Tempo, 123
Pitura Freska, 122, 145, 147
Pizzica, 77n33, 95n12, 101, 102, 105
Pizzutilo, Mimmo, 5, 38, 40, 45n1, 48–56, 48n3, 50n7, 54n10, 59, 60, 62, 63, 63n16, 67–69, 68n23, 71–73, 72n27, 75, 78, 79, 90, 93, 94, 104, 187
The Police, 40, 136, 138, 216
Popular culture, 18, 29, 38, 129, 181, 210
Portelli, Alessandro, 181
Posse era, 9, 10, 12, 85, 144, 171, 194, 203, 220, 223
Possessione, 149
Potter, Russell, 11n10, 23, 73, 88, 88n6, 89
Pozzi, Gloria, 128
Precarious, 58
Presley, Elvis, 22
Progetto Radio, 67
Proletarian youth, 31, 58, 60
Propaganda, 1, 31, 54
Provvedi, Marco, 68, 68n24, 69
Puff Bong, 40, 40n12, 69, 72n26
Pugliese, Joseph, 55, 56, 86, 94, 129, 157
Punk, 10, 11, 21n1, 36–40, 47, 48, 55–62, 62n15, 63n16, 64, 70, 106–108, 128–130, 132, 138

Q

Qawali, 153
Questione meridionale, 55, 86
Quilo (Sanna, Alessandro), 164, 170–174, 177–182, 185, 186, 194–196, 198–200, 202

R

Racism, 1, 6, 24, 38, 94, 103, 121, 129, 137–144, 150, 156, 158, 183, 195, 225–227

Radio, 9n7, 10, 12, 19, 20, 40, 48, 59, 60, 62, 66, 67, 67n22, 90, 93n11, 110, 111, 118, 123, 132, 132n2, 133

Radio programs
"Daje Pure Te," 132
"Funk Theology," 132
"Ganja University," 67, 90
"Rumori Molesti," 132

Radio stations
Blackout, 62
Dread Broadcasting Corporation (DBC), 59, 60, 67
Radio Alice, 66, 66n21, 106
Radio libere, 10, 12, 60, 66, 127–129, 131, 148
Radio Onda Rossa (*ROR*), 128, 130–137
Radio Torino Popolare, 141
Radio Underdog, 106
Radio Vecchia Savona, 93n11
Rebel Radio, 59

Rai, 26, 40, 118, 147

Randagiu Sardu, 12, 13, 164, 165, 187, 193–220, 229

Rankin, Chubby, 123

Ranking Sinyx, 93

Rap, 3, 9n7, 10, 10n9, 35, 54n10, 77, 88, 89, 93, 106–108, 108n23, 120, 123, 127, 129–132, 145–149, 153, 163–165, 168, 170, 170n1, 173, 177, 178, 181–183, 182n2, 186–188, 187n10, 194–197, 200, 201, 213, 220

Rappamuffin, 13, 194–213

Rastafari, 23n2, 24, 34, 57, 68

Rastafarian, 23, 23n2, 24, 27, 35, 36, 36n11, 40, 41, 41n14, 47, 53, 58n11, 65, 70, 73, 75n29, 91n8, 92, 224, 225, 225n1

Rebel music, 11, 17, 28

Reggae
dancehall, 3, 9n7, 203, 209n5
deejay style, 36, 93
dub, 3, 11, 34, 36, 64, 91n8, 107, 154, 156, 195
international, 27, 28, 34, 85, 118, 123
Italian, 6, 9, 9n7, 11, 20, 38–41, 48, 48n3, 57, 69, 90, 91, 106n21, 110, 129, 130, 141, 145, 150, 194, 202, 223–227, 230
raggamuffin, 3, 88, 130, 140
reggaetón, 203, 208–210, 209n5
roots, 3, 36, 41, 70, 90, 91n8, 203, 205, 227
rub-a-dub, 3, 93

Reggae National Tickets, 223

Reggae world fusion, 77, 78, 91, 229

Re Nudo, 30–32, 146

Rhizome, 3, 89

Rhythm'n'Blues (R&B), 208, 214

Rico, Don, 85n2, 110, 111, 114, 116

Riddims, 25, 63, 96, 97, 118, 118n26, 120, 142, 147, 224

Riflusso, 5, 12, 48, 51, 59, 61, 101

Rifondazione Comunista (Communist Refoundation Party), 144, 144n9, 152

Risorgimento, 7

Ritmo Vitale (record label), 122

Rizzoli, Angelo, 137

Roach, Max, 134n3

Rocchetta, Franco, 138

Rock Against Racism (RAR), 38, 39

Rockers beat, 74, 92

242 INDEX

Rockman, 9n7, 48n2, 65, 79n35, 90
Rocksteady, 3, 24, 25, 206, 208
Rolling Stones, 29, 38, 39
Rollo, Giovanni 'Papa Gianni,' 85n2, 96–98, 100, 101, 104
Roman Empire, 166
Romanticism, 180
Rome, 38, 49, 55, 57, 68–70, 72, 72n27, 102, 123, 130–132, 145, 146, 148, 157, 164, 175, 214, 225, 225n2
Rosapaeda (Di Domenico, Antonella), 50n7, 54, 67, 73, 74, 74n28, 78, 79, 230
Roxy club, 36
RTI Music, 148
Ruberti, Antonio, 131
Rude boy movement, 24
Ruido, 164, 196
Ruts, 39

S

Sacra Corona Unita, *see* Mafias
Salento Posse, 96, 128, 145
Salvatores, Gabriele, 149, 150
Sanluri, Battle of, 166, 199
Sanna, Alessandro, *see* Quilo
Santana, 38
Santoro, Marco, 10n8, 154
Saracens, 166
Sa Razza, 12, 145, 163–189, 194, 195, 202, 214
Sardinia
  Bronze Age, 166
  Quirra, 198
  Stone Age, 166
  Sulcis, 176, 177, 179
Sardu, *see* Language
Saturday Night Live, 39
Savona Posse, 70, 93, 93n11, 129
Schneider, Jane, 55, 94, 175
Scotti development company, 135

Selassie I, Haile, 23n2
Senese, James, 155n17, 157
Sepe, Daniele, 153
Sex Pistols 44, 36
Shabba Ranks, 122
Shaka, Jah, 74, 90, 91n8
Shakalab, 204
Sherwood, Adrian, 203, 204
Signorile, Nicola, 206
Simaryp, 24n3
Singjay style, 200, 206, 207
Ska, 3, 11n10, 20–26, 21n1, 132, 208
Skinheads, 24–26, 24n3, 26n5
Slits, 37
Small, Millie, 21
Smith, Patti, 36, 66
Soca, 203, 208
Socialist Party, 137, 146
Soft Machines, 50
Solaro, Alba, 51, 58, 60–62, 65, 66, 71, 72, 110, 135
Solaroli, Marco, 10n8, 154
Soul, 18, 66–71, 90, 107, 108n23, 153, 154, 171, 182, 203, 205, 216
Soul Boy, 122
Sound system, 3, 9n7, 11, 17, 19–21, 21n1, 28, 34, 35, 36n11, 48n3, 55, 59, 63, 64, 68, 89, 91–93, 91n8, 96, 99, 100n18, 105, 107, 144, 203, 227
Southern Question, *see Questione meridionale*
South Posse, 123, 204
Spanish Empire, 166
Spivak, Gyaltri, 88
Spliff a Dada Studio, 139
Spotify, 177, 193
SSS, *see* Sud Sound System
Stammer, Bertie, 72, 72n27, 75
Stampa Alternativa, 32
Steel Pulse, 37, 141
Stena, *see* Alborosie

Stifani, Luigi, 101
Stille, Alexander, 67n22, 77, 113n24, 137
Stitt, King, 35, 89n7
Stolfi, Pierluigi, 135, 135n4
Stormy Six, 33
Strage di Bologna, 135, 136
Strage di Ustica, 135
Stranglers, 37
Strategy of tension, 65, 65n19, 136, 152
Street, John, 52, 53
Struggle, 3, 8, 30, 31, 36n11, 56, 65, 71, 86, 90–94, 110, 154, 179, 199, 208
Subcultural theory, 47
Subnoise 130, 107
Sud Sound System (SSS), 12, 85–123, 128, 137n6, 138–140, 142, 144–147, 150, 150n12, 152, 155, 163, 164, 168, 170, 171, 187, 194, 228, 229
Suoni Mudù, 123
Suoni Uniti Differenti (S.U.D.), 123
Su Rais, 171–174
Swing, 136, 214
Syncretism, 142, 184n7

T
Tarantamuffin, 101–106
Taranto, 202, 209–213
Teatro Origine, 79
Teatro Tendastrisce, 68, 68n24
Terron Fabio, 97, 122
Terroni, 55, 56, 139
Tesone, Gennaro, 154, 154n16
Thriller Jenna, 123
Toasting, 3, 35, 93, 108, 120, 153, 205, 206
Torino Posse (TO.SSE), 127, 128, 140, 142, 147

Tosh, Peter, 17, 27n6, 38–40
Tozzi, Tommaso, 52
Train to Roots, 227, 228
Transculturation, 4, 6, 11, 17, 18, 20–28, 30, 47, 54, 60, 85, 91, 96–101, 105, 107, 115, 130, 150, 151, 163, 228
Trappavasciamuffin, 151, 152
Treble (Antonio Petrachi), 85n2, 90, 106–108, 111, 112, 114–116, 118, 119, 150n12
Trizta, 180
Trobamuffin, 103
Trojan Records, 26
Troso, Dario (Gopher D), 85n2, 106
Twelve Tribes of Israel, 225, 225n1, 225n2

U
Undafunk, 164, 180
UNESCO, 176
Unification, Italian, 1, 55, 86, 94, 169
Unprotected, *see Non-garantiti*
Urban, Maria Bonaria, 179, 180, 185, 197n2
U-Roy, 35

V
Vandals, 166
Veal, Michael, 17, 18, 35, 64, 64n18, 75
Velvet, 146
Venditti, Antonello, 2, 8
Verdicchio, Pasquale, 10n8, 55, 61, 86–88, 129, 139, 140, 157
Verdi, Giuseppe, 1
Vernacular
  hegemonic, 73, 88
  resistance, 73, 88, 88n6, 89, 97, 100, 120, 152

244 INDEX

Villa Ada Posse, 123
Virgin, 27, 50
   See also Branson, Richard
Virus, 62
Vox, Amedeo, 72, 78, 90
Vox Pop, label, 140

W

The Wailers, 11, 27, 27n6
   See also Marley, Rita
Wide Records, 138
Williams, Willie, 37
Winnie, Papa, 41, 41n15
Winspeare, Edoardo, 99, 101, 118
Wogs, 62n15
Woodstock, 32, 32n9
Workers' Movements, 6, 176, 181
   strikes, 176
Working class, British, 21, 21n1,
   23–26, 35
World fusion, 45

World music, 123, 153, 214, 215n6,
   230
Wyatt, Robert, 50

Y

Youth culture
   black, 21n1
   white, 25
Youth movements, 1, 4, 5, 23, 29, 38,
   49, 60, 123, 127
Youth politics
   anarchists, 49n6
   Lotta Continua, 49n6
   Stalinists, 49n6
   Trotskyites, 49n6
Youth unemployment, 95, 165,
   211

Z

Zorro Five, 26